1001 Quotes, Illustrations, and Humorous Stories for Preachers, Teachers, and Writers

1001 Quotes, Illustrations, and Humorous Stories for Preachers, Teachers, and Writers

Edward K. Rowell, Editor

BakerBooks
Grand Rapids, Michigan

Published by Baker Books
a division of Baker Publishing Group
P.O. Box 6287, Grand Rapids, MI 49516-6287
www.bakerbooks.com

Fourth printing, March 2006

Originally published as three books, *Quotes and Idea Starters for Preaching and Teaching* (© 1996), *Fresh Illustrations for Preaching and Teaching* (© 1997), and *Humor for Preaching and Teaching* (© 1996, with co-editor Bonne L. Steffen)

Printed in the United States of America

Library of Congress Cataloging-in-Publication Data is on file at the Library of Congress, Washington, D.C.

ISBN 10: 0-8010-9174-8
ISBN 978-0-8010-9174-2

Contents

Preface

To make this preaching resource even more useful and time-saving, we are providing:

1. *The right to copy.* The publisher grants you the right to copy the quotations, illustrations, and humor selections and file them in the way that best fits your system.
2. *Topical arrangements.* Quotation books indexed by author don't help unless you already have a quote in mind and know who said it. But with a topical approach, the quotation is easy to find. Likewise, we've filed each illustration and humor selection under the topics that come to mind during sermon study. You'll find fresh material for your next sermon on Anger, Salvation, or Worship.
3. *Alternate subjects and index.* Each quote, illustration, and humor selection is followed by two alternate subjects in parentheses. Since any good quotation or story has more than one application, you can find the reference you need indexed under at least three topics.

Quotes

The right quote is a pinch of spice for the sermon. It enhances the other ingredients. Its taste, whether pungent or sweet, can linger long after the preacher has closed the Bible and gone home.

For many years, *Leadership* has been gathering spicy quotes, as contemporary as today's sports page, as lasting as the church fathers. Our aim is to season both your sermons and your soul. A thoughtful phrase will often break the curse of "sermon block," highlighting your own experience and wisdom in a fresh way.

Some anonymous wag said, "Sermons affect different people in different ways: Some rise to go greatly strengthened; some awake greatly rested." The judicious use of catchy quotes and famous phrases will, at the very least, make the nappers wonder what they missed.

We're confident that "the use of this book will increase your effectiveness as you communicate the greatest message of all time."

You can quote me on that.

Edward K. Rowell

A

Ability

There is something that is much more scarce, something rarer than ability. It is the ability to recognize ability.

Robert Half

(Discernment, Gifts)

Abortion

When we consider that women are treated as property, it is degrading to women that we should treat our children as property to be disposed of as we wish.

Elizabeth Cady Stanton

(Women, Children)

Acceptance

The world has a philosophy that says, "What can't be cured must be endured." Christians have a philosophy that says, "What can't be cured can be enjoyed."

Joni Eareckson Tada

(Endurance, Suffering)

Do not wish to be anything but what you are, and try to be that perfectly.

Francis de Sales

(Contentment, Lifestyle)

In the world to come, I shall not be asked, "Why were you not Moses?" I shall be asked, "Why were you not Zusya?"

Rabbi Zusya

(Contentment, Envy)

Achievement

When you get to the top of the mountain, your first inclination is not to jump for joy, but to look around.

James Carville

(Evaluation, Success)

Action

If we are going to wait until every possible hindrance has been removed before we do a work for the Lord, we will never attempt to do anything.

T. J. Bach

(Mission, Boldness)

Advantage

To every disadvantage there is a corresponding advantage.

W. Clement Stone

(Disadvantage, Perspective)

Advent

The best way to prepare for the coming of Christ is never to forget the presence of Christ.

William Barclay

(Christmas, Second Coming)

Adversity

The good things which belong to prosperity are to be wished, but the good things which belong to adversity are to be admired.

Seneca

(Prosperity, Character)

Kites rise highest against the wind, not with it.

Winston Churchill

(Achievement, Success)

He knows not his own strength that hath not met adversity. Heaven prepares good men with crosses.

Ben Johnson

(Strength, Suffering)

Adversity is often the window of opportunity for change. Few people or organizations want to change when there is prosperity and peace. Major changes are often precipitated by necessity.

Leith Anderson

(Change, Opportunity)

God loves us in good times and bad . . . but he is even more real in our lives when we are having tough times.

Job Gibbs

(Trials, God's Love)

All the wrong people are against it, so it must be right.

James Carville

(Persecution, Opposition)

By the time I'm climbing back up from going down, I'm already thinking about the next play.

Joe Namath
Hall of Fame quarterback

(Courage, Discipline)

Age

The error of youth is to believe that intelligence is a substitute for experience, while the error of age is to believe that experience is a substitute for intelligence.

Lyman Bryson

(Intelligence, Experience)

Age is important no less than youth itself, though in another dress. And as the evening twilight fades away, the sky is filled with stars invisible by day.

Henry Wadsworth Longfellow

(Growth, Maturity)

Ambition

To be ambitious of true honor and of the real glory and perfection of our nature is the very principle and incentive of virtue; but to be ambitious of titles, place, ceremonial respects, and pageantry, is as vain and little as the things are which we court.

Sir Philip Sidney

(Honor, Virtue)

The kind of successor I may get may depend a great deal on the kind of predecessor I've been and how I've related to my own predecessor. To reject the past and ignore the future . . . is both selfish and foolish.

Warren W. Wiersbe

(Past, Future)

The slave has but one master, the ambitious man has as many as there are persons whose aid may contribute to the advancement of his fortunes.

Jean de la Bruyere

(Freedom, Slavery)

We all want to be great, but we don't want folks to know we want to be great.

Phil Lineberger

(Pride, Deception)

Keep away from people who try to belittle your ambitions. Small people always do that, but the really great make you feel that you, too, can become great.

Mark Twain

(Greatness, Criticism)

Anger

Speak when you're angry—and you'll make the best speech you'll ever regret.

Laurence J. Peter

(Self-control, Tongue)

Anxiety

Anxiety is the great modern plague. But faith can cure it.

Smiley Blanton

(Faith, Peace)

Apathy

Think about people who find themselves in religious ruts. They discover a number of things about themselves. They will find that they are getting older but not getting any holier. Time is their enemy, not their friend. . . . They were not any better last year than they had been the year before.

A. W. Tozer

(Holiness, Routine)

Assumptions

Unspoken premises direct the course of any civilization. The ideas which are not even argued are the building blocks of society.

James Newby

(Civilization, Ideas)

Attitude

It is not so important to be serious as it is to be serious about the important things. The monkey wears an expression of seriousness which would do credit to any scholar, but the monkey is serious because he itches.

Robert M. Hutchins

(Perspective, Importance)

There are no menial jobs, only menial attitudes.

William J. Bennett

(Work, Values)

B

Baptism

In baptism we are initiated, crowned, chosen, embraced, washed, adopted, gifted, reborn, killed, and thereby sent forth and redeemed. We are identified as one of God's own, then assigned our place and our job within the kingdom of God.

William Willimon

(Redemption, Kingdom of God)

Belief

Borrowed beliefs have no power.

James Black

(Convictions, Power)

Bible

I am a Christian because God says so, and I did what he told me to do, and I stand on God's Word, and if the Book goes down, I'll go with it.

Billy Sunday

(Word of God, Obedience)

It is better to pray over the Bible than to brood over the self.

P. T. Forsyth

(Prayer, Self)

The Bible was not given to increase our knowledge but to change our lives.

D. L. Moody

(Change, Knowledge)

The Bible is alive, it speaks to me; it has feet, it runs after me; it has hands, it lays hold of me.

Martin Luther

(Conviction, Inspiration)

The Bible is a stream of running water, where alike the elephant may swim, and the lamb walk without losing its feet.

Gregory the Great

(Knowledge, Simplicity)

Bitterness

Like the bee, we distill poison from honey for our self-defense—what happens to the bee if it uses its sting is well-known.

Dag Hammarskjöld

(Gossip, Slander)

Blessing

God is more anxious to bestow his blessings on us than we are to receive them.

Augustine

(Gifts, God)

Body of Christ

Alone I cannot serve the Lord effectively, and he will spare no pains to teach me this. He will bring things to an end, allowing doors to close and leaving me ineffectively knocking my head against a wall until I realize that I need the help of the body as well as of the Lord.

Watchman Nee

(Church, Self-reliance)

There are times when together we discover that we make up a single body, that we belong to each other and that God has called us to be together as a source of life for each other.

Jean Vanier

(Community, Unity)

Brevity of Life

For weeks after my last operation (for cancer)—frail and without energy, sleeping ten hours—I looked in my house at all the books I had not read and wept for my inability to read them. Or I looked at great books I had read too quickly in my avidity—telling myself I would return to them later. There is never a *later*, but for most of my life I have believed in *later*.

Donald Hall

(Time, Decisions)

We are always complaining that our days are few and acting as though there would be no end of them.

Seneca

(Death, Self-deception)

Busyness

If you have so much business to attend to that you have no time to pray, depend upon it, you have more business on hand than God ever intended you should have.

D. L. Moody

(Prayer, Disobedience)

Lord, I shall be very busy this day. I may forget Thee, but do not Thou forget me.

Sir Jacob Astley

(Devotion, Forgetfulness)

C

Calling

O ye gifted ones, follow your calling, let neither obstacles nor temptations induce you to leave it; bound along if you can; if not, on hands and knees follow it. Turn into other paths, and, for a momentary advantage or gratification, ye have sold your inheritance, your immortality.

George Borrow

(Gifts, Perseverance)

Calm

Christ's life outwardly was one of the most troubled lives that was ever lived: tempest and tumult, tumult and tempest, the waves breaking over it all the time. But the inner life was a sea of glass. The great calm was always there.

Henry Drummond

(Trouble, Christ)

Sometimes God calms the storm—and sometimes he lets the storm rage and calms his child.

Unknown

(Peace, Assurance)

Causes

When great causes are on the move in the world . . . we learn that we are spirits, not animals.

Winston Churchill

(Beliefs, Human Nature)

Chance

God does not play dice with the universe.

Albert Einstein

(God, Evolution)

Change

People wish to be settled; only as far as they are unsettled is there any hope for them.

Ralph Waldo Emerson

(Hope, Desire)

We trained hard . . . but every time we were beginning to form into teams we would be reorganized. I was to learn later in life that we tend to meet any new situation by reorganizing. And what a wonderful method it can be for creating the illusion of progress while producing inefficiency and demoralization.

Petronius

(Progress, Organization)

Character

What really matters is what happens in us, not to us.

James W. Kennedy

(Growth, Difficulty)

Ability will get you to the top, but it takes character to keep you there.

John Wooden

(Ability, Talent)

The ultimate measure of a man is not where he stands in moments of comfort and convenience, but where he stands at times of challenge and controversy.

Martin Luther King Jr.

(Adversity, Controversy)

So many missionaries, intent on doing something, forget that God's main work is to make something of them.

Jim Elliot

(Missions, Work)

No man can for any considerable time wear one face to himself and another to the multitude without finally getting bewildered as to which is the true one.

Nathaniel Hawthorne

(Deception, Honesty)

The proof of Christianity is not a book but a life. The power of Christianity is not a creed but a Christian character; and wherever you see life that has been transformed by the grace of God, you see a witness to the resurrection of Jesus.

William Woodfin

(Witness, Christianity)

It is easy in the world to live after the world's opinion. It is easy in solitude to live after one's own. But the great man is he who, in the midst of the crowd, keeps with perfect sweetness the independence of his character.

Ralph Waldo Emerson

(Peer Pressure, Independence)

People are like stained-glass windows. They sparkle and shine when the sun is out. But in the darkness, beauty is seen only if there is a light within.

Anonymous

(Perseverance, Beauty)

Character is what you are in the dark.

D. L. Moody

(Consistency, Perseverance)

Blessed is he who has learned to admire but not to envy, to follow but not imitate, to praise but not flatter, and to lead but not manipulate.

William Arthur Ward

(Virtue, Blessing)

Do not pray for easy lives; pray to be stronger people! Do not pray for tasks equal to your powers; pray for powers equal to your tasks. Then the doing of your work shall be no miracle but you shall be a miracle. Every day you shall wonder at yourself, at the richness of life which has come to you by the grace of God.

Phillips Brooks

(Strength, Perseverance)

When the rock is hard, we get harder than the rock.
When the job is tough, we get tougher than the job.

George Cullum Sr.

(Perseverance, Toughness)

I would rather be cheated a hundred times than develop a heart of stone.

Tim Stafford

(Forgiveness, Heart)

Cheerfulness

It is not fitting, when one is in God's service, to have a gloomy face or a chilling look.

Francis of Assisi

(Gloom, Depression)

Childlikeness

Now, as always, God [discloses] himself to "babes" and hides himself in thick darkness from the wise and the prudent. We must simplify our approach to him. We must strip down to essentials (and they will be found to be blessedly few). We must put away all effort to impress, and come with the guileless candor of childhood. If we do this, without doubt God will quickly respond.

A. W. Tozer

(Prayer, Devotion)

Children

People who do not like children are swine, dunces, and blockheads, not worthy to be called men and women, because they despise the blessing of God, the Creator and Author of marriage.

Martin Luther

(Marriage, Blessing)

Choices

Perpetual devotion to what man calls his business is only to be sustained by perpetual neglect of many other things.

Robert Louis Stevenson

(Devotion, Neglect)

We are ever being born, or dying, and the thrill of choosing which is ours. Only once must we be born without our own consent. Only once must we die without our own permission.

Calvin Miller

(Birth, Death)

Christ

We read not that Christ ever exercised force but once, and that was to drive profane ones out of his temple, and not to force them in.

John Milton

(Force, Restraint)

Two things there are which man has no arithmetic to reckon, and no lie to measure. One of these things is the extent of that man's loss who loses his own soul. The other is the extent of God's gift when he gave Christ to sinners. . . . Sin must indeed be exceeding sinful, when the Father must needs give his only Son to be the sinner's Friend!

J. C. Ryle

(Sin, Cross)

The supreme education of the soul comes through an intimate acquaintance with Jesus Christ of history.

Rufus M. Jones

(Education, Soul)

As every Scot knows, salt must be put into the oatmeal from the start, before cooking, not afterward. In a similar way, Christ can never be added as an afterthought to an already full and committed life. It's possible to attempt to use the Master and his power to fulfill our desires and plans for the people we love and still give him the one position he will not accept: second place.

Lloyd John Ogilvie

(Character, Commitment)

Christianity

The Christian ideal has not been tried and found wanting. It has been found difficult and left untried.

G. K. Chesterton

(Idealism, Difficulty)

Christianity is a demanding and serious religion. When it is delivered as easy and amusing, it is another kind of religion altogether.

Neil Postman

(Discipleship, Discipline)

Jesus promised his disciples three things; that they would be entirely fearless, absurdly happy, and that they would get into trouble.

W. Russell Maltby

(Discipleship, Peace)

Most of us spend the first six days of each week sowing wild oats; then we go to church on Sunday and pray for a crop failure.

Fred Allen

(Sin, Rebellion)

Church

Let none pretend that they love the brethren in general, and love the people of God, and love the saints, while their love is not fervently exercised towards those who are in the same church society with them. Christ will try your love at the last day by your deportment in that church wherein you are.

John Owen

(Love, Judgment)

The church should be a community of dates instead of pumpkins. Pumpkins you can harvest in six months. Dates have to be planted and tended by people who will not live to harvest them. Dates are for future generations.

George Chauncey

(Patience, Maturity)

It is not the business of the church to adapt Christ to men, but men to Christ.

Dorothy Sayers

(Christ, Change)

Away with those who want an entirely pure church! That is plainly the same thing as wanting no church at all.

Martin Luther

(Purity, Acceptance)

The first two laws of the church: (1) When other people have abandoned something, we discover it; (2) When people discover something wonderful that we have, we have just abandoned it.

Andrew Greeley

(Culture, Discovery)

The church must be reminded that it is not the master or the servant of the state, but rather the conscience of the state.

Martin Luther King Jr.

(Politics, Conscience)

The church is the glue that keeps us together when we disagree. It is the gasoline that keeps us going during the tough times. It is the guts that enables us to take risks when we need to.

Mary Nelson

(Community, Courage)

The church is the only cooperative society in the world that exists for the benefit of its nonmembers.

William Temple

(Evangelism, Outreach)

Anyone can love the ideal church. The challenge is to love the real church.

Bishop Joseph McKinney

(Idealism, Love)

It is of no avail to talk of the church in general, the church in the abstract, unless the concrete particular local church which the people attend can become a center of light and leading, of inspiration and guidance, for its specific community.

Rufus Jones

(Idealism, Community)

It was one of the Wesleys, I think, who said that the New Testament knows nothing of solitary religion. We are forbidden to neglect the assembling of ourselves together. Christianity is already institutional in the earliest of its documents.

C. S. Lewis

(Fellowship, Christianity)

We don't live alone. We are members of one body. We are responsible for each other. And I tell you that the time will soon come when, if men will not learn that lesson, then they will be taught it in fire and blood and anguish.

J. B. Priestley

(Community, Responsibility)

Church Growth

I have not followed a secret formula in the mighty church growth we are experiencing. There is no question in my mind that what has been done in Korea can also be duplicated in every part of the world. The key is prayer!

David Yonggi Cho

(Evangelism, Prayer)

Commitment

In our modern world, our real danger comes not from irreligion, but from mild religion.

D. Elton Trueblood

(Lukewarmness, Conviction)

You will invest your life in something, or you will throw it away on nothing.

Haddon Robinson

(Investment, Waste)

Community

A community is only a community when the majority of its members are making the transition from "the community for myself" to "myself for the community."

Jean Vanier

(Church, Fellowship)

The Bible is all about community: from the Garden of Eden to the City at the end.

George F. MacLeod

(Church, Fellowship)

If we don't accept Jesus in one another, we will not be able to give him to others.

Mother Teresa

(Acceptance, Jesus)

It takes a village to raise a child.

African proverb

(Fellowship, Children)

Compassion

Warmth, warmth, more warmth! For we are dying of cold and not of darkness. It is not the night that kills, but the frost.

Miguel DeUnamuno

(Apathy, Coldness)

Let my heart be broken by the things that break the heart of God.

Bob Pierce

(God, Heart)

Compromise

The swift wind of compromise is a lot more devastating than the sudden jolt of misfortune.

Charles Swindoll

(Misfortune, Commitment)

Condemnation

It's worth noting that Jesus didn't condemn bad people. He condemned "stiff" people. We condemn the bad ones and affirm the stiff ones.

Steve Brown

(Compassion, Acceptance)

Confession

We need not "sin that grace may abound." We are sinners and need only to confess that grace may abound.

C. FitzSimons Allison

(Sin, Grace)

Conflict

If two people agree on everything, you may be sure that one of them is doing all the thinking.

Anonymous

(Agreement, Thinking)

Figure out what went wrong, not who was wrong, when communication breaks down.

Tom Nash

(Communication, Blame)

The secret of every discord in Christian homes and communities and churches is that we seek our own way and our own glory.

Alan Redpath

(Home, Community)

Conscience

There is only one way to achieve happiness on this terrestrial ball. And that is to have either a clear conscience or none at all.

Ogden Nash

(Happiness, Guilt)

Contentment

Next to faith this is the highest art—to be content with the calling in which God has placed you. I have not learned it yet.

Martin Luther

(Calling, Faith)

One who makes it a rule to be content in every part and accident of life because it comes from God praises God in a much higher manner than one who has some set time for the singing of psalms.

William Law

(Praise, Acceptance)

Give a man everything he desires and yet at this very moment he will feel that everything is not everything.

Immanuel Kant

(Desire, Satisfaction)

A man looking at the present in light of the future, and taking his whole being into account, may be contented with his lot: That is Christian contentment. But if a man has come to that point where he is so content that he says "I do not want to know any more, or do any more, or be any more," he is in a state in which he ought to be changed into a mummy.

Henry Ward Beecher

(Growth, Knowledge)

It is right to be contented with what we have, never with what we are.

James Mackintosh

(Growth, Character)

Contentment consists not in adding more fuel, but in taking away some fire; not in multiplying of wealth, but in subtracting our desires.

Thomas Fuller

(Desire, Wealth)

Control

Dear God, I find it so easy to try to be the one in charge. I find it so painful to realize that I am not the one in control. Help me know when saying "I just work here" that it is a confession and not just a way of evading responsibility.

Dick Rasanen

(Prayer, Submission)

Conversion

Conversion is not implanting eyes, for they exist already; but giving them direction, which they have not.

Plato

(Vision, Direction)

My God, grant me the conversion of my parish; I am willing to suffer all my life whatsoever it may please thee to lay upon me; yes even for a hundred years am I prepared to endure the sharpest pains; only let my people be converted. My God, convert my parish.

Cure d'Ars

(Church, Prayer)

Conviction

When you read God's Word, you must constantly be saying to yourself, "It is talking to me, and about me."

Søren Kierkegaard

(Word of God, Application)

In matters of style, swim with the current. In matters of principle, stand like a rock.

Thomas Jefferson

(Principle, Style)

Too much of our orthodoxy is correct and sound, but like words without a tune, it does not glow and burn; it does not stir the heart; it has lost its hallelujah. One man with a genuine glowing experience with God is worth a library full of arguments.

Vance Havner

(Experience, Apologetics)

The Christian way is not the middle way between extremes, but the narrow way between precipices.

Donald Bloesch

(Extremes, Compromise)

Cooperation

What is most rewarding is doing something that really matters with congenial colleagues who share with us the firm conviction that it needs to be done.

Elton Trueblood

(Community, Conviction)

Our world has become a neighborhood without becoming a brotherhood.

Billy Graham

(Community, Love)

Coping

Coping with difficult people is always a problem, especially if the difficult person happens to be yourself.

Anonymous

(Self-awareness, Conflict)

Courage

Give us grace, O God, to do the deed which we will know cries to be done. Let us not hesitate because of ease, or the words of men's mouths, or our own lives. Mighty causes are calling us. . . . But they call with voices that mean work and sacrifice and death. Mercifully grant us, O God, the spirit of

Esther, that we say, "I will go unto the King and if I perish, I perish." Amen.

W. E. B. DuBois

(Conviction, Sacrifice)

Courage is being scared to death but saddling up anyway.

John Wayne

(Conviction, Sacrifice)

Courage is almost a contradiction in terms. It means a strong desire to live taking the form of a readiness to die.

G. K. Chesterton

(Life, Death)

I am in earnest; I will not equivocate; I will not excuse; I will not retreat a single inch; and I will be heard.

William Lloyd Garrison

(Social Protest, Speech)

Courage! I have shown it for years; think you I shall lose it at the moment when my sufferings are to end?

Marie Antoinette

(Suffering, Strength)

Courtesy

The test of good manners is to be able to put up pleasantly with bad ones.

Wendell Willkie

(Self-control, Conflict)

Covetousness

Covetousness is simply craving more of what you have enough of already.

Haddon Robinson

(Desire, Wealth)

Envy is thin because it bites but never eats.

Spanish proverb

(Envy, Gossip)

Creation

A number of materialistic thinkers have ascribed to blind evolution more miracles, more improbable coincidences and wonders, than all the teleologists could ever devise.

Isaac Bashevis Singer

(Evolution, Materialism)

If man is not a divinity, then man is a disease. Either he is the image of God or else he is the one animal which has gone mad.

G. K. Chesterton

(Human Nature, God's Image)

The sky is the daily bread of the eyes.

Ralph Waldo Emerson

(Beauty, Nature)

Spring is God's way of saying, "One more time!"

Robert Orben

(Nature, Seasons)

Creativity

What is there left in the world for original dissertation research?

Doctoral student at Princeton, 1952

(Learning, Education)

Credibility

The *how* of being people worth listening to is by letting our lives be filled with God himself. The *why* of being people worth listening to is because we are his, and he wants us to radiate him.

Carole Mayhall

(Character, Holy Spirit)

Crisis

Circumstances may appear to wreck our lives and God's plans, but God is not helpless among the ruins. Our broken lives are not lost or useless. God comes in and takes the calamity and uses it victoriously, working out his wonderful plan of love.

Eric Liddell

(Sovereignty, God's Plan)

Criticism

People ask you for criticism, but they only want praise.

W. Somerset Maugham

(Praise, Honesty)

Whatever you have to say to people, be sure to say it in words that will cause them to smile and you will be on pretty safe ground. And when you do find it necessary to criticize someone, put your criticism in the form of a question which the other fellow is practically sure to have to answer in a manner that he becomes his own critic.

John Wanamaker

(Speech, Discipleship)

Great spirits have always encountered violent opposition from mediocre minds.

Albert Einstein

(Opposition, Greatness)

The porcupine, whom we must handle gloved, may be respected, but is never loved.

Arthur Guiterman

(Love, Respect)

Criticism should not be querulous and wasting, all knife and root-puller, but guiding, instructive, inspiring—a south wind, not an east wind.

Ralph Waldo Emerson

(Gentleness, Discipleship)

The angry word is a blow struck at our brother, a stab at his heart: It seeks to hit, to hurt, and to destroy. A deliberate insult is worse, for we openly disgrace our brother in the eyes of the world, causing others to despise him.

Dietrich Bonhoeffer

(Anger, Insult)

If one man calls you a donkey, pay him no mind. If two men call you a donkey, look for hoofprints. If three call you a donkey, get a saddle.

Unknown

(Accountability, Listening)

Get your friends to tell you your faults, or better still, welcome an enemy who will watch you keenly and sting you savagely. What a blessing such an irritating critic will be to a wise man, what an intolerable nuisance to a fool!

Charles Spurgeon

(Accountability, Enemies)

I would rather be disagreed with by someone who understands me, than to be agreed with by someone who does not understand me.

James D. Glasse

(Agreement, Understanding)

The defects of a preacher are soon spied. Let him be endowed with ten virtues and have but one fault, and that one fault will eclipse and darken all his virtues and gifts, so evil is the world in these times.

Martin Luther

(Gossip, Preaching)

To avoid criticism, say nothing, do nothing, be nothing.

Fred Shero

(Courage, Leadership)

Cross

If thou bear the cross cheerfully, it will bear thee.

Thomas à Kempis

(Cheerfulness, Suffering)

This only we may be assured of, that if tomorrow brings a cross, He who sends it can and will send grace to bear it.

J. C. Ryle

(Grace, Assurance)

My wife is . . . a mirror. When I have sinned against her, my sin appears in the suffering of her face. . . . The passion of Christ . . . is such a mirror. Are the tears of my dear wife hard to look at? Well, the pain in the face of Jesus is harder. . . . Nevertheless, I will not avoid this mirror! No, I will carefully rehearse, again this year, the passion of my Jesus—with courage, with clarity and faith; for this is the mirror of dangerous grace, purging more purely than any other.

Walter Wangerin Jr.

(Grace, Sin)

The story we're called to tell and live and die by is one of risk confronted, death embraced. What's more, Jesus calls us to walk the narrow way, take up a cross with him, daily. It's terribly risky business. Ask that bright company of martyrs that quite recklessly parted with goods, security, and life itself, preferring to be faithful in death rather than safe in life.

William H. Willimon

(Risk, Martyrdom)

[Jesus] rose up from the place where the kingdoms of the world shimmered before him, where crowns flashed and banners rustled, and hosts of enthusiastic people were ready to acclaim him, and quietly walked the way of poverty and suffering to the cross.

Helmut Thielicke

(Suffering, Sacrifice)

If that was God on that cross, then the hill called Skull is a granite studded with stakes to which you can anchor.

Max Lucado

(Trust, Good Friday)

It's easiest to see the cross on Jesus' shoulders. It's a bit harder with our neighbor's cross. Most difficult of all is seeing our own cross.

Mieczyslaw Malinski

(Suffering, Responsibility)

Culture

There's a lot more money to be made on Wall Street. If you want real power, go to Washington. If you want sex, go into the fashion business. But if you want the whole poison cocktail in one glass—go to Hollywood.

Alec Baldwin

(Money, Power, Sex)

Dostoyevsky reminded us in *The Brothers Karamazov* that "if God does not exist, everything is permissible." We are now seeing "everything." And much of it is not good to get used to.

William J. Bennett

(Sin, God)

The only effective response to our nation's crime problem is spiritual revival.

N. Lee Cooper

(Crime, Revival)

Man creates culture and through culture creates himself.

Pope John Paul II

(Influence, Sin)

We live in a strange society where we make documentaries of serial killers, movie idols out of organized crime members, authors out of political crooks, and role models out of criminals who beat the system. . . . I don't know when crime went from being news to entertainment, but somehow it's made the transition.

Erma Bombeck

(Crime, Entertainment)

Cynicism

Cynicism has gone too far. We are becoming what the history books tell us late Rome was like: mired in decadent self-absorption and lacking virtue.

Oliver Stone

(Decadence, Virtue)

D

Death

Why is it that we rejoice at a birth and grieve at a funeral? It is because we are not the person involved.

Mark Twain

(Birth, Grief)

We come into this world with our fingers curled and only slowly, by repeated practice, do we learn to open our hands. It takes a great deal of dying to get us ready to live.

Virginia Stem Owens

(Openness, Growth)

If you attempt to talk with a dying man about sports or business, he is no longer interested. He now sees other things as more important. People who are dying recognize what we often forget, that we are standing on the brink of another world.

William Law

(Eternity, Priorities)

If you live wrong, you can't die right.

Billy Sunday

(Righteousness, Life)

Deception

We can easily forgive a child who is afraid of the dark; the real tragedy of life is when men are afraid of the light.

Plato

(Sin, Darkness)

An error is the more dangerous the more truth it contains.

Henri-Frederic Amiel

(Truth, Danger)

Decisions

Ideally when Christians meet as Christians to take counsel together, their purpose is not—or should not be—to ascertain what is in the mind of the majority but what is in the mind of the Holy Spirit—something which may be quite different.

Margaret Thatcher

(Church, Holy Spirit)

Depravity

I think it says something that the only form of life that we have created so far [computer viruses] is purely destructive. Talk about creating life in our own image.

Stephen W. Hawking

(Human Nature, Creativity)

One of the enduring images in Christian culture is the praying hypocrite—the slave trader who reads the Bible in the hull of the ship; the preacher whose prayers bring him wealth; the convicted criminal who suddenly embraces religion. But don't we all have a bit of the hypocrite or con artist in us? Don't we all sometimes overlook our faults as we pray with the seemingly uninformed heart of a child? Prayer doesn't fail us; we fail prayer.

Jay Copp

(Hypocrisy, Prayer)

Desire

We are disgusted by the things that we desire, and we desire what disgusts us.

Mario Cuomo

(Disgust, Covetousness)

Destiny

Destiny is not a matter of chance; it is a matter of choice.

William Jennings Bryan

(Choices, Change)

Devil

The devil is like a mad dog that is chained up. He is powerless to harm us when we are outside his reach, but once we enter his circle we expose ourselves again to injury or harm.

Augustine

(Harm, Protection)

The devil's most beautiful ruse is to convince us that he does not exist.

Pierre Baudelaire

(Doubt, Deception)

Devotion

Keep us, Lord, so awake in the duties of our calling that we may sleep in thy peace and wake in thy glory.

John Donne

(Duty, Calling)

If life is to have meaning, and if God's will is to be done, all of us have to accept who we are and what we are, give it back to God, and thank him for the way he made us. What I am is God's gift to me; what I do with it is my gift to him.

Warren W. Wiersbe

(Acceptance, Giving)

Devotional Life

How many Christians look upon it as a burden and a duty and a difficulty to get alone with God! That is the great hindrance to our Christian life everywhere.

Andrew Murray

(Prayer, Duty)

The Word of God is demanding. It demands a stretch of time in our day—even though it be a very modest one—in which it is our *only* companion. . . . God will not put up with being fobbed off with prayers in telegram style and cut short like a troublesome visitor for whom we open the door just a crack to get rid of him as quickly as possible.

Helmut Thielicke

(Word of God, Time)

If you've made a habit of communing with God when the sun is shining, you'll find it much easier to sing in the rain.

Bill Pannell

(God, Difficulty)

Difficulty

What we do in the crisis always depends on whether we see the difficulties in the light of God, or God in the shadow of the difficulties.

G. Campbell Morgan

(Crisis, God)

Looking back, [my wife] Jan and I have learned that the wilderness is part of the landscape of faith, and every bit as essential as the mountaintop. On the mountaintop we are overwhelmed by God's presence. In the wilderness we are overwhelmed by his absence. Both places should bring us to our knees; the one, in utter awe; the other, in utter dependence.

Dave Dravecky

(God, Faith)

Bad times have a scientific value. These are occasions a good learner would not miss.

Ralph Waldo Emerson

(Learning, Suffering)

With me a change of trouble is as good as a vacation.

David Lloyd George

(Change, Refreshment)

We are too little to be able always to rise above difficulties. Well, then, let us pass beneath them quite simply.

Therese of Lisieux

(Humility, Perseverance)

The difficult we do immediately; the impossible takes a little longer.

U.S. Navy Seabees slogan, World War II

(Challenge, Teamwork)

Discernment

God never gives us discernment in order that we may criticize, but that we may intercede.

Oswald Chambers

(Criticism, Intercession)

The great thing is to get the true picture, whatever it is.

Winston Churchill

(Truth, Learning)

Reading God's hand into circumstances can be an evasion of genuine commitment to being his person in them. It can be an insidious alternative to giving him your heart—because it keeps your attention directed outward rather than inward, where his chisel bites. . . . We have elevated coincidence to the status of miracle, and the interpretation of coincidence to gospel. We can routinely ask God to intervene in our circumstances while hoping he'll keep his nose out of inner things like our spiritual indifference and pride.

John Boykin

(Submission, Miracles)

Discipleship

Full-grown oaks are not produced in three years; neither are servants of God.

Douglas Rumford

(Growth, Patience)

We teach what we know; we reproduce what we are.

Robert Schmidgall

(Education, Change)

In a church in Verona stands, or rather sits, a wooden image of St. Zeno, an ancient bishop, with knees so ludicrously short that there is no lap on which a baby could be held. He was not the first nor the last ecclesiastic who has been utterly incapable of being a nursing father to the church. It would be good if all ministers had a heavenly instinct for the nourishing and bringing up of the Lord's little ones, but this quality is sadly lacking.

Charles Spurgeon

(Compassion, Ministry)

Discipline

Liberty is the right to discipline ourselves in order not to be disciplined by others.

Clemenceau

(Liberty, Self-control)

Discipline begets abundance. Abundance, unless we use utmost care, destroys discipline. Discipline in its fall pulls down with it abundance.

Anonymous

(Abundance, Self-control)

Discipline is the refining fire by which talent becomes ability.

Roy L. Smith

(Talent, Ability)

To live a disciplined life, and to accept the result of that discipline as the will of God—that is the mark of a man.

Tom Landry

(Character, Manhood)

Discretion

Discretion is leaving a few things unsaid.

Elbert Hubbard

(Tact, Speech)

Duty

The greatest thing is to be found at one's post as a child of God, living each day as though it were our last, but planning as though our world might last a hundred years.

C. S. Lewis

(Planning, Responsibility)

Every generation is strategic. We are not responsible for the past generation, and we cannot bear full responsibility for the next one; but we do have our generation. God will hold us responsible as to how well we fulfill our responsibilities to this age and take advantage of our opportunities.

Billy Graham

(Opportunity, Responsibility)

Many people neglect the task that lies at hand and are content with having wished to do the impossible.

Teresa of Avila

(Neglect, Idealism)

Now my heart is troubled, and what shall I say? "Father, save me from this hour"? No, it was for this very reason I came to this hour.

Jesus Christ (John 12:27)

(Dedication, Courage)

E

Easter

The preacher brings a report from the battlefield of the conflict between Christ and Satan. The news is that for the whole of humankind Jesus Christ has won the victory in his death and resurrection.

James W. Cox

(Spiritual Warfare, Resurrection)

When death stung Jesus Christ, it stung itself to death.

Peter Joshua

(Death, Victory)

Easter suffers from acute holiday envy. Its egg hunts and rabbit have never had the commercial appeal of Santa's bounty and eight tiny reindeer. Let's face it, cattle lowing and a baby who doesn't cry is money in the bank compared to a homeless thirty-year-old dangling from a cross.

Joey Earl Horstmann

(Christmas, Cross)

I cannot give in to the devil's principle, deceitful tactic which makes so many Christians satisfied with an "Easter celebration" instead of experiencing the power of Christ's resurrection. It is the devil's business to keep Christians mourning and weeping with pity beside the cross instead of demonstrating that Jesus Christ is risen, indeed.

A. W. Tozer

(Power, Resurrection)

Many think the Christian religion has run its course and that the gloom of Good Friday is now settling over the long history of the church. But they are wrong. The reality of the resurrection cannot so easily be undone. In truth, it is the world of unbelievers that remains on notice of judgment.

Carl F. H. Henry

(Resurrection, Judgment)

Ego

Arrogant, pompous, obnoxious, vain, cruel, verbose, a show-off. I have been called all of these. Of course, I am.

Howard Cosell

(Pride, Self-evaluation)

Emotion

If choice must be made between rationality and fervor, men will choose fervor.

George A. Buttrick

(Rationalism, Enthusiasm)

Encouragement

A pat on the back is only a few vertebrae removed from a kick in the pants, but is miles ahead in results.

Ella Wheeler Wilcox

(Motivation, Criticism)

Enemies

Friends may come and go, but enemies accumulate.

David Belasic

(Friendship, Criticism)

Envy

The man who keeps busy helping the man below him won't have time to envy the man above him.

Henrietta Mears

(Service, Contentment)

Eternal Life

Nations, cultures, arts, civilizations—these are mortal, and their life is to ours as the life of a gnat. But it is immortals whom we joke with, work with, marry, snub, and exploit—immortal horrors or everlasting splendors.

C. S. Lewis

(Human Nature, Immortality)

We take excellent care of our bodies, which we have for only a lifetime; yet we shrivel our souls, which we will have for eternity.

Billy Graham

(Soul, Body)

Ethics

The world has achieved brilliance without conscience. Ours is a world of nuclear giants and ethical infants.

Omar Bradley

(Conscience, Progress)

The church is uncommonly vocal about the subject of bedrooms and as singularly silent on the subject of boardrooms!

Dorothy L. Sayers

(Leadership, Unity)

Evangelism

Saving knowledge is diffused over the earth, not like sunlight but like torchlight, which is passed from hand to hand.

James Strachan

(Witness, Relationships)

I would rather fail in the cause that some day will triumph than triumph in a cause that some day will fail.

Woodrow Wilson

(Missions, Church)

There is a subtle false teaching that says we can be evangelical without being evangelistic. It has us believe we "go" to church rather than we "are" the church.

Chris A. Lyons

(Church, Missions)

The church that does not evangelize will fossilize.

Oswald J. Smith

(Church, Apathy)

The gospel is good news only if it arrives in time.

Carl F. H. Henry

(Gospel, Time)

I feel that God has put me beside a cliff where people dance close to the edge. I say to them, "Look, if I were you I wouldn't get so close. I have seen people go over, and they always get hurt. Some of them get killed." And they say, "I really appreciate your telling me that. I didn't realize it was so dangerous." And then they jump! I feel so responsible for the pain. And the Father reminds me through his Word, "Son, you are not responsible for the jumping; you are responsible for the telling. As long as you are faithful, you don't have to play God."

Steve Brown

(Responsibility, Choices)

It is our privilege to have world evangelism as a passion, not our responsibility to have as a burden.

Mary Nordstrom

(Passion, Burden)

The world has more winnable people than ever before . . . but it is possible to come out of a ripe field empty-handed.

Donald McGavran

(Missions, Opportunity)

The gospel must be preached afresh and told in new ways to every generation, since every generation has its own unique questions. The gospel must constantly be forwarded to a new address, because the recipient is repeatedly changing his place of residence.

Helmut Thielicke

(Gospel, Creativity)

The idea is not to get the word out, but to let the Word out.

Dick Rasanen

(Witness, Word of God)

Consumers want to know not only what they're buying, but *who* they're buying it from. . . . Consumer relationship development is as important as product development.

Frank P. Perdue

(Witness, Relationships)

It could be that one of the greatest hindrances to evangelism today is the poverty of our own experience.

Billy Graham

(Experience, Hypocrisy)

Evil

Once we assuage our conscience by calling something a "necessary evil," it begins to look more and more necessary and less and less evil.

Sydney J. Harris

(Conscience, Deception)

Why did Jesus Christ not remain alive and eliminate, generation by generation, all the evils which harass humanity? Simply because he was the Great Physician, and in the finest tradition of medical science, he was unwilling to remain preoccupied with the symptoms when he could destroy the disease. Jesus Christ was unwilling to settle for anything less than elimination of the cause of all evil in history.

Richard C. Halverson

(Christ, Cross)

Men never do evil so completely and cheerfully as when they do it from religious conviction.

Blaise Pascal

(Religion, Conviction)

When a man is getting better, he understands more and more clearly the evil that is still left in him. When a man is getting worse, he understands his own badness less and less.

C. S. Lewis

(Self-deception, Good)

Example

God has no more precious gift to a church or an age than a man who lives as an embodiment of his will, and inspires those around him with the faith of what grace can do.

Andrew Murray

(Grace, Inspiration)

Excellence

The society which scorns excellence in plumbing because plumbing is a humble activity, and tolerates shoddiness in philosophy because it is an exalted activity, will have neither good plumbing nor good philosophy. Neither its pipes nor its theories will hold water.

John Gardner

(Shoddiness, Tolerance)

Badness you can get easily, in quantity: The road is smooth and lies close by. But in front of excellence the immortal gods have put sweat, and long and steep is the way to it, and rough at first. But when you come to the top, then it is easy, even though it is hard.

Hesiod

(Difficulty, Work)

Excuses

Never excuse. Never explain. Never complain.

Motto of the British Foreign Service

(Leadership, Character)

Expectations

Treat a man as he appears to be, and you make him worse. But treat a man as if he already were what he potentially could be, and you make him what he should be.

Johann Wolfgang Goethe

(Growth, Motivation)

Attempt great things for God. Expect great things from God.

William Carey

(Ambition, Motivation)

It is a fundamental principle in the life and walk of faith that we must always be prepared for the unexpected when we are dealing with God.

D. Martyn Lloyd-Jones

(Sovereignty, Trials)

I always prefer to believe the best of everybody—it saves so much trouble.

Rudyard Kipling

(Church, Community)

F

Failure

We fight for lost causes because we know that our defeat and dismay may be the preface for our successor's victory.

T. S. Eliot

(Causes, Victory)

One reason God created time was so there would be a place to bury the failures of the past.

James Long

(Time, Past)

Take away my ability to fail and I would not know the meaning of success. Let me be immune to rejection and heartbreak and I could not know the glory of living.

Ross W. Marrs

(Success, Pain)

I cannot give you the formula for success, but I can give you the formula for failure, which is: Try to please everybody.

Herbert Bayard Swope

(Success, Peer Pressure)

The increase of suicides, alcoholics, and even some forms of nervous breakdowns is evidence that many people are training for success when they should be training for failure. Failure is far more common than success; poverty is more prevalent than wealth, and disappointment more normal than arrival.

J. Wallace Hamilton

(Success, Perseverance)

Whenever you fall, pick up something.

Oswald Avery

(Learning, Growth)

We never see God in failure, but only in success—a strange attitude for people who have the cross as the center of their faith.

Cheryl Forbes

(Success, Cross)

A moment of conscious triumph makes one feel that after this nothing will really matter; a moment of realized disaster makes one feel that this is the end of everything. But neither feeling is realistic, for neither event is really what it is felt to be.

J. I. Packer

(Success, Perspective)

Faith

Faith like Job's cannot be shaken because it is the result of having been shaken.

Abraham Heschel

(Certainty, Difficulty)

What else will do *except* faith in such a cynical, corrupt time? When the country goes temporarily to the dogs, cats must learn to be circumspect, walk on fences, sleep in trees, and have faith that all this woofing is not the last word.

Garrison Keillor

(Cynicism, World)

A weak faith is weakened by predicaments and catastrophes whereas a strong faith is strengthened by them.

Victor Frankl

(Trials, Strength)

Jesus holds the answers to all of the everyday problems that you face. I am talking about an acceptance and belief in Jesus, heaven, and God. I guess you can deal with your problems on your own without these beliefs, but it's much, much tougher. With those beliefs, you realize how insignificant the budget deficit debate is in comparison with the big picture.

Rush Limbaugh

(Jesus, Problems)

Faith means trusting in advance what will only make sense in reverse.

Philip Yancey

(Vision, Trust)

Faith must never be counter to reason; yet it must always go beyond reason, for the nature of man is more than rationalism. Faith is emotion as well as reason.

George A. Buttrick

(Reason, Emotion)

That you are sitting before me in this church is a fact. That I am standing and speaking to you from this pulpit is a fact. But it is only faith that makes me believe anyone is listening.

Anonymous preacher

(Fact, Belief)

Faith is not belief without proof but trust without reservation.

Elton Trueblood

(Trust, Belief)

It is a fatal error to mistake mere historical belief for saving faith. A man may firmly believe his religion historically, and yet have no part nor portion therein practically and savingly. He must not only believe his faith, he must believe *in* his faith.

Thomas More

(Belief, Religion)

True faith goes into operation when there are no answers.

Elisabeth Elliot

(Difficulty, Doubt)

Faith does not operate in the realm of the possible. There is no glory for God in that which is humanly possible. Faith begins where man's power ends.

George Müller

(Power, Glory)

Our faith becomes practical when it is expressed in two books: the date book and the checkbook.

Elton Trueblood

(Time, Money)

Hope is hearing the melody of the future. Faith is to dance to it.

Rubem Alves

(Hope, Future)

I prayed for faith, and thought that some day faith would come down and strike me like lightning. But faith did not seem to come. One day I read in the tenth chapter of Romans, "Now faith cometh by hearing, and hearing by the Word of God." I had closed my Bible, and prayed for faith. I now opened my Bible, and began to study, and faith has been growing ever since.

D. L. Moody

(Bible, Study)

Faith is to believe what we do not see, and the reward of this faith is to see what we believe.

Augustine

(Vision, Belief)

Nothing worth doing is completed in one lifetime: Therefore we must be saved by hope. Nothing true or beautiful makes complete sense in any context of history: Therefore we must be saved by faith. Nothing we do, no matter how virtuous, can be accomplished alone: Therefore we are saved by love.

Reinhold Niebuhr

(Hope, Love)

False Teachers

False teachers invite people to come to the Master's table because of what's on it, not because they love the Master.

Hank Hanegraaff

(Leadership, Teaching)

Fame

Don't confuse fame with success. Madonna is one, and Helen Keller is the other.

Erma Bombeck

(Success, Character)

The fame of great men should always be judged by the methods they employed to achieve it.

Francois de la Rochefoucauld

(Character, Achievement)

Family

Abraham was chosen to be a blessing to the whole earth, but his vocation was to begin to take effect in the simplest way. He was called to teach his own household, who again would hand down the truth to their households. His being a blessing to the world depended on his being a blessing to his own home.

James Strachan

(Blessing, Home)

The Christian home is the Master's workshop where the processes of character molding are silently, lovingly, faithfully, and successfully carried on.

Lord Houghton

(Character, Home)

The tragedy of my life is that although I've led thousands of people to Jesus Christ, my own sons are not saved.

Billy Sunday

(Children, Salvation)

Fanaticism

A fanatic is a person who can't change his mind and won't change the subject.

Winston Churchill

(Conviction, Change)

Our trouble with earnestness is that those who are possessed by it so often take it as proof certain that they are on God's side.

Eliot Porter

(Conviction, Humility)

Fatalism

I'm not a fatalist. And even if I were, what could I do about it?

Emo Philips

(Will, Freedom)

Fatherhood of God

We want, in fact, not so much a Father in heaven as a grandfather in heaven—a senile benevolence who, as they say, "liked to see young people enjoying themselves" and whose plan for the universe was simply that it might be truly said at the end of each day, "a good time was had by all."

J. B. Phillips

(Theology, Indulgence)

Faultfinding

The initial temptation to try and fill one's predecessor's shoes is soon followed by another—the temptation to fill them with clay.

Dick Rasanen

(Criticism, Envy)

Fear

Not to fear is the armor.

Ulrich Zwingli

(Courage, Protection)

No one loves the man whom he fears.

Aristotle

(Love, Relationships)

Fear knocked at the door. Faith answered. No one was there.

Unknown

(Faith, Courage)

Fear of God

Erase all thought and fear of God from a community, and selfishness and sensuality would trample in scorn on the restraints of human laws. Virtue, duty, and principle would be mocked as unmeaning sounds.

William Ellery Channing

(Selfishness, Virtue)

The remarkable thing about fearing God is that when you fear God you fear nothing else, whereas if you do not fear God you fear everything else.

Oswald Chambers

(Courage, Devotion)

Fellowship

People join churches more because they want warmth than light. . . . Sermons may get them into church the first time, but what keeps them coming are friendships that foster inward awareness and support.

Jack R. Van Ens

(Church, Friendship)

Flattery

Flattery, provided that it be disguised as something other than flattery, is infinitely sweet. So Brutus says of Caesar: "But when I tell him he hates flatterers, he says he does, being then most flattered."

Richard John Neuhaus

(Deception, Motivation)

Forgiveness

The wonder of forgiveness has become a banality. It can be the death of our faith if we forget that it is literally a miracle.

Helmut Thielicke

(Miracles, Faith)

What I envy most about you Christians is your forgiveness; I have nobody to forgive me.

Marghanita Laski
secular humanist and novelist, before her death in 1988

(Witness, Guilt)

We pardon in the degree that we love.

Francois de la Rochefoucauld

(Love, Pardon)

Free Will

If there are a thousand steps between us and God, he will take all but one. He will leave the final one for us. The choice is ours.

Max Lucado

(Evangelism, Salvation)

Freedom

I have on my table a violin string. It is free. I twist one end of it and it responds. It is free. But it is not free to do what a violin string is supposed to do—to produce music. So I take it, fix it in my violin, and tighten it until it is taut. Only then is it free to be a violin string.

Sir Rabindranath Tagore

(Self-restraint, Duty)

Friendship

Oh, the inexpressible comfort of feeling safe with a person; having neither to weigh thoughts nor measure words, but to pour them all out, just as they are, chaff and grain together, knowing that a faithful hand will take and sift them, keep what is worth keeping, and then, with the breath of kindness, blow the rest away.

George Eliot

(Listening, Kindness)

We love those who know the worst of us and don't turn their faces away.

Walker Percy

(Love, Devotion)

Future

We should all be concerned about the future because we will have to spend the rest of our lives there.

Charles F. Kettering

(Concern, Life)

G

Gifts

God does not require that each individual shall have capacity for everything.

Richard Rothe

(Limitations, Acceptance)

I have known projects abandoned for lack of funds, but not for lack of the gifts of the Spirit. Provided the human resources are adequate we take the spiritual for granted.

John V. Taylor

(Holy Spirit, Self-reliance)

Giving

You give but little when you give of your possessions. It is when you give of yourself that you truly give.

Kahlil Gibran

(Possessions, Stewardship)

Glory

God is looking for men in whose hands his glory is safe.

A. W. Tozer

(God, Humility)

Resolved: that all men should live for the glory of God. Resolved second: that whether others do or not, I will.

Jonathan Edwards

(Determination, Purpose)

Your great glory is not to be inferior to what God has made you.

Pericles

(Acceptance, Gifts)

God

If God exists, everything is possible; if there is no God, everything is permitted.

Fyodor Dostoyevsky

(Sin, Possibilities)

One can be a good Jew, or a good Christian, with God or against God, but not without God.

Elie Wiesel

(God's Presence, Faith)

God's might to direct me
God's power to protect me
God's wisdom for learning
God's eye for discerning
God's ear for my hearing
God's Word for my clearing.

Saint Patrick

(Word of God, Power)

If you can explain what God is doing in your ministry, then God is not really in it.

Warren W. Wiersbe

(Ministry, Understanding)

To know and to serve God, of course, is why we're here, a clear truth that, like the nose on your face, is near at hand and easily discernible but can make you dizzy if you try to focus on it hard. But a little faith will see you through.

Garrison Keillor

(Knowledge, Service)

Let us think often that our only business in this life is to please God.

Brother Lawrence

(Discipleship, Devotion)

God's Knowledge

Nothing will more quickly rid us of laziness and coldness, of hypocrisy, cowardice, and pride than the knowledge that God sees, hears, and takes account.

John R. W. Stott

(Motivation, Sin)

Though you are one of the teeming millions in this world, and though the world would have you believe that you do not count and that you are but a speck in the mass, God says, "I know you."

D. Martyn Lloyd-Jones

(Value, Worth)

God's Will

O Lord, grant that I may do thy will as if it were my will; so that thou mayest do my will as if it were thy will.

Augustine

(Obedience, Surrender)

Never confuse the will of the majority with the will of God.

Charles Colson

(Peer Pressure, Obedience)

To what are we to be consecrated? Not to Christian work, but to the will of God, to be and to do whatever he requires.

Watchman Nee

(Ministry, Obedience)

I have found that the most extravagant dreams of boyhood have not surpassed the great experience of being in the will of God, and I believe that nothing could be better.

Jim Elliot

(Reward, Satisfaction)

Spread out your petition before God, and then say, "Thy will, not mine, be done." The sweetest lesson I have learned in God's school is to let the Lord choose for me.

D. L. Moody

(Prayer, Sovereignty)

I believe the will of God prevails; without him all human reliance is vain; without the assistance of that Divine Being I cannot succeed; with that assistance I cannot fail.

Abraham Lincoln

(Self-reliance, Success)

Four questions a Christian might ask when making a career decision: (1) Is this a realistic opportunity? (2) Am I reasonably prepared to meet the challenge? (3) What is the counsel of godly men I respect? (4) What is the leading of the Holy Spirit?

Ed MacAteer

(Guidance, Decisions)

God's Work

To have God do his own work through us, even once, is better than a lifetime of human striving.

Watchman Nee

(Sovereignty, Submission)

I used to ask God to help me. Then I asked if I might help him. I ended up asking him to do his work through me.

J. Hudson Taylor

(Service, Ministry)

God's Wrath

God's wrath is his utter intolerance of whatever degrades and destroys. He hates iniquity as a mother hates the polio that would take the life of the child.

A. W. Tozer

(Sin, Holiness)

Good Works

We can't save ourselves by pulling on our bootstraps, even when the bootstraps are made of the finest religious leather.

Eugene Peterson

(Salvation, Self-reliance)

Do all the good you can,
By all the means you can,
In all the ways you can,
In all the places you can,
At all the times you can,
To all the people you can,
As long as ever you can.

John Wesley

(Service, Missions)

The person who looks for quick results in the seed planting of well-doing will be disappointed. If I want potatoes for dinner tomorrow, it will do me little good to plant them in my garden tonight. There are long stretches of darkness and invisibility and silence that separate planting and reaping.

Eugene Peterson

(Patience, Results)

A do-gooder is a person trying to live beyond his spiritual income.

H. A. Williams

(Character, Maturity)

Gospel

The resurrection is not only the Good News, it is the best news imaginable.

Ray C. Stedman

(Resurrection, Easter)

Gossip

One of the striking differences between a cat and a lie is a cat only has nine lives.

Mark Twain

(Truth, Lying)

Loose lips sink ships.

World War II poster

(Speech, Self-control)

It takes two years to learn to talk and seventy years to learn to control your mouth.

Unknown

(Speech, Truth)

Government

Just be glad you're not getting all the government you're paying for.

Will Rogers

(Politics, Corruption)

The whole art of government consists in being honest.

Thomas Jefferson

(Honesty, Leadership)

Grace

Those who would avoid the despair of sinfulness by staying far from God find they have also missed the forgiving grace of God.

Charles E. Wolfe

(Sin, Forgiveness)

Cheap grace is the grace we bestow on ourselves. Cheap grace is the preaching of forgiveness without requiring repentance, baptism without church discipline, Communion without confession. Cheap grace is grace without discipleship, grace without the cross, grace without Jesus Christ, living and incarnate.

Dietrich Bonhoeffer

(Repentance, Discipline)

Remember the great need you have of the grace and assistance of God. You should never lose sight of him—not for a moment.

Andrew Murray

(God, Vision)

Saving grace makes a man as willing to leave his lusts as a slave is willing to leave his galley, or a prisoner his dungeon, or a thief his bolts, or a beggar his rags.

Thomas Brooks

(Repentance, Change)

Greatness

It is a rough road that leads to the heights of greatness.

Seneca

(Trials, Character)

Those who aim at great deeds must also suffer greatly.

Plutarch

(Suffering, Achievement)

Growth

Growth for the sake of growth is the ideology of the cancer cell.

Edward Abbey

(Maturity, Evangelism)

If you have the Spirit without the Word, you blow up. If you have the Word without the Spirit, you dry up. If you have both the Word and the Spirit, you grow up.

Don Lyon

(Holy Spirit, Word of God)

The Christian walk is much like riding a bicycle; we are either moving forward or falling off.

Robert Tuttle

(Progress, Backsliding)

Guilt

I find it impossible to avoid offending guilty men, for there is no way of avoiding it but by our silence or their patience; and silent we cannot be because of God's command, and patient they cannot be because of their guilt.

Martin Luther

(Truth, Conviction)

Happiness

The grand essentials of happiness are: something to do, something to love, and something to hope for.

Thomas Chalmers

(Purpose, Hope)

When one door of happiness closes, another opens; but often we look so long at the closed door that we do not see the one which has been opened for us.

Helen Keller

(Faith, Perspective)

There are three kinds of people: those who have sought God and found him, and these are reasonable and happy; those who seek God and have not yet found him, and these are reasonable and unhappy; and those who neither seek God nor find him, and these are unreasonable and unhappy.

Blaise Pascal

(God, Satisfaction)

If your happiness (or health) depends on what somebody else says (or does), I guess you do have a problem.

Richard Bach

(Acceptance, Peer Pressure)

I think we have lost the old knowledge that happiness is overrated. . . . Our ancestors believed in two worlds, and understood this to be the solitary, poor, nasty, brutish, and short one. We are the first generation of man that actually expected to find happiness here on earth, and our search for it has caused such unhappiness.

Peggy Noonan

(Eternity, Contentment)

Feeling better has become more important to us than finding God.

Larry Crabb

(Feelings, Faith)

Hatred

Hate is born when men call evil good. And like an infant serpent bursting from its small, confining shell, it can never be cased so small again.

Calvin Miller

(Evil, Sin)

I hate everybody. I know they say, "Now, you can't hate the world; don't be bitter." But I just hate everybody.

Mike Tyson

(Bitterness, Anger)

Heart

Out in front of us is the drama of men and of nations, seething, struggling, laboring, dying . . . but within the silences of the souls of men an eternal drama is ever being enacted. . . . On the outcome of this inner drama rests, ultimately, the outer pageant of history.

Thomas Kelly

(Eternity, Purpose)

Heaven

The great thing in this world is not so much where we stand as in what direction we are moving. To reach the port of heaven, we must sail sometimes with the wind and sometimes against it—but we must sail, not drift, nor lie at anchor.

Oliver Wendell Holmes

(Progress, Eternity)

We are afraid that heaven is a bribe, and that if we make it our goal we shall no longer be disinterested. It is not so. Heaven offers nothing that a mercenary soul can desire. It is safe to tell the pure in heart that they shall see God, for only the pure in heart want to.

C. S. Lewis

(Eternity, Hope)

We see heaven more clearly through the prism of tears.

Robertson McQuilken

(Sorrow, Eternity)

Hell

The one principle of hell is "I am my own!"

George MacDonald

(Self-reliance, Pride)

The mind is its own place, and in itself
Can make a Heav'n of Hell, a Hell of Heav'n.

John Milton

(Heaven, Mind)

Heroism

True heroism is remarkably sober, very undramatic. It is not the urge to surpass all others at whatever cost, but the urge to serve others at whatever cost.

Arthur Ashe

(Service, Sacrifice)

Being positive is part of being a hero—maybe the hardest part, because if you are a hero you're smart enough to know all the reasons why you should be discouraged.

Michael Dorris

(Optimism, Discouragement)

Holiness

Am I becoming more and more in love with God as a holy God, or with the conception of an amiable being who says, "Oh, well, sin doesn't matter much"?

Oswald Chambers

(God, Sin)

In our age, as in every age, people are longing for happiness, not realizing that what they are looking for is holiness.

Jerry L. Walls

(Happiness, Longing)

Some people get so caught up in their own holiness that they look at the Trinity for a possible vacancy.

John MacArthur

(Self-righteousness, Pride)

The world and the Cross do not get along too well together, and comfort and holiness do not share the same room.

Carlo Carretto

(Discipleship, Sacrifice)

All the holy men seem to have gone off and died. There's no one left but us sinners to carry on the ministry.

Jamie Buckingham

(Discipleship, Service)

Holy Spirit

We have given too much attention to methods and to machinery and to resources, and too little to the Source of Power, the filling with the Holy Ghost.

J. Hudson Taylor

(Power, Unction)

Nothing is more dangerous than to put a wedge between the Word and the Spirit, to emphasize either one at the expense of the other. It is the Spirit and the Word, the Spirit upon the Word, and the Spirit in us as we read the Word.

D. Martyn Lloyd-Jones

(Word of God, Bible)

The church wants not more consecrated philanthropists, but a disciplined priesthood of theocentric souls who shall be tools and channels of the Spirit of God.

Evelyn Underhill

(Stewardship, Obedience)

I have a glove here in my hand. The glove cannot do anything by itself, but when my hand is in it, it can do many things. True, it is not the glove, but my hand in the glove that acts.

We are gloves. It is the Holy Spirit in us who is the hand, who does the job. We have to make room for the hand so that every finger is filled.

Corrie ten Boom

(Obedience, Sanctification)

Every time we say, "I believe in the Holy Spirit," we mean that we believe that there is a living God able and willing to enter human personality and change it.

J. B. Phillips

(Change, Faith)

Home

Home is where people go when they're tired of being nice.

Anonymous

(Family, Relationships)

Honesty

To be persuasive, we must be believable. To be believable, we must be credible. To be credible, we must be truthful.

Edward R. Murrow

(Credibility, Truth)

Do not expect God to cover what you are not willing to uncover.

Duncan Campbell

(Confession, Truth)

If we are honest, we must admit that much of our time is spent pretending. But when we turn to God in prayer, we must present our real selves, candidly acknowledging our strengths and weaknesses and our total dependence on him.

Anonymous

(Prayer, Confession)

The elegance of honesty needs no adornment.

Merry Browne

(Truth, Speech)

Hope

Hope has two beautiful daughters. Their names are anger and courage; anger at the way things are, and courage to see that they do not remain the way they are.

Augustine

(Anger, Courage)

Man is a creature of hope and invention, both of which belie the idea that things cannot be changed.

Tom Clancy

(Despair, Courage)

Human Nature

God had enough for a saint and a devil, and he put it all in me.

Johann Wolfgang Goethe

(Self-evaluation, Depravity)

So far I have never met a man who wanted to be bad. The mystery of man is that he is bad when he wants to be good.

George MacLeod

(Depravity, Goodness)

Human nature is like a drunk peasant. Lift him into the saddle on one side, over he topples on the other side.

Martin Luther

(Sin, Extremes)

Humility

Spiritual things are not to be boasted of. One can boast of worldly riches, and the paper money will not fly away unspent nor will the amount magically decrease, but the spiritual riches you boast of vanish with the telling.

Watchman Nee

(Wealth, Maturity)

Until a man is nothing, God can make nothing out of him.

Martin Luther

(God, Discipleship)

If we are sure of our God we are free to laugh at ourselves.

Madeleine L'Engle

(Laughter, Certainty)

Humility means two things. One, a capacity for self-criticism. . . . The second feature is allowing others to shine, affirming others, empowering and enabling others. Those who lack humility are dogmatic and egotistical. That masks a deep sense of insecurity. They feel the success of others is at the expense of their own fame and glory.

Cornel West

(Confidence, Affirmation)

I may have my faults, but being wrong ain't one of them.

Jimmy Hoffa

(Self-deception, Pride)

When a little child becomes conscious of being a little child, the child-likeness is gone; and when a saint becomes conscious of being a saint, something has gone wrong.

Oswald Chambers

(Pride, Self-awareness)

The man who knows his sins is greater than one who raises a dead man by his prayer. He who sighs and grieves within himself for an hour is greater than one who teaches the entire universe. He who follows Christ, alone and contrite, is greater than one who enjoys the favor of crowds in the churches.

Isaac the Syrian

(Contrition, Popularity)

All men are ordinary men; the extraordinary men are those who know it.

G. K. Chesterton

(Self-awareness, Pride)

A man is humble when he stands in the truth with a knowledge and appreciation for himself as he really is.

The Cloud of Unknowing

(Self-awareness, Truth)

If you see another stumble or fall, let your first thought be that, of all men, you are most likely to stumble or fall in that same manner.

Thomas à Kempis

(Self-awareness, Empathy)

Lord, when we are wrong, make us willing to change. And when we are right, make us easy to live with.

Peter Marshall Sr.

(Change, Graciousness)

Humor

Anyone without a sense of humor is at the mercy of everyone else.

William Rotsler

(Attitude, Community)

Hypocrisy

What was so bad about [the Pharisees'] hypocrisy? . . . They were using God and the things of God as a means to some other end. "They do all their deeds to be noticed by men" (Matt. 23:5 NASB). . . . Better to ignore God altogether than to exploit him as a means to something else you value more highly.

John Boykin

(God, Sin)

I

Imitation

Christian literature, to be accepted and approved by evangelical leaders of our time, must follow very closely the same train of thought, a kind of "party line" from which it is scarcely safe to depart. A half-century of this in America has made us smug and content. We imitate each other with slavish devotion. Our most strenuous efforts are put forth to try to say the same thing everyone around us is saying—and yet to find an excuse for saying it, some little safe variation on the approved theme or, if no more, at least a new illustration.

A. W. Tozer

(Truth, Art)

Individuals

The greatest works are done by the ones. The hundreds do not often do much—the companies never. It is the units, the single individuals, that are the power and the might.

Charles Spurgeon

(Power, Good Works)

Influence

If you wish to enrich days, plant flowers; If you wish to enrich years, plant trees; If you wish to enrich Eternity, plant ideals in the lives of others.

S. Truett Cathy

(Eternity, Character)

He who has influence upon the heart of God rules the world.

Helmut Thielicke

(Prayer, God)

Insight

A new insight is quite sound when a master uses it, cheapens as it becomes popular, and is unendurable when it is merely fashionable.

Charles Williams

(Popularity, Knowledge)

The situation today is:
Lots of knowledge, but little understanding.
Lots of means, but little meaning.
Lots of know-how, but little know-why.
Lots of sight, but little insight.

Robert Short

(Wisdom, Knowledge)

Integrity

Integrity is keeping my commitment even if the circumstances when I made the commitment have changed.

David Jeremiah

(Character, Perseverance)

Introspection

Look outward. You have been rightly taught Socrates' dictum that the unexamined life is not worth living. I would add: The too examined life is not worth living either.

Charles Krauthammer

(Life, Perspective)

J

Jesus

Jesus is all we have; he is all we need and all we want. We are shipwrecked on God and stranded on omnipotence!

Vance Havner

(Dependence, Christ)

Follow me; I am the way, the truth, and the life.
Without the way there is no going;
Without the truth there is no knowing;
Without the life there is no living.

Thomas à Kempis

(Christ, Truth)

To tie Jesus Christ to the very best human system is to tie a star, light years distant, to a dead horse here on earth. Neither the star nor Christ will thus be bound.

Joe Bayly

(Christ, Politics)

Jesus Christ turns life right-side-up, and heaven outside-in.

Carl F. H. Henry

(Christ, Heaven)

Joy

Surely there can be no deeper joy than that of saving souls.

Lottie Moon

(Evangelism, Missions)

To pursue joy is to lose it. The only way to get it is to follow steadily the path of duty, without thinking of joy, and then, like sheep, it comes most surely, unsought, and we "being in the way," the angel of God, fair-haired joy, is sure to meet us.

Alexander MacLaren

(Duty, Devotion)

Joy bursts in on our lives when we go about doing the good at hand and not trying to manipulate things and times to achieve joy.

C. S. Lewis

(Manipulation, Ministry)

Joy is never in our power and pleasure often is.

C. S. Lewis

(Christ, Pleasure)

This is the land of sin and death and tears . . . but up yonder is unceasing joy!

D. L. Moody

(Heaven, Sorrow)

Judgment

I shall tell you a great secret, my friend. Do not wait for the Last Judgment. It takes place every day.

Albert Camus

(Eschatology, Conviction)

To sensible men, every day is a day of reckoning.

John W. Gardner

(Reason, Accountability)

K

Kindness

Kindness is more important than wisdom, and the recognition of this is the beginning of wisdom.

Theodore Isaac Rubin, M.D.

(Wisdom, Love)

Kingdoms

The fundamental biblical opposition is not between flesh and Spirit, creature and Creator, but between the Creator of the flesh and its destroyer, between God and the devil, Christ and Satan, the Holy Spirit and the unholy.

Philip S. Watson

(Spiritual Warfare, Satan)

Knowing God

You will never be satisfied just to know *about* God. Really knowing God only comes through experience as he reveals himself to you.

Henry Blackaby

(Worship, Obedience)

Our soundest knowledge is to know that we know God not as indeed he is, neither can we know him; and our safest eloquence concerning him is our silence, when we confess, without confession, that his glory is inexplainable, his greatness above our capacity and reach.

Richard Hooker

(Worship, Omnipotence)

Knowledge

The experts don't know for sure how old or how big the universe is. They don't know what most of it is made of. They don't know in any detail how it began or how it will end.

Time *magazine*

(Science, Creation)

I use not only all the brains I have, but all I can borrow.

Woodrow Wilson

(Thinking, Learning)

The beautiful, the good, the true cannot be weighed and measured. True knowledge is spiritual knowledge, which is beyond the reach of the world of quantity and therefore is disregarded by our civilization.

Paul Tournier

(Wisdom, Virtue)

L

Labels

It seems that more than ever the compulsion today is to identify, to reduce someone to what is on the label. To identify is to control, to limit.

To love is to call by name, and so open the wide gates of creativity.

Madeleine L'Engle

(Stereotyping, Love)

Labor

He who labors diligently need never despair; for all things are accomplished by diligence and labor.

Menander

(Work, Despair)

Laziness

When all is said and done, as a rule, more is said than done.

Lou Holtz

(Work, Talk)

Leadership

The job of a football coach is to make men do what they don't want to do, in order to achieve what they've always wanted to be.

Tom Landry

(Discipleship, Teamwork)

Alexander, Caesar, and Hannibal conquered the world but they had no friends. . . . Jesus founded his empire upon love, and at this hour millions would die for him. . . . He has won the hearts of men, a task a conqueror cannot do.

Napoleon Bonaparte

(Devotion, Motivation)

Why have we no great men? We have no great men chiefly because we are always looking for them. We are connoisseurs of greatness, and connoisseurs can never be great. . . . When anybody goes about on his hands and knees looking for a great man to worship, he is making sure that one man at any rate shall not be great.

G. K. Chesterton

(Character, Humility)

The pioneers are the guys with the arrows in their backs.

Erwin Potts

(Vision, Criticism)

The best decision makers are those who are willing to suffer the most over their decisions but still retain their ability to be decisive.

M. Scott Peck

(Compassion, Conviction)

At the end of the days of truly great leaders, the people will say about them, "We did it ourselves."

Lao-Tzu

(Empowerment, Discipleship)

Our task is not to bring order out of chaos, but to get work done in the midst of chaos.

George Peabody

(Productivity, Focus)

Qualifications of a pastor: He must have the mind of a scholar, the heart of a child, and the hide of a rhinoceros.

Stuart Briscoe

(Gentleness, Courage)

There they go, I must hurry, I am their leader.

Anonymous

(Vision, Pace setting)

He who thinketh he leadeth and hath no one following him is only taking a walk.

Benjamin L. Hooks

(Pace setting, Vision)

A Christian who is ambitious to be a star disqualifies himself as a leader.

David Watson

(Humility, Character)

One of the tests of leadership is to recognize a problem before it becomes an emergency.

Arnold H. Glasow

(Foresight, Wisdom)

General Eisenhower used to demonstrate the art of leadership with a simple piece of string. He'd put it on a table and say: "Pull it, and it'll follow wherever you wish. Push it and it will go nowhere at all."

Dwight D. Eisenhower

(Motivation, Discipleship)

Disturbers are to be rebuked, the low-spirited to be encouraged, the infirm to be supported, objectors confuted, the treacherous guarded against, the unskilled taught, the lazy aroused, the contentious restrained, the haughty repressed, litigants pacified, the poor relieved, the oppressed liberated, the good approved, the evil borne with, and all are to be loved.

Augustine

(Ministry, Preaching)

The trouble with being a leader today is that you can't be sure whether people are following you or chasing you.

Bits & Pieces

(Criticism, Courage)

It indeed seems that the Christian leader is first of all the artist who can bind together many people by his courage in giving expression to his most personal concern.

Henri Nouwen

(Honesty, Courage)

An organization can be filled by appointments, but a team must be built by a leader.

Carl Combs

(Teamwork, Discipleship)

Life

Life is the art of drawing without an eraser.

John Christian

(Consequences, Decisions)

The monotony of life, if life is monotonous to you, is in you and not in the world.

Phillips Brooks

(Boredom, Creation)

You must live with people to know their problems, and live with God in order to solve them.

P. T. Forsyth

(Ministry, Discipleship)

Seek to live with such lucidity that the clarity of your motives becomes a lens which projects the image of Christ upon the screens of others' lives.

David Augsburger

(Christlikeness, Character)

If God does not enter your kitchen, there is something wrong with your kitchen. If you can't take God into your recreation, there is something wrong with your play. . . . We all believe in the God of the heroic. What we need most these days is the God of the humdrum—the commonplace, the everyday.

Peter Marshall

(Discipleship, God's Presence)

Listening

The most important thing in communication is to hear what isn't being said.

Peter Drucker

(Communication, Relationships)

He who can no longer listen to his brother will soon no longer be listening to God, either.

Dietrich Bonhoeffer

(Communication, Relationships)

Loneliness

The biggest disease today is not leprosy or cancer. It's the feeling of being uncared for, unwanted—of being deserted and alone.

Mother Teresa

(Disease, Compassion)

Longsuffering

To become longsuffering one has to be long-bothered.

Manford George Gutzke

(Patience, Character)

Lordship

To love and admire anything outside yourself is to take one step away from utter spiritual ruin; though we shall not be well so long as we love and admire anything more than we love and admire God.

C. S. Lewis

(Devotion, Idolatry)

Love

When we preach atonement, it is atonement planned by love, provided by love, given by love, finished by love, necessitated because of love. When we preach the resurrection of Christ, we are preaching the miracle of love. When we preach the return of Christ, we are preaching the fulfillment of love.

Billy Graham

(Atonement, Salvation)

God loves us the way we are, but he loves us too much to leave us that way.

Leighton Ford

(Change, Acceptance)

When [Jesus] wrapped a towel around his waist, poured water into a basin, and began to wash his disciples' feet (see John 13:4–5), Simon Peter objected that this was beneath the dignity of the Master. We the disciples are to be the servants, I want to insist along with Peter. But Jesus answered him, "If I do not wash you, you have no part in me." This is a stunning and stupendous thought. Unless I can believe in this much love for me, unless I can and will accept him with faith as my servant as well as my God, unless I truly know that it's my good he seeks, not his glory . . . then I cannot have his companionship. What an amazing revelation!

Catherine Marshall

(Service, Devotion)

How do I want to be remembered? Not primarily as a Christian scholar but rather as a loving person. This can be the goal of every individual.

Elton Trueblood

(Legacy, Goals)

More people have been brought into the church by the kindness of real Christian love than by all the theological arguments in the world, and more people have been driven from the church by the hardness and ugliness of so-called Christianity than by all the doubts in the world.

William Barclay

(Christianity, Church)

The height of our love for God will never exceed the depth of our love for one another.

Patrick Morley

(Fellowship, Community)

Love should cast out terror, but not awe. True love must include awe. This is one of the great truths about sex and marriage that our age has tragically forgotten: awe at the great mystery that is sex. . . . God is love. But love is not *luv.* Love is not *nice.* Love is a fire, storm, earthquake, volcano, lightning, and hurricane. Love endured the hell of the cross.

Peter Kreeft

(Sex, Awe)

A man is only as good as what he loves.

Saul Bellow

(Character, Devotion)

I have found the paradox that if I love until it hurts, then there is no more hurt, but only more love.

Mother Teresa

(Sacrifice, Suffering)

Love is never lost. If not reciprocated, it will flow back and soften and purify the heart.

Washington Irving

(Character, Sanctification)

If you're going to care about the fall of the sparrow you can't pick and choose who's going to be the sparrow.

Madeleine L'Engle

(Servanthood, Compassion)

Love is . . . a free gift. . . . And it is most itself, most free when it is offered in spite of suffering, of injustice, and of death.

Archibald MacLeish

(Sacrifice, Servanthood)

People need love, especially when they don't deserve it.

Unknown

(Devotion, Compassion)

Christians state glibly that they love the whole world, while they permit themselves animosities within their immediate world. . . . But loving the world at large can only be done by loving face-to-face the world that is not so distant.

Calvin Miller

(Compassion, World)

Lying

A lie is like a snowball. The longer it is rolled on the ground the larger it becomes.

Martin Luther

(Consequences, Sin)

M

Marriage

The difficulty with marriage is that we fall in love with a personality but must live with a character.

Peter DeVries

(Family, Love)

In domestic affairs, I am led by Katie [my wife]. In all other matters, I am led by the Holy Ghost.

Martin Luther

(Holy Spirit, Submission)

Marriage is somewhat like undertaking a Lego project without instructions.

Ammunni Bala Subramanian

(Husbands, Wives)

The concept of two people living together for twenty-five years without a serious dispute suggests a lack of spirit only to be admired in sheep.

Walter Lippman

(Conflict, Timidity)

Martyrdom

The blood of the martyrs is the seed of the church.

Tertullian

(Sacrifice, Church)

Materialism

The late Bishop Edwin Hughes once delivered a rousing sermon on "God's Ownership" that offended a rich parishioner. The wealthy man took the bishop off for lunch, and then walked him through his elaborate gardens, woodlands, and farm. "Now are you going to tell me," he demanded when the tour was completed, "that all this land does not belong to me?" Bishop Hughes smiled and suggested, "Ask me that same question a hundred years from now."

(Eternity, Greed)

The essence of life today is not having—it is having to have.

David Hansen

(Greed, Lifestyle)

The world would be better off if people tried to become better. And people would become better if they stopped trying to become better off. For when everybody tries to become better off, nobody becomes better off. But when everybody tries to become better, everybody is better off.

Peter Maurin

(Service, Greed)

Media

I keep reading between the lies.

Goodman Ace

(Deception, Culture)

Meditation

A garment that is double dyed, dipped again and again, will retain the color a great while; so a truth which is the subject of meditation.

Philip Henry

(Truth, Study)

Meekness

The meek man is not a human mouse afflicted with a sense of his own inferiority. Rather, he may be in his moral life as bold as a lion and as strong as Samson; but he has stopped being fooled about himself. He has accepted God's estimate of his own life. He knows he is as weak and helpless as God has declared him to be, but paradoxically, he knows at the same time that he is, in the sight of God, more important than angels.

A. W. Tozer

(Courage, Self-evaluation)

Memories

You can close your eyes to reality but not to memories.

Stanislaw J. Lee

(Deception, Denial)

Men

There is one unmistakable lesson in American history: A community that allows a large number of young men to grow up in broken families, dominated by women, never acquiring any stable relationship to male authority, never acquiring any set of rational expectations about the future—that community asks for and gets chaos. Crime, violence, unrest, disorder—most particularly the furious, unrestrained lashing out at the whole social structure—that is not only to be expected; it is very near to inevitable.

Daniel Patrick Moynihan

(Family, Society)

Mercy

We are God's tenants here, and yet here he, our landlord, pays us rents—not yearly, nor quarterly, but hourly and quarterly; every minute he renews his mercy.

John Donne

(Grace, Hope)

Ministry

If you are Christian, then you are a minister. A nonministering Christian is a contradiction in terms.

D. Elton Trueblood

(Lifestyle, Example)

The three qualifications for the ministry are the grace of God, knowledge of the sacred Scriptures, and gumption.

Samuel Johnson

(Scripture, Character)

Our office is a ministry of grace and salvation. It subjects us to great burdens and labors, dangers and temptations, with little reward or gratitude from the world. But Christ himself will be our reward if we labor faithfully.

Martin Luther

(Sacrifice, Servanthood)

It is one of the ironies of the ministry that the very man who works in God's name is often hardest put to find time for God. The parents of Jesus lost him at church, and they were not the last ones to lose him there.

Vance Havner

(Time, Priorities)

A pastor needs three bones to remain upright, a backbone, a wishbone, and a funny bone.

Anonymous

(Courage, Hope)

Shun, as you would the plague, a cleric who from being poor has become wealthy, or who from being nobody has become a celebrity.

Jerome

(Fame, Pride)

Ministers are like trumpets, which make no sound if breath be not breathed into them. Or like Ezekiel's wheels, which move not unless the Spirit move them. Or like Elisha's servants whose presence does no good unless Elisha's spirit be there also.

John Flavel

(Holy Spirit, Unction)

When a minister is "too charming," he is always in demand for events of small spiritual significance.

Paul M. Schmidt

(Character, Leadership)

Ministers cannot walk on water; but they can learn to swim.

Edward Bratcher

(Leadership, Discipleship)

God makes his ministers a flame of fire. Am I ignitable? God, deliver me from the dread asbestos of "other things." Saturate me with the oil of thy Spirit that I may be a flame. Make me thy fuel, Flame of God.

Jim Elliot

(Holy Spirit, Unction)

Misfortune

Mishaps are like knives, that either serve us or cut us, as we grasp them by the blade or the handle.

James Russell Lowell

(Perspective, Pain)

Missions

We are all missionaries. Wherever we go, we either bring people nearer to Christ, or we repel them from Christ.

Eric Liddell

(Evangelism, Example)

We have a whole Christ for our salvation, a whole Bible for our staff, a whole church for our fellowship, and a whole world for our parish.

John Chrysostom

(Evangelism, Salvation)

The mission of the church is missions.

Unknown

(Church, Goals)

Mistakes

Strong people make as many and as ghastly mistakes as weak people. The difference is that strong people admit them, laugh at them, learn from them. That is how they become strong.

Richard J. Needham

(Failure, Maturity)

Money

For every verse in the Bible that tells us the benefits of wealth, there are ten that tell us the danger of wealth.

Haddon Robinson

(Materialism, Greed)

Money will buy a bed but not sleep; books but not brains; food but not appetite; finery but not beauty; a house but not a home; medicine but not health; luxuries but not culture; amusements but not happiness; religion but not salvation—a passport to everywhere but heaven.

Voice in the Wilderness

(Materialism, Satisfaction)

God entrusts us with money as a test; for like a toy to the child, it is training for handling things of more value.

Fred Smith

(Testing, Character)

Satan now is wiser than of yore. And tempts by making rich, not by making poor.

Alexander Pope

(Materialism, Wealth)

When a fellow says, "It isn't the money but the principle of the thing"—it's the money.

Kin Hubbard

(Integrity, Lying)

Jesus talked much about money. Sixteen of the thirty-eight parables were concerned with how to handle money and possessions. In the Gospels, an amazing one out of ten verses deal directly with the subject of money. The Bible offers 500 verses on prayer, less than 500 verses on faith, but more than 2,000 verses on money and possessions.

Howard L. Dayton Jr.

(Bible, Materialism)

There is no dignity quite so impressive, and no independence quite so important, as living within your means.

Calvin Coolidge

(Stewardship, Giving)

He that serves God for money will serve the devil for better wages.

Sir Robert L'Estrange

(Devil, Service)

Get all you can.
Save all you can.
Give all you can.

John Wesley

(Saving, Giving)

Nothing that is God's is obtainable by money.

Tertullian

(Wealth, Salvation)

Almost all reformers, however strict their social conscience, live in houses as big as they can pay for.

Logan Pearsall Smith

(Conscience, Materialism)

Mothers

Let France have good mothers and she will have good sons.

Napoleon

(Sons, Parenting)

All I am my mother made me.

John Quincy Adams

(Parenting, Character)

I believe in the love of all mothers,
and its importance in the lives of the children they bear.
It is stronger than steel, softer than down,
and more resilient than a green sapling on the hillside.
It closes wounds, melts disappointments,
and enables the weakest child to stand tall
and straight in the fields of adversity.
I believe that this love, even at its best,
is only a shadow of the love of God. . . .
And I believe that one of the most beautiful sights
in the world is a mother who lets this greater love
flow through her to her child,
blessing the world with the tenderness of her touch
and the tears of her joy.

John Killinger

(Love, Sacrifice)

Motivation

The oilcan is mightier than the sword.

Everett Dirksen

(Complaining, Leadership)

Motives

No man knows what he is living for until he knows what he'll die for.

Peter Pertocci

(Causes, Courage)

God uses lust to impel man to marriage, ambition to office, avarice to earning, and fear to faith.

Martin Luther

(Sin, Character)

Music

The devil should not be allowed to keep all the best tunes for himself.

Martin Luther

(Devil, Worship)

Next after theology, I give to music the highest place and the greatest honor.

Martin Luther

(Theology, Worship)

N

Narcissism

You cannot at the same time show that Christ is wonderful—and you are clever.

Principal Denny of Scotland

(Witness, Christ)

Christ sends none away empty but those who are full of themselves.

Donald Gray Barnhouse

(Emptiness, Gifts)

Nature

Nature is the art of God.

Thomas Brown

(Creation, Art)

Neglect

The untended garden will soon be overrun with weeds; the heart that fails to cultivate truth and root out error will shortly be a theological wilderness.

A. W. Tozer

(Error, Truth)

Neighbors

The Bible tells us to love our neighbors, and also to love our enemies; probably because generally they are the same people.

G. K. Chesterton

(Love, Enemies)

New Age

I don't . . . think any real journey is beginning with the New Age movement. I think it's more a detour, a truck stop on the way to the Rockies.

Peggy Noonan

(Religion, Mysticism)

O

Obedience

If God be God over us, we must yield him universal obedience in all things. He must not be over us in one thing, and under us in another, but he must be over us in everything.

Peter Bulkeley

(Sovereignty, Submission)

The fruit of the Spirit grows only in the garden of obedience.

Terry Fullam

(Lifestyle, Character)

Do not quench the Spirit. . . . When it moves and stirs in you, be obedient; but do not go beyond, nor add to it, nor take from it.

George Fox

(Holy Spirit, Devotion)

All the good maxims have been written. It only remains to put them into practice.

Blaise Pascal

(Lifestyle, Action)

It is our business to see that we do right; God will see that we come out right.

Donald Gray Barnhouse

(Discipleship, Character)

He that cannot obey, cannot command.

Benjamin Franklin

(Leadership, Character)

Opposition

We are so outnumbered there's only one thing to do. We must attack.

Sir Andrew Cunningham

(Courage, Trials)

P

Parables

You cannot tell people what to do, you can only tell them parables; and that is what art really is, particular stories of particular people and experiences.

W. H. Auden

(Preaching, Communication)

Parenting

The parent who exerts his or her power most drastically over children loses all power over them, except the power to twist and hurt and destroy.

Garry Wills

(Power, Children)

My major effort must be devoted to my children. If Caroline and John turn out badly, nothing I could do in the public eye would have any meaning.

Jacqueline Kennedy Onassis
Shortly after she entered the White House in 1960

(Children, Fame)

Passion

The core problem is not that we are too passionate about bad things, but that we are not passionate enough about good things.

Larry Crabb

(Conviction, Goodness)

Patience

Second only to suffering, waiting may be the greatest teacher and trainer in godliness, maturity, and genuine spirituality most of us ever encounter.

Richard Hendrix

(Maturity, Godliness)

God's Word often refers to the Christian experience as a walk, seldom as a run, and never as a mad dash.

Steven J. Cole

(Stress, Burnout)

He is not truly patient who will suffer only as much as he pleases or from whom he pleases. A truly patient man gives no heed from whom he suffers, whether from his superior or from his equal or from someone below him.

Thomas à Kempis

(Suffering, Surrender)

Peace

Have peace in your heart, and thousands will be saved around you.

Seraphin of Sarov

(Salvation, Witness)

Peace is not the absence of trouble. Peace is the presence of God.

Unknown

(God's Presence, Difficulty)

God . . . "works always in tranquility." Fuss and feverishness, anxiety, intensity, intolerance, instability, pessimism and wobble, and every kind of hurry and worry—these, even on the highest levels, are signs of the self-made and self-acting soul; the spiritual parvenu. The saints are never like that. They share the quiet and noble qualities of the great family to which they belong.

Evelyn Underhill

(Self-reliance, Stress)

Persecution

The greatest criticism of the church today is that no one wants to persecute it: because there is nothing very much to persecute it about.

George F. MacLeod

(Church, Conviction)

Perseverance

To cling to God and to the things of God—this must be our major effort, this must be the road that the heart follows.

John Cassian

(God, Heart)

Never, never, never, never give up.

Winston Churchill

(Quitting, Endurance)

The woman who stayed behind to seek Christ was the only one to see him. For perseverance is essential to any good deed, as the voice of truth tells us: "Whosoever perseveres to the end will be saved."

Gregory the Great

(Good Works, Christ)

Let me tell you the secret that has led me to my goal. My strength lies solely in my tenacity.

Louis Pasteur

(Tenacity, Success)

Perspective

My grandmother used to tell me that every boss is temporary, that every rainy day is temporary, that every hardship is temporary. She used to tell me, "Son, every good-bye ain't gone. Just hold on—there's joy coming in the morning."

James Melvin Washington

(Difficulty, Hope)

If the only tool you have is a hammer, you tend to see every problem as a nail.

Abraham Maslow

(Leadership, Solutions)

You are given a situation. What you are determines what you see; what you see determines what you do.

Haddon Robinson

(Solutions, Leadership)

The young man who has not wept is a savage, and the old man who will not laugh is a fool.

George Santayana

(Grief, Laughter)

The greatest thing a human soul ever does in this world is to see something and tell what it saw in a plain way. Hundreds of people can talk for one who can think, but thousands can think for one who can see. To see clearly is poetry, prophecy, and religion, all in one.

John Ruskin

(Leadership, Vision)

Politics

Too many of us Christians confuse political convictions with spiritual convictions. Insecure with ambiguity, we assume people of one Lord, one faith, and one baptism must also promote one political agenda. That assumption leads the church into trouble. First, it prompts us to make judgments about people that ought to be left to God. . . . Second, when the church confuses spiritual and political convictions it is tempted to use political power to forward a "spiritual" agenda.

Don Ratzlaff

(Judgment, Conviction)

What's real in politics is what the voters decide is real.

Ben J. Wattenberg

(Truth, Values)

Popularity

To set one's heart on being popular is fatal to the preacher's best growth. It is the worst and feeblest part of your congregation that makes itself heard in vociferous applause, and it applauds that in you which pleases it.

Phillips Brooks

(Pride, Deception)

We honor God when we ask for great things. It is a humiliating thing to think that we are satisfied with very small results.

D. L. Moody

(Honor, Satisfaction)

Prayer

Heaven is full of answers to prayers for which no one ever bothered to ask.

Billy Graham

(Heaven, Apathy)

I am often, I believe, praying for others when I should be doing things for them. It's so much easier to pray for a bore than to go and see him.

C. S. Lewis

(Action, Good Works)

Souls without prayer are like people whose bodies or limbs are paralyzed: They possess feet and hands but they cannot control them.

Teresa of Avila

(Growth, Self-control)

In prayer it is better to have a heart without words than words without heart.

John Bunyan

(Sincerity, Conviction)

I have often learned more in one prayer than I have been able to glean from much reading and reflection.

Martin Luther

(Study, Learning)

He who prays fervently knows not whether he prays or not, for he is not thinking of the prayer which he makes, but of God, to whom he makes it.

Francis de Sales

(Devotion, Submission)

As we are involved in unceasing thinking, so we are called to unceasing prayer.

Henri Nouwen

(Spirituality, Devotion)

I have been driven many times to my knees by the overwhelming conviction that I had nowhere else to go. My wisdom, and that of all about me, seemed insufficient for the day.

Abraham Lincoln

(Seeking God, Submission)

In prayer, we are aware that God is in action and that when the circumstances are ready, when others are in the right place, and when our hearts are prepared, he will call us into the action. Waiting in prayer is a disciplined refusal to act before God acts.

Eugene Peterson

(Waiting, Trust)

Not to want to pray is the sin behind sin.

P. T. Forsyth

(Prayerlessness, Sin)

To pray is the greatest thing we can do, and to do it well, there must be calmness, time, and deliberation.

E. M. Bounds

(Time, Devotion)

The penalty of not praying is the loss of one's capacity to pray.

Edward J. Farrell

(Spiritual Neglect, Apathy)

Pray the largest prayers. You cannot think a prayer so large that God, in answering it, will not wish you had made it larger. Pray not for crutches but for wings!

Phillips Brooks

(Faith, Hope)

We are too busy to pray, and so we are too busy to have power. We have a great deal of activity but we accomplish little; many services but few conversions; much machinery but few results.

R. A. Torrey

(Power, Results)

Preaching

O God, let me preach with enthusiasm because of what Christ did, not because of what the crowds think . . . because of the salvation we have, not the size of the group we have. Use me, O God, not because it's the hour for the message, but because you've given me a message for the hour.

Ed Towne

(Conviction, Obedience)

No man is fit to preach the gospel, seeing the whole world is set against it, save only he who is armed to suffer.

John Calvin

(Suffering, Opposition)

If you ask me how you may shorten your sermons, I should say, study them better. Spend more time in the study that you may need less in the pulpit. We are generally longest when we have least to say.

Charles Spurgeon

(Study, Speech)

Those who make comfort the great subject of their preaching seem to mistake the end of their ministry. Holiness is the great end. There must be a struggle and trial here. Comfort is a cordial, but no one drinks cordials from morning to night.

John Henry Newman

(Holiness, Prophetic Voice)

To be always relevant, you have to say things which are eternal.

Simone Weil

(Eternity, Relevance)

It is not necessary for a preacher to express all his thoughts in one sermon. A preacher should have three principles, first, to make a good beginning and not spend time with many words before coming to the point; secondly, to say that which belongs to the subject in chief, and avoid strange and foreign thought; thirdly, to stop at the proper time.

Martin Luther

(Brevity, Speech)

I've heard a lot of sermons in the past ten years or so that made me want to get up and walk out. They're secular, psychological, self-help sermons. Friendly, but of no use. They didn't make you straighten up. They didn't give you anything hard. . . . At some point and in some way, a sermon has to direct people toward the death of Christ and the campaign that God has waged over the centuries to get our attention.

Garrison Keillor

(Conviction, Cross)

To preach more than half an hour, a man should be an angel himself or have angels for hearers.

George Whitefield

(Brevity, Longsuffering)

When pride has written the sermon, it goes with us to the pulpit.

Richard Baxter

(Pride, Motives)

To love to preach is one thing—to love those to whom we preach, quite another.

Richard Cecil

(Compassion, Motives)

Surely the preacher's greatest sin is to put people to sleep with the greatest story ever told.

Bruce W. Thielemann

(Boredom, Gospel)

Preaching is not the art of making a sermon and delivering it. Preaching is the art of making a preacher and delivering him.

Bishop Quayle

(Sanctification, Holiness)

All preachers must struggle for that magical note somewhere between a trumpet of uncertain sound that brings no one to battle and the tin horn that thinks itself to be Gabriel's.

Robert N. Schaper

(Conviction, Pride)

The test of a preacher is that his congregation goes away saying, not "What a lovely sermon!" but "I will do something."

Francis de Sales

(Action, Persuasion)

The true function of a preacher is to disturb the comfortable and to comfort the disturbed.

Chad Walsh

(Complacency, Comfort)

Preparation

A lasting work requires extensive preparation.

Douglas Rumford

(Endurance, Work)

Pressure

When three are shut into a furnace and three become four, that is enlargement through pressure.

Watchman Nee

(Difficulty, God's Presence)

The intensity of pressure doesn't matter as much as its location. Does it come between you and God, or does it press you closer to him?

Unknown

(Devotion, Rebellion)

Pride

A man is never so proud as when striking an attitude of humility!

C. S. Lewis

(Humility, Self-deception)

I define ego as Edging God Out.

Kenneth Blanchard

(God, Self-reliance)

It's like the beaver told the rabbit as they stared up at the immense wall of Hoover Dam, "No, I didn't actually build it myself. But it was based on an idea of mine."

Charles H. Townes,
Nobel Prize winner in laser technology

(Humility, Ambition)

Priorities

We must first be committed to Christ, then to one another in Christ, and finally to the work of Christ in the world.

Ray Ortlund

(Goals, Commitment)

Whenever we place a higher priority on solving our problems than on pursuing God, we are immoral.

Larry Crabb

(Problem solving, Immorality)

Think of only three things—your God, your family, and the Green Bay Packers—in that order.

Vince Lombardi

(God, Family)

Problems

There are three kinds of people in our society: those who can't see or refuse to see the problems; those who see the problems and because they didn't personally create them are content to blame someone else; and those who see the problems and though they didn't create them are willing to assume personal responsibility for solving them.

John Perkins

(Servanthood, Ministry)

Prosperity

Prosperity has not been kind to the American family. It breeds short, shallow roots. Fragile anchors. It's not that prosperity and wealth are inherently evil. They aren't. But their presence constantly tempts us to believe we are secure without God and that money can be an adequate substitute for real family values.

Robert Lewis

(Security, Materialism)

Protection

God has promised to keep his people, and he will keep his promise.

Charles Spurgeon

(Promises, God)

Provision

God's work done in God's way will never lack God's supply.

J. Hudson Taylor

(God, Ministry)

Purity

The pastor should always be pure in thought, inasmuch as no impurity ought to pollute him who has undertaken the office of wiping away the stains of pollution in the hearts of others . . . for the hand that would cleanse from dirt must be clean, lest, being itself sordid with clinging mire, it soil whatever it touches all the more.

Gregory the Great

(Ministry, Example)

Purpose

Great minds have purposes; others have wishes.

Washington Irving

(Vision, Wishful Thinking)

Two centuries ago, when a great man appeared, people looked for God's purpose in him. Today we look for his press agent.

Daniel Boorstin

(Fame, Popularity)

Q

Questions

God will answer all our questions in one way and one way only—namely, by showing us more of his Son.

Watchman Nee

(Jesus, Revelation)

When somebody says, "That's a good question," you can be pretty sure it's a lot better than the answer you're going to get.

Franklin P. Jones

(Certainty, Truth)

It is harder to ask a sensible question than to supply a sensible answer.

Persian proverb

(Wisdom, Knowledge)

Quitting

It is always too soon to quit.

V. Raymond Edman

(Faithfulness, Integrity)

Quitting is usually a long-term solution to a short-term problem.

Anonymous

(Conflict, Faithfulness)

R

Reconciliation

One sign and wonder . . . that alone can prove the power of the Gospel is that of reconciliation . . . Hindus can produce as many miracles as any Christian miracle worker. Islamic saints in India can produce and duplicate every miracle that has been produced by Christians. But they cannot duplicate the miracle of black and white together, of racial injustice being swept away by the power of the Gospel.

Vinay Samuel

(Miracles, Racial Injustice)

Religion

It is a great mistake to think that God is chiefly interested in religion.

William Temple

(God, Faith)

If your religion does not change you, then you should change your religion.

Elbert Hubbard

(Change, Faith)

Religion is, at its heart, a way of denying the authority of the rest of the world.

Stephen Carter

(Culture, Authority)

Religion is the best armor a man can have, but it is the worst cloak.

John Bunyan

(Hypocrisy, Strength)

Men will wrangle for religion; write for it; fight for it; die for it; anything but live for it.

C. C. Colton

(Lifestyle, Faith)

It is no disgrace to Christianity, it is no disgrace to any great religion, that its counsels of perfection have not made every single person perfect. If, after centuries, a disparity is still found between its ideal and its followers, it only means that the religion still maintains the ideal, and the followers still need it.

G. K. Chesterton

(Christianity, Perfection)

History shows that when religion wanes in any country, it is not replaced by popular rationalist philosophy that leads to a universal happiness and peace. . . . The vacuum left by the waning of religion in western countries has been filled by an army of superstitious cults and beliefs. Perfect secularism by no means casts out fear.

David H. C. Read

(Superstition, Secularism)

Religious Freedom

I have learned that the important thing for the church is not to have leaders and parish buildings, but to have Christians in the individual parishes who take the Gospel and the sacraments seriously. . . . This was a lesson for us. We had always had the church as an institution. The pastor would go to the mayor and ask for money to fix the roof. The pastor got his money and had a lifelong job; he could lose it only for reasons of immorality. . . . In the Confessing Church, we learned to give all this up—and to learn this in only twelve years is a great gift.

Pastor Friedemann M.,
remembering his years under Hitler

(Separation, Sacrifice)

Renewal

We're in need of a spiritual revival.

Norman Lear

(Revival, Awakening)

Repentance

A salty pagan, full of the juices of life, is a hundred times dearer to God, and also far more attractive to men, than a scribe who knows his Bible . . . in whom none of this results in repentance, action, and above all, death of the self. A terrible curse hangs over the know-it-all who does nothing.

Helmut Thielicke

(Hypocrisy, Apathy)

Reputation

Be more concerned with your character than with your reputation, because your character is what you really are, while your reputation is merely what others think you are.

John Wooden

(Character, Lifestyle)

Rest

I used to say that the devil never takes a vacation, so why should I?—and I never stopped to think that the devil wasn't to be my example.

Anonymous

(Devil, Vacation)

When I rest, I rust.

Martin Luther

(Lethargy, Work)

Resurrection

Jesus' resurrection makes it impossible for man's story to end in chaos—it has to move inexorably towards light, towards life, towards love.

Carolo Carretto

(Hope, Eternal Life)

Revelation

I lay it down as a foundation principle . . . that [God's] voice will always be in harmony with itself, no matter in how many different ways he may speak. The voices may be many, the message can be but one. If God tells me in one voice to do or to leave undone anything, he cannot possibly tell me the opposite in another voice. . . . Therefore my rule for distinguishing the voice of God would be to bring it to the test of this harmony.

Hannah Whitall Smith

(Guidance, God's Will)

Risk

He who deliberates fully before taking a step will spend his entire life on one leg.

Chinese proverb

(Cowardice, Timidity)

Strangely, the expounders of many of the great new ideas of history were frequently considered on the lunatic fringe for some or all of their lives. If one stands up and is counted, from time to time one may get knocked down. But remember this: A man flattened by an opponent can get up again. A man flattened by conformity stays down for good.

Thomas J. Watson Jr.

(Failure, Peer Pressure)

Take calculated risks. That is quite different from being rash.

George S. Patton

(Rashness, Reason)

Shoot for the moon. Even if you miss it, you will land among the stars.

Les Brown

(Achievement, Results)

Rumor

Rumor travels faster, but it don't stay put as long as truth.

Will Rogers

(Truth, Gossip)

S

Sabbath

All days are holy, but some are more so; all moments can be sacred, but not unless we set some aside to be intensely so.

Karen Mains

(Holiness, Time)

I can't be teaching kids how to keep the Lord's Day holy while my cash registers are ringing.

S. Truett Cathy,
Chick-Fil-A restaurant chain owner and Sunday school teacher, whose stores close on Sundays

(Example, Work)

He who wants to enter the holiness of the day must first lay down the profanity of clattering commerce, of being yoked to toil. He must go away from the screech of dissonant days, from the nervousness and fury of acquisitiveness and the betrayal in embezzling his own life. He must say farewell to manual work and learn to understand that the world has already been created.

Abraham Joshua Heschel

(Profanity, Holiness)

Sacrifice

A life without sacrifices is abomination.

Annie Dillard

(Discipleship, Lifestyle)

We all have some dying to do. Jesus showed us how it should be done.

Stephen Neill

(Servanthood, Death)

The pendulum is swinging back from self-expression to self-discipline. But if we are serious about this, it means we will have to sacrifice some measure of the freedom we now have to do anything we want if it feels good.

Michael Horowitz

(Indulgence, Self-discipline)

The willing sacrifice of the innocent is the most powerful answer yet conceived by God or man to insolent tyranny.

Mohandas Gandhi

(Tyranny, Social Justice)

Salvation

If we or the world could be saved through human kindness or clear thinking, Jesus either would have formed a sensitivity group and urged us to share our feelings or would have founded a school and asked us to have discussions. But knowing the ways of God, the way of the world, and the persistence of human sin, he took up the cross, called disciples, gathered the church, and bade us follow him down a different path of freedom.

William H. Willimon

(Sin, Cross)

Salvation isn't what liberals or conservatives in this country think it is. It's about getting my life straight. It's not about ultimate significance. Salvation is about an adventure that was made possible through the death and resurrection of Jesus of Nazareth, through which I am made part of a community who will tell me who I am. You are not free to make up your life as a Christian. Your life is not like a gift, your life is a gift. That is a very important grammatical point. Until you learn to receive your life gift, you are lost. And people are lost.

Stanley Hauerwas

(Life, Gifts)

You can become a Christian by going to church just about as easily as you can become an automobile by sleeping in a garage.

Vance Havner

(Lifestyle, Church)

Sanctification

O Lord, make the bad people good and the good people nice.

Prayer of a young girl

(Hypocrisy, Meanness)

A saint is someone whose life makes it easier to believe in God.

William Barclay

(Witness, Example)

God creates out of nothing. Wonderful, you say. Yes, to be sure, but he does what is still more wonderful: He makes saints out of sinners.

Søren Kierkegaard

(Sin, Creation)

A walloping great congregation is fine, and fun, but what most communities really need is a couple of saints.

Martin Thornton

(Church, Holiness)

Satan

We may not pay [Satan] reverence, for that would be indiscreet, but we can at least respect his talents. A person who has for untold centuries maintained the imposing position of spiritual head of four-fifths of the human race, and political head of the whole of it, must be granted the possession of executive abilities of the loftiest order.

Mark Twain

(Sin, Evil)

Satisfaction

I have never met a soul who has set out to satisfy the Lord and has not been satisfied himself.

Watchman Nee

(Contentment, Lordship)

Science

We have grasped the mystery of the atom and rejected the Sermon on the Mount.

Omar Bradley

(Atomic Age, Ethics)

Scripture

My conscience has been taken captive by the Word of God, and to go against conscience or Scripture is neither right nor safe.

Martin Luther

(Conscience, Obedience)

To hear the voice of God in Holy Scripture oneself, and to help others to hear it, is a worthy cause to which to devote one's resources. To be commissioned to this cause is a sacred trust, not to be undertaken lightly, not to be refused irresponsibly, but to be fulfilled thankfully.

F. F. Bruce

(God's Voice, Calling)

Most people are bothered by those Scripture passages which they cannot understand. But for me, the passages in Scripture which trouble me most are those which I do understand.

Mark Twain

(Understanding, Obedience)

Ignorance of the Scriptures is ignorance of Christ.

Jerome

(Christ, Ignorance)

If someone considers the prophetic writings with all the diligence and reverence they are worth, while he reads and examines with great care, it is certain that in that very act he will be struck in his mind and senses by some more divine breath and will recognize that the books he reads have not been produced in a human way, but are words of God.

Origen

(Revelation, Conviction)

Second Coming

I wish I could be alive when Christ returns because I would like to be the first earthly monarch to take my crown and lay it at his feet.

Elizabeth I of England

(Worship, Majesty)

Self-control

Be not angry that you cannot make others as you wish them to be, since you cannot make yourself as you wish to be.

Thomas à Kempis

(Change, Acceptance)

O God, help us to be masters of ourselves that we may be servants of others.

Sir Alec Paterson

(Discipline, Ministry)

Self-deception

Knowing your own strength is a fine thing. Recognizing your own weakness is even better. What is really bad, what hurts and finally defeats us, is mistaking a weakness for a strength.

Sydney J. Harris

(Discernment, Strength)

You never find yourself until you face the truth.

Pearl Bailey

(Truth, Discernment)

Self-examination

It is when we face ourselves and face Christ, that we are lost in wonder, love, and praise. We need to rediscover the almost lost discipline of self-examination; and then a reawakened sense of sin will beget a reawakened sense of wonder.

Andrew Murray

(Wonder, Sin)

Self-fulfillment

The search for self-fulfillment is endless, and endlessly frustrating.

James Hitchcock

(Frustration, Service)

Living for his own pleasure is the least pleasurable thing a man can do; if his neighbors don't kill him in disgust, he will die slowly of boredom and lovelessness.

Joy Davidman

(Selfishness, Pride)

Self-love

The labor of self-love is a heavy one indeed. Think for yourself whether much of your sorrow has not arisen from someone speaking slightly of you. As long as you set yourself up as a little god to which you must be loyal, there will be those who will delight to offer affront to your idol. How then can you hope to have inward peace? The heart's fierce effort to protect itself from every slight, to shield its touchy honor from the bad opinion of friend and enemy, will never let the mind rest.

A. W. Tozer

(Pride, Idolatry)

The reigning cliché of the day is that in order to love others one must first learn to love oneself. This formulation—love thyself, then thy neighbor—is a license for unremitting self-indulgence, because the quest for self-love is endless. By the time you have finally learned to love yourself, you'll find yourself playing golf at Leisure World.

Charles Krauthammer

(Self-indulgence, Love)

The smallest package I ever saw was a man wrapped up wholly in himself.

Billy Graham

(Selfishness, Arrogance)

Self-reliance

You cannot help men permanently by doing for them what they could and should do themselves.

Abraham Lincoln

(Independence, Ministry)

O what a giant is man when he fights against himself, and what a dwarf when he needs or exercises his own assistance for himself. . . . Man hath no center but misery; there, and only there, he is fixed, and sure to find himself.

John Donne

(Misery, Human Nature)

Service

Teach us, Lord, to serve you as you deserve, to give and not to count the cost, to fight and not to heed the wounds, to toil and not to seek for rest, to labor and not to ask for any reward save that of knowing that we do your will.

Ignatius Loyola

(Discipleship, Sacrifice)

Beware of anything that competes with loyalty to Jesus Christ. The greatest competitor of devotion to Jesus is service for him.

Oswald Chambers

(Loyalty, Christ)

Sex

You mustn't force sex to do the work of love, or love to do the work of sex.

Mary McCarthy

(Love, Marriage)

Sickness

God is often (in some senses) nearer to us, and more effectually present with us, in sickness than in health. . . . He often sends diseases of the body to cure those of the soul. Comfort yourself with the sovereign Physician of both the soul and the body.

Brother Lawrence

(Healing, Soul)

Silence

To preserve the silence within—amid all the noise. To remain open and quiet, a moist humus in the fertile darkness where the rain falls and the grain ripens—no matter how many tramp across the parade ground in whirling dust under an arid sky.

Dag Hammarskjöld

(Contemplation, Prayer)

To sin by silence when they should protest makes cowards out of men.

Abraham Lincoln

(Protest, Cowardice)

Speech is silver, silence is gold.

Proverb

(Speech, Values)

Sin

Many Christians define sin as the sum total of acts which they themselves do not commit.

Carlyle Marney

(Self-evaluation, Pride)

I have more trouble with D. L. Moody than any other man I know.

D. L. Moody

(Self-awareness, Character)

You can't repent of confusion of psychological flaws inflicted by your parents—you're stuck with them. But you can repent of sin. Sin and repentance are the only grounds for hope and joy. The grounds for reconciled, joyful relationships. You can be born again.

John Alexander

(Repentance, Confession)

Contrary to popular opinion, sin is not what you want to do but can't; it is what you should not do because it will hurt you—and hurt you bad. . . . God is not a policeman; he is a Father concerned about his children. When a child picks up a snake and the father says, "Put that down right this minute!" the child thinks he's losing a toy. The fact is, he is not losing a toy; he is losing a snake.

Steve Brown

(Discipline, Correction)

People in general, Christian people in particular, tend to divide sins into two categories: their sins and our sins. The Bible, of course, knows no such distinction. Sin is sin, without partiality shown to the sins of God's people—our sins.

Joe Bayly

(Judgment, Guilt)

Whenever God touches sin it is independence that is touched, and that awakens resentment in the human heart. Independence must be blasted clean out, there must be no such thing left, only freedom, which is very different. Freedom is the ability not to insist on my rights, but to see that God gets his.

Oswald Chambers

(Independence, Freedom)

Solitude

We seem so frightened today of being alone that we never let it happen. Instead of planting our solitude with our own dream blossoms, we choke the space with continuous music, chatter, and companionship to which we do not even listen. When the noise stops there is no inner music to take its place.

Anne Morrow Lindbergh

(Quiet, Fear)

Sorrow

There is no despair so absolute as that which comes with the first moments of our first great sorrow, when we have not yet known what it is to have suffered and be healed, to have despaired and recovered hope.

George Eliot

(Grief, Suffering)

Soul

The meaning of earthly existence lies, not as we have grown used to thinking, in prospering, but in the development of the soul.

Aleksandr Solzhenitsyn

(Prosperity, Character)

The soul is the place where man's supreme and final battles are fought.

Abraham Neuman

(Character, Sin)

In a certain sense, every single human soul has more meaning and value than the whole history with its empires, its wars and revolutions, its blossoming and fading civilizations.

Nicholas Berdyaev

(Evangelism, Human Nature)

What lies behind us and what lies before us are tiny matters compared to what lies within us.

Ralph Waldo Emerson

(Past, Future)

Speech

When the heart is afire, some sparks will fly out of the mouth.

Thomas Fuller

(Passion, Unction)

I have learned this art: When I have nothing more to say, I stop talking.

Martin Luther

(Preaching, Self-control)

Spiritual Disciplines

Most of the significant things done in the world were done by persons who were either too busy or too sick! There are few ideal and leisurely settings for the disciplines of growth.

Robert Thornton Henderson

(Growth, Difficulty)

Spiritual Gifts

Some people have the notion that following your spiritual gifts is spending the days and years of your life doing only those things which come naturally, easily, with no effort, discipline, or practice.

Wesley Tracy

(Discipline, Growth)

Spirituality

Spirituality is a slippery term, but the phenomenon itself is not new. Christian spirituality is nothing other than life in Christ by the presence and power of the Spirit: being conformed to the person of Christ, and being united in communion with God and with others. Spirituality is not an aspect of Christian life, it is the Christian life.

Michael Downey

(Christianity, Holiness)

Success

Those who know how to win are much more numerous than those who know how to make proper use of their victories.

Polybius

(Victory, Responsibility)

While no man has succeeded . . . without some spark of divine fire, many have succeeded better by taking precious good care of a precious small spark than others, who have been careless with a generous flame.

Henry Holt

(Responsibility, Carelessness)

There is nothing so weak, for working purposes, as this enormous importance attached to immediate victory. There is nothing that fails like success.

G. K. Chesterton

(Victory, Failure)

Nothing fails quite so totally as success without God.

Vic Pentz

(Failure, God)

I don't think God is too interested in our success. He is interested in our maturity.

Fred Smith

(Growth, Maturity)

Suffering

He who can't endure the bad will not live to see the good.

Yiddish proverb

(Trials, Misfortune)

People get very upset by the idea that their children might have to suffer. Well, why . . . are you having children? You want them to be Christians, don't you? If they are going to be Christians, they are going to suffer. That is what life is about.

Stanley Hauerwas

(Children, Parenting)

We do not want suffering; we want success. We identify not with those who are low and hurt but with those who are high and healthy. We don't like lepers or losers very well; we prefer climbers and comers. For Christians, the temptation to be conformed to this world is desperately sweet and strong. Yet, says the apostle Paul, we are children of God if we suffer with Christ.

Cornelius Plantinga Jr.

(Success, Conformity)

Preach to the suffering, and you will never lack a congregation. There is a broken heart in every pew.

Joseph Parker

(Ministry, Compassion)

Perhaps the main task of the minister is to prevent people from suffering for the wrong reasons.

Henri Nouwen

(Ministry, Prevention)

It is a fact of Christian experience that life is a series of troughs and peaks. In his efforts to get permanent possession of a soul, God relies on the troughs more than the peaks. And some of his special favorites have gone through longer and deeper troughs than anyone else.

Peter Marshall Sr.

(Difficulty, Trials)

Supernatural

Surely we cannot take an open question like the supernatural and shut it with a bang, turning the key of the madhouse on all the mystics of history. You cannot take the region called the unknown and calmly say that though you know nothing about it, you know that all the gates are locked.

G. K. Chesterton

(Agnosticism, Faith)

Surrender

One does not surrender a life in an instant. That which is lifelong can only be surrendered in a lifetime.

Jim Elliot

(Life, Endurance)

I became my own only when I gave myself to Another.

C. S. Lewis

(Devotion, Allegiance)

T

Teaching

Becoming an effective teacher is simple. You just prepare and prepare until drops of blood appear on your forehead.

Marlene LeFever

(Preparation, Devotion)

Teamwork

"What makes a good manager?" someone asked Yogi Berra. "A good ball club," Yogi replied.

(Leadership, Church)

None of us is as smart as all of us.

Unknown

(Community, Church)

If the team wins, we all had a good year; if we don't win, then it doesn't matter who had a good year.

Paul O'Neill,
1994 American League batting champion

(Winning, Success)

Television

The answer [to television] is not censorship, but more citizenship in the corporate boardroom and more active families who will turn off the trash, boycott the sponsors, and tell the executives that you hold them personally responsible for making money from glorifying violence and human degradation.

Bill Bradley

(Violence, Responsibility)

Temptation

The trouble with trouble is that it usually starts out as a whole lot of fun.

Anonymous

(Sin, Entertainment)

An untempted minister will never do us any good, and an untried man will talk over our heads.

Joseph Parker

(Character, Preaching)

Tenderness

The higher people are in the favor of God, the more tender they are.

Martin Luther

(Compassion, Mercy)

Good Friday came after Christmas, but the angels still sang at the manger. In the midst of the hardest reality of life, there is always a welcome for tenderness and beauty.

Bruce W. Thielemann

(Easter, Christmas)

Testimony

Preach the Gospel at all times. If necessary, use words.

Francis of Assisi

(Righteousness, Lifestyle)

Time

Don't let yesterday use up too much of today.

Will Rogers

(Regret, Busyness)

Time is life—nothing more, nothing less. The way you spend your hours and your days is the way you spend your life.

John Boykin

(Stewardship, Faithfulness)

The management of time is the management of self; therefore, if you manage time with God, he will begin to manage you.

Jill Briscoe

(Self-control, Devotional Life)

I have this minute in my control. It is all I really do have to work with. It is as magnificent or drab or vile as the thoughts which fill it. I fear our most common sin is empty minutes.

Frank Laubach

(Stewardship, Sin)

Today

One today is worth two tomorrows.

Benjamin Franklin

(Present, Future)

Tongue

Ninety percent of the friction of daily life is caused by the wrong tone of voice.

Francois de la Rochefoucauld

(Speech, Attitude)

The tongue of man is a twisty thing.

Homer

(Deception, Speech)

Trials

We grow and mature spiritually through adversity—not when everything is going smoothly. . . . [I]n a time of adversity or trouble, the Christian has the opportunity to know God in a special and personal way.

C. Everett Koop

(Adversity, Growth)

These are just speed bumps on the highway of life.

Andrew Wainrib,
Los Angeles restaurant owner who lost a nightclub in the Rodney King verdict riots, a Malibu home in the fires, and a beachside cafe in the earthquake

(Adversity, Attitude)

I have nothing to offer but blood, toil, tears, and sweat.

Winston Churchill

(Sacrifice, Work)

Trouble

Trouble shared is trouble halved.

Dorothy Sayers

(Friendship, Grief)

Sentimentalism is born among the flowers; noble sentiment is born among the snows.

John Henry Jowett

(Wisdom, Sentimentalism)

Truth

He who begins by loving Christianity better than truth will proceed by loving his own sect or church better than Christianity, and end in loving himself better than all.

Samuel Taylor Coleridge

(Devotion, Christianity)

The truth does not change according to our ability to stomach it.

Flannery O'Connor

(Courage, Relativity)

The very amount of information that computers make available threatens us with cognitive overload: Overwhelmed with facts, people tend to mistake data for truth, knowledge for wisdom. With a mind-set fixed on information, our attention span shortens. We collect fragments. We become mentally poorer in overall meaning.

Michiko Katkutani

(Significance, Information)

Hard are the ways of truth, and rough to walk.

John Milton

(Courage, Honesty)

I never give 'em hell. I just tell the truth, and they think it's hell.

Harry S. Truman

(Speech, Honesty)

Truth does not blush.

Tertullian

(Conviction, Honesty)

Western culture has made a fundamental change in its religious base. We have exchanged that one who said, "I am the Truth" (John 14:6) for the incredibly expensive doctrine of Freud and the words of all his various disciples. Our new religion says with Pontius Pilate, "What is truth?" and teaches that our status is one of "original victim" rather than "original sin."

Carol Tharp

(Religion, Blame)

A man can't be always defending the truth; there must be a time to feed on it.

C. S. Lewis

(Spiritual Growth, Apologetics)

You shall know the truth, and the truth shall make you mad.

Aldous Huxley

(Honesty, Anger)

Peace, if possible, but the truth at any rate.

Martin Luther

(Peace, Honesty)

Unbelievers

God is not hostile to sinners, but only to unbelievers.

Martin Luther

(Sin, Grace)

Understanding

Understanding someone properly involves learning from him, and learning from someone properly involves changing oneself.

Hans Küng

(Change, Learning)

God, help us not to despise or oppose what we do not understand.

William Penn

(Unity, Acceptance)

Unity

Talk about *what* you believe and you have disunity. Talk about *who* you believe in and you have unity.

E. Stanley Jones

(Belief, Conflict)

Unselfishness

What does the Lord do to help broaden my horizons and assist me in seeing how selfish I am? Very simple: He gives me four busy kids who step on shoes, wrinkle clothes, spill milk, lick car windows, and drop sticky candy on the carpet. . . . Being unselfish in attitude strikes at the very core of our being. It means we are willing to forgo our own comfort, our own preferences, our own schedule, our own desires for another's benefit. And that brings us back to Christ.

Charles Swindoll

(Parenting, Grace)

V

Values

Even those who have renounced Christ's way and attack it, in their innermost being still follow Christ's ideals, for hitherto neither their subtlety nor the ardor of their hearts has been able to create a higher idea of man and of virtue than the ideal given by Christ of old. When it has been attempted, the result has been only grotesque.

Fyodor Dostoyevsky

(Christianity, Ideals)

People do not value sunsets because they cannot pay for them.

Oscar Wilde

(Materialism, Money)

Virtue

He who is not angry at sin is not in love with virtue.

James Strachan

(Anger, Sin)

I must be poor and in want, before I can exercise the virtue of gratitude; miserable and in torment, before I can exercise the virtue of patience.

John Donne

(Gratitude, Patience)

How commonly vices pass themselves off as virtues. Inordinate laxity is believed to be loving-kindness, and unbridled wrath is accounted the virtue of spiritual zeal. Hence it is necessary for the ruler of souls to distinguish with vigilant care between virtues and vices.

Gregory the Great

(Anger, Laziness)

Vision

People grow old only by deserting their ideals. Years may wrinkle the skin, but to give up interest wrinkles the soul. Worry, self-doubt, self-distrust, fear and despair; these are the long, long years that bow the head and turn the growing spirit back to dust.

Douglas MacArthur

(Age, Attitude)

We are like dwarfs, seated on the shoulders of giants. We see more things than the Ancients, things more distant, but it is due neither to the sharpness of our sight nor the greatness of our stature. It is simply because they have lent us their own.

Bernard of Chartres

(Church, Saints)

Leaders do not have to be the greatest visionaries themselves. The vision may come from anyone. The leaders do have to state the vision, however. Leaders also have to keep the vision before the people and remind them of the progress that is being made to achieve the vision. Otherwise, the people might assume that they are failing and give up.

Ezra Earl Jones

(Leadership, Communication)

The real danger in our situation lies in the fact that so many people see clearly what they are revolting from and so few see at all what they are revolting to.

Harry Emerson Fosdick

(Revolt, Conformity)

W

Waiting

Don't wait for your ship to come in; swim out to it.

Unknown

(Risk, Achievement)

Wealth

Wealth takes away the sharp edges of our moral sensitivities and allows a comfortable confusion about sin and virtue.

Henri Nouwen

(Materialism, Deception)

I continually find it necessary to guard against that natural love of wealth and grandeur which prompts us always, when we come to apply our general doctrine to our own case, to claim an exception.

William Wilberforce

(Possessions, Materialism)

Will

The receiving of the Word consists of two parts: attention of mind and intention of will.

William Ames

(Word of God, Obedience)

Winning

About the only problem with success is that it doesn't teach you how to deal with failure.

Tommy Lasorda

(Failure, Success)

Often the best way to win is to forget to keep score.

Marianne Espinosa

(Competition, Cooperation)

Wisdom

Whatever withdraws us from the power of our senses; whatever makes the past, the distant, the future, predominate over the present, advances us in the dignity of thinking beings.

Samuel Johnson

(Past, Future)

I do not feel obliged to believe that the same God who has endowed us with sense, reason, and intellect has intended us to forgo their use.

Galileo

(Reason, Apologetics)

God's wisdom is not first counsel on how to practice family values or to use common sense. It is the wisdom of his plan of grace, the wisdom of the Cross. That wisdom is foolishness to the calculations of prudence.

Edmund P. Clowney

(Grace, Sacrifice)

A man has made at least a start on discovering the meaning of human life when he plants shade trees under which he knows full well he will never sit.

D. Elton Trueblood

(Patience, Service)

Witness

Lord, shine in me and so be in me that all with whom I come in contact may know thy presence in my soul. Let them look up and see no longer me but only Jesus.

John Henry Newman

(God's Presence, Jesus)

Some of us who have already begun to break the silence of the night have found that the calling to speak is often a vocation of agony, but we must speak. We must speak with all the humility that is appropriate to our limited vision, but we must speak.

Martin Luther King Jr.

(Preaching, Social Action)

Women

Men are like the earth and we are like the moon; we turn always one side to them and they think there is no other.

Olive Schreiner

(Marriage, Men)

Woman—last at the cross, and earliest at the grave.

E. S. Barrett

(Easter, Devotion)

Whatever women do they must do twice as well as men to be thought half as good. Luckily, this is not difficult.

Charlotte Whitton

(Work, Marriage)

A woman with a woman's viewpoint is of more value than when she forgets she's a woman and begins to act like a man.

Nelly Ptaschkina

(Identity, Culture)

Wonder

The world is not lacking in wonders, but in a sense of wonder.

G. K. Chesterton

(Miracles, Creation)

Faith is the inborn capacity to see God behind everything, the wonder that keeps you an eternal child. Wonder is the very essence of life. Beware always of losing the wonder, and the first thing that stops wonder is religious conviction. Whenever you give a trite testimony, the wonder is gone. The evidence of salvation is that the sense of wonder is developing.

Oswald Chambers

(Testimony, Faith)

Word of God

When the hot Word of God is poured over a cold, cold world, things break, and it is into that brokenness that we are called, into whatever big or small piece we find in front of us, with fire in our bones, to show a frightened world that it is not the heat of the fire that we fear, but the chill that lies ahead if the fire goes out.

Barbara Brown Taylor

(Courage, Conviction)

When the soul is suffering . . . there is great need of the Word.

John Chrysostom

(Suffering, Discipleship)

Words

If a man's life be lightning, his words are thunder.

Medieval proverb

(Spiritual Power, Character)

A man of words and not of deeds
Is like a garden full of weeds.

Anonymous

(Good Works, Hypocrisy)

Work

There is a danger of doing too much as well as of doing too little. Life is not for work, but work for life, and when it is carried to the extent of undermining life or unduly absorbing it, work is not praiseworthy but blameworthy.

Ralph Turnbull

(Balance, Life)

The best kept secret in America today is that people would rather work hard for something they believe in than enjoy a life of pampered idleness.

John W. Gardner

(Idleness, Purpose)

Do not confound work and fruit. There may be a good deal of work for Christ that is not the fruit of the heavenly Vine.

Andrew Murray

(Fruitfulness, Busyness)

Choose that employment or calling in which you may be most serviceable to God. Choose not that in which you may be most rich or honorable in the world; but that in which you may do most good, and best escape sinning.

Richard Baxter

(Lifestyle, Vocation)

The highest reward for man's toil is not what he gets for it, but what he becomes by it.

John Ruskin

(Character, Reward)

Thanks be to God for a life full-packed with things that matter crying to be done—a life, thank God, of never-ending strife against the odds. . . . Just enough time to do one's best, and then pass on, leaving the rest to him.

John Oxenham

(Stress, Significance)

It is possible to be so active in the service of Christ as to forget to love him. Many a man preaches Christ but gets in front of him by the multiplicity of his own works. . . . Christ can do without your works; what he wants is you. Yet if he really has you, he will have all your works.

P. T. Forsyth

(Good Works, Devotion)

O Lord, renew our spirits and draw our hearts unto thyself, that our work may not be to us a burden, but a delight; and give us such a mighty love to thee as may sweeten all our obedience.

Benjamin Jenks

(Love, Obedience)

Most middle-class Americans tend to worship their work, to work at their play, and to play at their worship.

Gordon Dahl

(Priorities, Worship)

Disciplined reflection does not take time away from work; it sustains the spirit and increases the intensity and quality of work.

Kesharan Nair

(Discipline, Reflection)

Work as if you were to live 100 years; pray as if you were to die tomorrow.

Benjamin Franklin

(Prayer, Future)

I long to accomplish a great and noble task; but it is my chief duty and joy to accomplish humble tasks as though they were great and noble. The world is moved along, not only by the mighty shoves of its heroes, but also by the aggregate of the tiny pushes of each honest worker.

Helen Keller

(Community, Humility)

If a man is to be called to be a streetsweeper, he should sweep streets even as Michelangelo painted, or Beethoven composed music, or Shakespeare wrote poetry. He should sweep streets so well that all the hosts of heaven and earth will pause to say, "Here lived a great streetsweeper who did his job well."

Martin Luther King Jr.

(Vocation, Devotion)

World

The world is poor because her fortune is buried in the sky and all her treasure maps are of the earth.

Calvin Miller

(Heaven, Eternity)

He who marries the spirit of the age soon becomes a widower.

Dean Inge

(Culture, Devotion)

We have a society which is psychiatrized in the same sense in which medieval European society was Christianized, religionized—everything was a matter of religion. Now everything is a matter of psychiatry, from homosexuality, to heroin, to murder.

Thomas Szasz

(Psychology, Blame)

Worry

The eagle that soars in the upper air does not worry itself how it is to cross rivers.

Gladys Aylward

(Trust, Spiritual Power)

Three things sap a man's strength: worry, travel, and sin.

Jewish proverb

(Travel, Sin)

When you have accomplished your daily task, go to sleep in peace; God is awake.

Victor Hugo

(Rest, Faith)

Worship

If worship is just one thing we do, everything becomes mundane. If worship is the one thing we do, everything takes on eternal significance.

Timothy J. Christenson

(Priorities, Significance)

Our greatest claim to nobility is our created capacity to know God, to be in personal relationship with him, to love him and to worship him. Indeed, we are most truly human when we are on our knees before our Creator.

John Stott

(God, Creation)

Worship does not satisfy our hunger for God; it whets our appetite.

Eugene H. Peterson

(Longing, Devotion)

I sit for six days a week like a weaver behind his loom, busily fingering the threads of an intricate pattern. On the seventh day, the church in its worship calls me around in front of the loom to look at the pattern on which I have been working. It bids me compare the design of my days with the pattern shown me on Mount Sinai and the Mount of Olives. Some threads thereupon I have to cut, others I pull more tightly, and most of all, I renew my picture of the whole plan.

Ralph W. Sockman

(Perspective, Holiness)

Worship is a stairway on which there is movement in two directions; God comes to man, and man goes to God.

Daniel Baumann

(God, Human Nature)

Worship renewal does not consist of moving chairs in a circle, rearranging the order of worship, or finding new gimmicks. The heart of worship renewal is a recovery of the power of the Holy Spirit, who enables the congregation to offer praise and thanksgiving to God.

Robert Webber

(Holy Spirit, Renewal)

Somehow, about forty percent of churchgoers seem to have picked up the idea that "singing in church is for singers." The truth is that "singing is for believers." The relevant question is not "Do you have a voice?" but "Do you have a song?"

Donald Hustad

(Music, Reverence)

There are entire congregations who worship praise and praise worship but who have not yet learned to praise and worship God in Jesus Christ. The song, the dance, the banners have been accepted as worship instead of being seen as a means of expressing worship.

Judson Cornwall

(Music, Renewal)

Idolatry is worshiping anything that ought to be used, or using anything that is meant to be worshiped.

Augustine

(Idolatry, Respect)

Y

Youth

We are only young once. That is all society can stand.

Bob Bowen

(Maturity, Growth)

I was born in the wrong generation. When I was a young man, no one had any respect for youth. Now I am an old man and no one has any respect for age.

Bertrand Russell

(Age, Respect)

You are only young once, but you can be immature your whole life.

A bumper sticker

(Immaturity, Wisdom)

Today's accent may be on youth, but the stress is still on the parents.

Earl Wilson

(Age, Wisdom)

As I approve of the youth that has something of the old man in him, so am I no less pleased with an old man that has something of the youth.

Cicero

(Age, Wisdom)

Z

Zeal

Fanaticism consists of redoubling your efforts when you have forgotten your aim.

George Santayana

(Fanaticism, Enthusiasm)

Illustrations

I was sitting with a bunch of magazine editors recently, listening to Sharon Grigsby, editor of the award-winning religion section of the *Dallas Morning News*. She was encouraging us to focus our magazines, not on the issues editors care about, rather on the issues *readers* care about. She told a story to make her point.

The editors of the *Dallas Morning News* foods section love exotic recipes requiring rare ingredients, high levels of culinary skill, and hours of preparation and presentation. Though the editors win awards for photography and journalism, many of their page-one selections are out of the reach of most cooks.

These food editors were shocked when a reader survey revealed that the highest-rated article of the past year had been a short, non-feature piece on "What to Do with Stale Bread."

Grigsby concluded: "Whatever else you provide for your readers, be sure and tell them how to use their stale bread."

Her skillful use of a simple story introduced a new term into our vocabulary. When I talked recently with another editor from that conference, she told me about the forthcoming "stale bread" story in her magazine. A simple story helps her remember to ask how she can serve her reader's daily, practical needs.

We preachers often lament that people forget our carefully crafted exposition and remember our simple stories. I contend that's not a problem—if we tell the right stories.

This "Illustrations" section offers you a storehouse of powerful, contemporary stories that will cause your listeners to remember your next sermon or talk.

Give these simple stories a try. And while you're at it, why not preach a "stale bread" sermon next Sunday?

Ed Rowell

Abundant Life

A university professor tells of being invited to speak at a military base one December and there meeting an unforgettable soldier named Ralph. Ralph had been sent to meet him at the airport. After they had introduced themselves, they headed toward the baggage claim.

As they walked down the concourse, Ralph kept disappearing. Once to help an older woman whose suitcase had fallen open. Once to lift two toddlers up to where they could see Santa Claus, again to give directions to someone who was lost. Each time he came back with a smile on his face.

"Where did you learn that?" the professor asked.

"What?" Ralph said.

"Where did you learn to live like that?"

"Oh," Ralph said, "during the war, I guess." He then told the professor about his tour of duty in Vietnam, how it was his job to clear minefields, how he watched his friends blow up before his eyes, one after another.

"I learned to live between steps," he said. "I never knew whether the next one would be my last, so I learned to get everything I could out of the moment between when I picked up my foot and when I put it down again. Every step I took was a whole new world, and I guess I've been that way ever since."

The abundance of our lives is not determined by how long we live, but by how well we live.

Barbara Brown Taylor

(Fulfillment, Serving)

Dates used:____________

Acceptance

In *The Whisper Test*, Mary Ann Bird writes:

I grew up knowing I was different, and I hated it. I was born with a cleft palate, and when I started school, my classmates made it clear to me how I looked to others: a little girl with a misshapen lip, crooked nose, lopsided teeth, and garbled speech.

When schoolmates asked, "What happened to your lip?" I'd tell them I'd fallen and cut it on a piece of glass. Somehow it seemed more acceptable to have suffered an accident than to have been born different. I was convinced that no one outside my family could love me.

There was, however, a teacher in the second grade whom we all adored—Mrs. Leonard. She was short, round, happy—a sparkling lady.

Annually we had a hearing test. . . . Mrs. Leonard gave the test to everyone in the class, and finally it was my turn. I knew from past years that as we stood against the door and covered one ear, the teacher sitting at her desk would whisper something, and we would have to repeat it back—things like "The sky is blue" or "Do you have new shoes?" I waited there for those words that God must have put into her mouth, those seven words that changed my life. Mrs. Leonard said, in her whisper, "I wish you were my little girl."

God says to every person deformed by sin, "I wish you were my son" or "I wish you were my daughter."

(Encouragement, Love)

Dates used:____________

Accountability

Jawanza Kunjufu, in his book *Restoring the Village*, writes:

When I was a fourteen-year-old high school freshman, school was dismissed early for a teachers' meeting. I conveniently neglected to tell my parents about the change and arranged to bring my girlfriend over to my house. We weren't planning to study.

As we were going up the steps, my neighbor, Mrs. Nolan, poked her head out of a window and said, "You're home awfully early, Jerome."

"Yes, Ma'am," I said, improvising a lame story about how we planned to review algebra problems.

"Does your mother know you're home this early," Mrs. Nolan persisted, "and do you want me to call her?"

I gave up. "No, Ma'am. I'll go inside and call her while Kathy sits on the porch."

Mrs. Nolan saved our careers that day. If Kathy had gotten pregnant, she might not have become the doctor she is today. And my father had warned me that if I made a baby, the mutual fund he set up for me to go to college or start a business would have gone to the child. I'm glad Mrs. Nolan was at her window, looking out for me.

(Abstinence, Neighbors)

Dates used:____________

On February 26, 1995, Barings, the oldest bank in Britain, announced it was seeking bankruptcy protection after losing nearly one billion dollars in a stock gamble, according to *Time* magazine.

In late 1994, the chief trader at Barings's Singapore office began betting big on Japan's Nikkei market. Then disaster struck. An earthquake hit Kobe, Japan, and on January 23, 1995, the Nikkei plunged more than one thousand points.

Barings Bank lost big money. But instead of cutting his losses, Barings's Singapore trader doubled his investment, apparently hoping that the Nikkei would rebound. It didn't. Barings's London office put up nearly $900 million to support its falling position on the Singapore investments. Finally, Barings ran out of capital and declared bankruptcy.

How could one 28-year-old trader in Singapore lose nearly a billion dollars and ruin a 233-year-old British bank? According to *Time*, the problem was lack of supervision.

"London allowed [the Singapore trader] to take control of both the trading desk and the backroom settlement operation in Singapore. It is a mix that can be—and in this case was—toxic. . . . A trader keeping his own books is like a schoolboy grading his own tests; the temptation to cheat can be overwhelming, particularly if the stakes are high enough."

Craig Brian Larson
Contemporary Illustrations for Preachers, Teachers, and Writers

(Risk, Temptation)

Dates used:____________

Anger

In a 1994 article, "Wars' Lethal Leftovers Threaten Europeans," Associated Press reporter Christopher Burns writes:

The bombs of World War II are still killing in Europe. They turn up—and sometimes blow up—at construction sites, in fishing nets, or on beaches fifty years after the guns fell silent.

Hundreds of tons of explosives are recovered every year in France alone. Thirteen old bombs exploded in France in 1993, killing twelve people and wounding eleven.

"I've lost two of my colleagues," said Yvon Bouvet, who heads a government team in the Champagne-Ardennes region that defuses explosives from both World War I and II. "Unexploded bombs become more dangerous with time. With the corrosion inside, the weapon becomes more unstable, and the detonator can be exposed."

What is true of lingering bombs is also true of lingering anger. Buried anger will explode when we least expect it.

Barry McGee

(Resentment, Temper)

Dates used:____________

In his autobiography, *Number 1,* Billy Martin told about hunting in Texas with Mickey Mantle. Mickey had a friend who would let them hunt on his ranch. When they reached the ranch, Mickey told Billy to wait in the car while he checked in with his friend.

Mantle's friend quickly gave them permission to hunt, but he asked Mickey a favor. He had a pet mule in the barn who was going blind, and didn't have the heart to put him out of his misery. He asked Mickey to shoot the mule for him.

When Mickey came back to the car, he pretended to be angry. He scowled and slammed the door. Billy asked him what was wrong, and Mickey said his friend wouldn't let them hunt. "I'm so mad at that guy," Mantle said, "I'm going out to his barn and shoot one of his mules!"

Martin protested, "We can't do that!"

But Mickey was adamant. "Just watch me."

He jumped out of the car with his rifle, ran inside the barn, and shot the mule. As he was leaving, though, he heard two shots. He saw that Martin had taken out his rifle, too.

"What are you doing, Martin?" he yelled.

Martin yelled back, face red with anger, "We'll show that son of a gun! I just killed two of his cows!"

Anger can be dangerously contagious. As Proverbs puts it, "Do not make friends with a hot-tempered man . . . or you may learn his ways" (Prov. 22:24–25).

Scott Bowerman

(Rage, Relationships)

Dates used:____________

The *Arizona Republic* (4/25/95) reported that when Steve Tran of Westminster, California, closed the door on twenty-five activated bug bombs, he thought he had seen the last of the cockroaches that shared his apartment. When the spray reached the pilot light of the stove, it ignited, blasting his screen door across the street, breaking all his windows, and setting his furniture ablaze.

"I really wanted to kill all of them," he said. "I thought if I used a lot more, it would last longer." According to the label, just two canisters of the fumigant would have solved Tran's roach problem.

The blast caused over $10,000 damage to the apartment building. And the cockroaches? Tran reported, "By Sunday, I saw them walking around."

As Proverbs 29:11 says, only "a fool gives full vent to his anger."

(Foolishness, Overkill)

Dates used:____________

Assisted Suicide

Alva B. Weir, an oncologist in Germantown, Tennessee, told this true story:

I was awakened from sleep by the telephone. On the other end of the line, a distraught woman told me that her son, a cancer patient of one of my partners, was unconscious, breathing badly, with an empty bottle of pills at his bedside. I inquired further and learned this patient had recently discovered that his cancer had metastasized to his bone.

Along with his pain, he had lost control of his bowels. He could not tolerate the thought of pain and incontinence with no hope of cure. He had decided to end his life and appeared close to succeeding.

The mother did not know what to do. I convinced her to bring him to the hospital where we could evaluate him.

I met them in the emergency room. The mother, brother, and sister were there. The patient was breathing badly and looked as if he were dying from the overdose. I examined the patient, checked the laboratory results, and recommended that we lavage his stomach and place him on a ventilator until the drugs left his system.

The mother was uncertain; the brother took charge, suggesting that the patient desired suicide and that they should honor his wishes and let him die in peace rather than bring him through to face life with cancer. They insisted on taking him home with no therapy.

I worked with them for some time, and they compromised by allowing me to admit him to the hospital with only oxygen and intravenous fluid support, but no tubes and no ventilator. They consented mainly because of logistical and legal complications produced by a patient dying at home of suicide.

I admitted him, expecting him to die. His care was resumed by his physician, my partner. The following weekend I was rounding for my group and was surprised to find this patient's name on my list. I walked into the room to find a beaming mother and an alert patient. With the minimal support, he had survived his overdose. After another week, he was walking with his pain improved, bowels controlled, and depression diminished.

I realized that this man and his family, who had chosen for him the absence of life forever, were experiencing precious moments together of unfathomable value. . . . There is no one this side of heaven who has the ability to make the correct decision regarding when our life should be extinguished.

Today's Christian Doctor *(Spring 1997)*

(Death, Life)

Dates used:____________

LAVAGE — TO WASH OUT (SOMETHING) WITH WATER.

Blood of Christ

Jeffrey Ebert shares this story:

When I was five years old, before factory-installed seat belts and automobile air bags, my family was driving home at night on a two-lane country road. I was sitting on my mother's lap when another car, driven by a drunk driver, swerved into our lane and hit us head-on. I don't have any memory of the collision. I do recall the fear and confusion I felt as I saw myself literally covered with blood from head to toe.

Then I learned that the blood wasn't mine at all, but my mother's. In that split second when the two headlights glared into her eyes, she instinctively pulled me closer to her chest and curled her body around mine. It was her body that slammed against the dashboard, her head that shattered the windshield. She took the impact of the collision so that I wouldn't have to. It took extensive surgery for my mother to recover from her injuries.

In a similar, but infinitely more significant way, Jesus Christ took the impact for our sin, and his blood now permanently covers our lives.

(Atonement, Sacrifice)

Dates used:____________

Christmas

A few years ago, Alex Dovales was drifting to Miami on a rickety boat with twenty-seven other Cubans. A year later, he was an angel.

Fourteen exhausted and penniless Cuban rafters washed ashore on Key Largo. The rafters had spent four days huddled in an eighteen-foot raft with little water and a few rusted cans filled with meat. Dovales looked at them—"and felt like I had just arrived here myself."

The twenty-five-year-old, who clears $197 per week as a dishwasher, walked home and gathered all the presents from under his Christmas tree. He gave the gifts—each containing shirts and other clothing—to the new arrivals. "They were wet and cold," said Henry Paez, Dovales's roommate. "Alex took off his shirt and gave it to them."

Dovales said he didn't give it a second thought. "They had nothing," he said.

Telegraph Herald

(Empathy, Generosity)

Dates used:____________

Church

In Hot Springs, Arkansas, you'll find the Morris Antique Mall. Nothing on the inside distinguishes this antique store from dozens like it in town. There's a musty smell and dusty relics from the past.

But if you look closely at the outside of the Morris Antique Mall, you'll see something that makes it distinct: Before it was an antique store, it was a church building.

A focus on the future prevents a church from becoming a resting place for dusty relics.

Michael A. Howe

(Future, Vision)

Dates used:____________

Commitment

In *Living Above the Level of Mediocrity,* Chuck Swindoll writes:

On Sunday, believers arrived at a house church in the Soviet Union in small groups throughout the day so as not to arouse the suspicion of KGB informers. They began by singing a hymn quietly. Suddenly, in walked two soldiers with loaded weapons at the ready. One shouted, "If you wish to renounce your commitment to Jesus Christ, leave now!"

Two or three quickly left, then another. After a few more seconds, two more.

"This is your last chance. Either turn against your faith in Christ," he ordered, "or stay and suffer the consequences."

Two more slipped out into the night. No one else moved. Parents with children trembling beside them looked down reassuringly, fully expecting to be gunned down or imprisoned.

The other soldier closed the door, looked back at those who stood against the wall and said, "Keep your hands up—but this time in praise to our Lord Jesus Christ. We, too, are Christians. We were sent to another house church several weeks ago to arrest a group of believers. . . ."

The other soldier interrupted, "But, instead, we were converted! We have learned by experience, however, that unless people are willing to die for their faith, they cannot be fully trusted."

David Waggoner

(Faith, Trust)

Dates used:____________

Communion

Henri J. M. Nouwen writes in the March 1994 *New Oxford Review*:

A few years ago Bob, the husband of a friend of mine, died suddenly of a heart attack. My friend decided to keep her two young children away from the funeral. She thought it would be too hard for them to see their father put in the ground. For years after Bob's death, the cemetery remained a fearful and a dangerous place for them.

One day, my friend asked me to visit the grave with her, and invited the children to come along. The elder one was too afraid to go, but the younger one decided to come with us. When we came to the place where Bob was buried, the three of us sat down on the grass around the stone engraved with the words, A KIND AND GENTLE MAN.

I said: "Maybe one day we should have a picnic here. This is not only a place to think about death, but also a place to rejoice in our life. Bob will be most honored when we find new strength, here, to live."

At first it seemed a strange idea: having a meal on top of a tombstone. But isn't that similar to what Jesus told his disciples to do when he asked them to share bread and wine in his memory?

A few days later my friend took her elder child to the grave, the younger one having convinced his sister that there was nothing to fear. Now they often go to the cemetery and tell each other stories about Bob.

(Celebration, Resurrection)

Dates used:____________

Community

A few winters ago, heavy snows hit North Carolina. Following a wet, six-inch snowfall, it was interesting to see the effect along Interstate 40.

Next to the highway stood several large groves of tall, young pine trees. The branches were bowed down with the heavy snow—so low that branches from one tree were often leaning against the trunk or branches of another.

Where trees stood alone, however, the effect of the heavy snow was different. The branches had become heavier, but without other trees to lean against, the branches snapped. They lay on the ground, dark and alone in the cold snow.

When the storms of life hit, we need to be standing close to other Christians. The closer we stand, the more we will be able to hold up.

Carl G. Conner

(Fellowship, Support)

Dates used:____________

Compassion

A student asked anthropologist Margaret Mead for the earliest sign of civilization in a given culture. He expected the answer to be a clay pot or perhaps a fish hook or grinding stone.

Her answer was: "A healed femur."

Mead explained that no mended bones are found where the law of the jungle, survival of the fittest, reigns. A healed femur shows that someone cared. Someone had to do that injured person's hunting and gathering until the leg healed. The evidence of compassion is the first sign of civilization.

R. Wayne Willis

(Caring, Civilization)

Dates used:____________

On Monday, August 9, 1993, a thirty-one-year-old woman, Sophia White, burst into the hospital nursery at UCLA Medical Center in Los Angeles, wielding a .38-caliber handgun. She had come gunning for Elizabeth Staten, a nurse whom she accused of stealing her husband. White fired six shots, hitting Staten in the wrist and stomach.

Staten fled, and White chased her into the emergency room, firing once more. There, with blood on her clothes and a hot pistol in her hand, the attacker was met by another nurse, Joan Black, who did the unthinkable. Black walked calmly to the gun-toting woman, hugged her, and spoke comforting words.

The assailant said she didn't have anything to live for, that Staten had stolen her family.

"You're in pain," Black said. "I'm sorry, but everybody has pain in their lives. . . . I understand, and we can work it out."

As they talked, the hospital invader kept her finger on the trigger. Once she began to lift the gun as if to shoot herself. Nurse Black just pushed her arm down and continued to hold her. At last Sophia White gave the gun to the nurse.

She was disarmed by a hug. It's amazing what compassion can do.

Tom Tripp

(Courage, Empathy)

Dates used:____________

In 1975 a child named Raymond Dunn Jr. was born in New York State. *The Associated Press* reports that at his birth, a skull fracture and oxygen deprivation caused severe retardation. As Raymond grew, the family discovered further impairments. His twisted body suffered up to twenty seizures per day. He was blind, mute, immobile. He had severe allergies that limited him to only one food: a meat-based formula made by Gerber Foods.

In 1985, Gerber stopped making the formula that Raymond lived on. His mother scoured the country to buy what stores had in stock, accumulating cases and cases, but in 1990 her supply ran out. In desperation, she appealed to Gerber for help. Without this particular food, Raymond would starve to death.

The employees of the company listened. In an unprecedented action, volunteers donated hundreds of hours to bring out old equipment, set up production lines, obtain special approval from the USDA, and produce the formula—all for one special boy.

In January 1995, Raymond Dunn Jr. known as the Gerber Boy, died from his physical problems. But during his brief lifetime he called forth a wonderful thing called compassion.

Larry A. Payne

(Service, Teamwork)

Dates used:____________

Confession

In January 1697, on a day of fasting called to remember the Salem witch trials, Samuel Sewall slipped a document into the hands of his pastor, Samuel Willard, at Boston's Old South Meeting House.

Sewall, one of the seven judges who had sentenced twenty people to death in Salem five years earlier, stood silent before the congregation as Willard read: "Samuel Sewall, sensible of the reiterated strokes of God upon himself and family . . . desires to take the blame and shame of it, asking pardon of men, and especially desiring prayers that God, who has an unlimited authority, would pardon that sin and his other sins. . . ."

Sewall believed that eleven of his fourteen children had died as divine punishment for his involvement in the witch trials. His only spiritual hope was confession as public as his sin.

Yankee *(1/97)*

(Repentance, Responsibility)

Dates used:____________

In *The Essential Calvin and Hobbes* by Bill Watterson, the cartoon character Calvin says to his tiger friend, Hobbes, "I feel bad that I called Susie names and hurt her feelings. I'm sorry I did it."

"Maybe you should apologize to her," Hobbes suggests.

Calvin ponders this for a moment and replies, "I keep hoping there's a less obvious solution."

When we want to restore our relationship with God, we need to remember that he has a liking for the obvious solution.

Norm Langston

(Apologies, Restoration)

Dates used:____________

Early in 1993, British police accused two ten-year-old boys of the brutal murder of two-year-old James Bulger. The two boys pleaded innocence.

During the two-week trial the young defendants responded to police questioning with noticeable inconsistency. The climax of the trial came when the parents of one of the boys assured him that they would always love him. Confronted with irrefutable evidence linking him with the crime and the assurance of his parents' love, the boy confessed in a soft voice, "I killed James."

The miracle of God's love is that he knows how evil we are, yet he loves us. We can confess our worst sins to him, confident that his love will not diminish.

Greg Asimakoupoulos

(God's Love, Guilt)

Dates used:____________

Conflict

Research indicates that the spotted owls' greatest threat may be not logging, but one of its relatives. For the past fifteen years, the barred owl has migrated westward rapidly. Barred owls, which used to live exclusively east of the Mississippi, compete for the same food as spotted owls but are more aggressive and adaptable.

Sometimes our greatest conflict comes not from outside culture, but from other Christians.

Newsweek *(11/25/96)*

(Competition, Culture)

Dates used:____________

The *Fort Worth Star-Telegram* reported that firefighters in Genoa, Texas, were accused of deliberately setting more than forty destructive fires. When caught, they stated, "We had nothing to do. We just wanted to get the red lights flashing and the bells clanging."

The job of firefighters is to put out fires, not start them. The job of Christians is to help resolve conflict (Matt. 5:9), not start more of it.

Gerald Cornelius

(Boredom, Peace)

Dates used:____________

Conscience

Many electronic fire alarms have an internal switch triggered by a beam of light. As long as light is received unbroken by the photosensitive receiver, the detector is quiet. But if smoke, moisture, or an insect obstructs the beam for even a split second, the alarm sounds.

Our conscience resembles such an alarm. When sin obstructs our connection with the light of God's Spirit, the conscience signals us that there's life-threatening danger.

A. D. Sterner

(Holy Spirit, Sin)

Dates used:____________

Contentment

In *Our Daily Bread*, Philip Parham tells the story of a rich industrialist who was disturbed to find a fisherman sitting lazily beside his boat.

"Why aren't you out there fishing?" he asked.

"Because I've caught enough fish for today," said the fisherman.

"Why don't you catch more fish than you need?" the rich man asked.

"What would I do with them?"

"You could earn more money," came the impatient reply, "and buy a better boat so you could go deeper and catch more fish. You could purchase nylon nets, catch even more fish, and make more money. Soon you'd have a fleet of boats and be rich like me."

The fisherman asked, "Then what would I do?"

"You could sit down and enjoy life," said the industrialist.

"What do you think I'm doing now?" the fisherman replied.

Scott Minnich

(Ambition, Greed)

Dates used:____________

The *Hope Health Letter* (10/95) included this story:

Once upon a time, there was a man who lived with his wife, two small children, and his elderly parents in a tiny hut. He tried to be patient and gracious, but the noise and crowded conditions wore him down.

In desperation, he consulted the village wise man. "Do you have a rooster?" asked the wise man.

"Yes," he replied.

"Keep the rooster in the hut with your family, and come see me again next week."

The next week, the man returned and told the wise elder that living conditions were worse than ever, with the rooster crowing and making a mess of the hut.

"Do you have a cow?" asked the wise elder. The man nodded fearfully. "Take your cow into the hut as well, and come see me in a week."

Over the next several weeks, the man—on the advice of the wise elder—made room for a goat, two dogs, and his brother's children.

Finally, he could take no more, and in a fit of anger, kicked out all the animals and guests, leaving only his wife, his children, and his parents. The home suddenly became spacious and quiet, and everyone lived happily ever after.

(Attitude, Family)

Dates used:____________

The comedy film *Cool Runnings* is about the first Jamaican bobsled team to go to the Olympics. John Candy plays a former American gold medalist who becomes a coach to the Jamaican team. The players grow to like the American coach and affectionately dub him "Sled-god."

Later in the story, the coach's dark history comes out. In an Olympics following his gold medal performance, he broke the rules by weighting the U.S. sled, bringing disgrace on himself and his team.

One of the Jamaican bobsledders could not understand why anyone who had already won a gold medal would cheat. Finally he nervously asked the coach to explain.

"I had to win," he said. "I learned something. If you are not happy without a gold medal, you won't be happy with it."

Randall Bergsma

(Happiness, Motive)

Dates used:____________

Courage

In *A Pretty Good Person,* Lewis Smedes writes:

A federal judge had ordered New Orleans to open its public schools to African-American children, and the white parents decided that if they had to let black children in, they would keep their children out. They let it be known that any black children who came to school would be in for trouble. So the black children stayed home too.

Except Ruby Bridges. Her parents sent her to school all by herself, six years old.

Every morning she walked alone through a heckling crowd to an empty school. White people lined up on both sides of the way and shook their fists at her. They threatened to do terrible things to her if she kept coming to their school. But every morning at ten minutes to eight Ruby walked, head up, eyes ahead, straight through the mob; two U.S. marshals walked ahead of her and two walked behind her. Then she spent the day alone with her teachers inside that big silent school building.

Harvard professor Robert Coles was curious about what went into the making of courageous children like Ruby Bridges. He talked to Ruby's mother and, in his book *The Moral Life of Children,* tells what she said: "There's a lot of people who talk about doing good, and a lot of people who argue about what's good and what's not good," but there are other folks who "just put their lives on the line for what's right."

Bob Campbell

(Action, Racial Reconciliation)

Dates used:____________

Creativity

Helen Prejean, the nun whose experiences with death-row inmates led to the movie *Dead Man Walking*, talked recently about creativity:

"In creating, we imitate God. . . . To be a creator is part of what it means to be a human being. I met a guy on death row in Arizona who had nothing. . . . So he would unravel his socks and weave little necklaces with crosses out of the threads. The first time I visited another death-row inmate, he gave me a picture frame he'd made out of gum wrapper foils.

"These men were locked in a small cell 23 out of 24 hours a day; they had absolutely nothing, and still they were reaching out to create something of beauty and worth."

Inklings *(Vol. 2, No. 3)*

(Beauty, Creation)

Dates used:____________

Criticism

Colonel George Washington Goethals, the man responsible for the completion of the Panama Canal, had big problems with the climate and the geography. But his biggest challenge was the growing criticism back home from those who predicted he'd never finish the project.

Finally, a colleague asked him, "Aren't you going to answer these critics?"

"In time," answered Goethals.

"When?" his partner asked.

"When the canal is finished."

(Accomplishment, Challenges)

Dates used:____________

Cross

In the 1993 movie *In the Line of Fire*, Clint Eastwood played Secret Service agent Frank Horrigan. Horrigan had protected the life of the president for more than three decades, but he was haunted by the memory of what had happened thirty years before. Horrigan was a young agent assigned to President Kennedy on that fateful day in Dallas in 1963. When the assassin fired, Horrigan froze in shock.

For thirty years afterward, he wrestled with the ultimate question for a Secret Service agent: Can I take a bullet for the president?

In the climax of the movie, Horrigan did what he had been unable to do earlier—he threw himself into the path of an assassin's bullet to save the chief executive.

Secret Service agents are willing to do such a thing because they believe the president is so valuable to our country and the world that he is worth dying for. Obviously they would not take a bullet for just anyone.

At Calvary the situation was reversed. The President of the Universe actually took a bullet for each of us. At the Cross we see how valuable we are to God.

Douglas G. Pratt

(Atonement, Substitution)

Dates used:____________

Tim Miller writes:

My nine-year-old daughter Jennifer was looking forward to our family's vacation. But she became ill, and a long anticipated day at Sea World was replaced by an all-night series of CT scans, X-rays, and blood work at the hospital.

As morning approached, the doctors told my exhausted little girl that she would need to have one more test, a spinal tap. The procedure would be painful, they said. The doctor then asked me if I planned to stay in the room. I nodded, knowing I couldn't leave Jennifer alone during the ordeal.

The doctors gently asked Jennifer to remove all her clothing. She looked at me with childlike modesty as if to ask if that were all right. They had her curl into a tiny ball. I buried my face in hers and hugged her.

When the needle went in, Jennifer cried. As the searing pain increased, she sobbingly repeated, "Daddy, Daddy, Daddy," her voice becoming more earnest with each word. It was as if she were saying, "Oh Daddy, please, can't you do something?"

My tears mingled with hers. My heart was broken. I felt nauseated. Because I loved her, I was allowing her to go through the most agonizing experience of her life, and I could hardly stand it.

In the middle of that spinal tap, my thoughts went to the cross of Christ. What unspeakable pain both the Son and the Father went through—for our sake.

(Empathy, Pain)

Dates used:____________

Death

Bob Russell, senior minister of Southeast Christian Church in Louisville, Kentucky, told this story:

When my father died, there was too much snow at our home in Pennsylvania to have a funeral procession. At the end of the service, the funeral director said, "I'll take your dad's body to the grave." I felt we were leaving something undone, so I gathered five of my relatives, and we piled into a four-wheel-drive vehicle, plowed through ten inches of snow into the cemetery, and got about fifty yards from my dad's grave.

The wind was blowing about twenty-five miles an hour. The six of us lugged that casket down to the grave site. We watched as his body was lowered into that grave.

I wanted to pray before we left. "Lord, this is such a cold, lonely place." I got choked up and battled to keep my composure. Finally I just whispered, "But I thank you that to be absent from the body is to be present in your warm arms. Amen."

Preaching Today

(Heaven, Hope)

Dates used:___________

ok 26

A boy and his father were driving down a country road on a beautiful spring afternoon, when a bumblebee flew in the car window. The little boy, who was allergic to bee stings, was petrified. The father quickly reached out, grabbed the bee, squeezed it in his hand, and then released it.

The boy grew frantic as it buzzed by him. Once again the father reached out his hand, but this time he pointed to his palm. There stuck in his skin was the stinger of the bee. "Do you see this?" he asked. "You don't need to be afraid anymore. I've taken the sting for you."

We do not need to fear death anymore. Christ has died and risen again. He has taken the sting from death.

Adrian Uieleman

(Father's Love, Sacrifice)

Dates used:____________

In the movie *Casualties of War*, Michael J. Fox plays Private Erikson, a soldier in Vietnam who is part of a squad that abducts and rapes a young Vietnamese girl. He didn't participate in the crime.

Afterward, as he struggles with what has happened, he says to the other men in his squad, "Just because each of us might at any second be blown away, we're acting like we can do anything we want, as though it doesn't matter what we do. I'm thinking it's just the opposite. Because we might be dead in the next split second, maybe we gotta be extra careful what we do. Because maybe it matters more. Maybe it matters more than we ever know."

Death, for all of us, is a breath away. And the nearer death is, the closer we are to answering to God for all we have said and done.

Joel Sarrault

(Conscience, Consequences)

Dates used:____________

Determination

Guideposts (9/95) published the story of Jim Stovall, who became totally blind at age twenty-nine. While he still had partial vision, he volunteered at a school for the blind. He was assigned to help a four-year-old boy, blind and severely handicapped. Stovall spent considerable time trying to convince the boy he could tie his own shoes or climb stairs in spite of his limitations.

"No, I can't!" the boy insisted.

"Yes, you can," Stovall replied.

"No, I can't!" The verbal battle went on.

Meanwhile, Stovall fought his own limitations. Because of his deteriorating vision, he decided he had to quit his college courses. On his way to withdraw from college, he decided to resign his volunteer position as well.

"It's just too tough," he explained. "I can't do it."

"Yes, you can!" said a little voice beside him. It was the four-year-old who refused to tie his shoes.

"No, I can't!" said Stovall with conviction.

"Yes, you can!"

Stovall realized if he didn't continue, the child would give up too. So Stovall stayed in school and graduated three-and-a-half years later. The same week he graduated, his little friend tied his shoes and climbed a flight of stairs.

Philippians tell us we "can do all things through Christ who gives us strength."

David Chotka

(Example, Perseverance)

Dates used:____________

Discipleship

From time to time, lobsters have to leave their shells in order to grow. They need the shell to protect them from being torn apart, yet when they grow, the old shell must be abandoned. If they did not abandon it, the old shell would soon become their prison—and finally their casket.

The tricky part for the lobster is the brief period of time between when the old shell is discarded and the new one is formed. During that terribly vulnerable period, the transition must be scary to the lobster. Currents gleefully cartwheel them from coral to kelp. Hungry schools of fish are ready to make them a part of their food chain. For awhile at least, that old shell must look pretty good.

We are not so different from lobsters. To change and grow, we must sometimes shed our shells—a structure, a framework—we've depended on. Discipleship means being so committed to Christ that when he bids us to follow, we will change, risk, grow, and leave our "shells" behind.

Brent Mitchell

(Growth, Transitions)

Dates used:____________

Distractions

In one scene of the popular movie *Robin Hood, The Prince of Thieves,* Kevin Costner as Robin comes to a young man taking aim at an archery target. Robin asks, "Can you shoot amid distractions?"

Just before the boy releases the string, Robin pokes his ear with the feathers of an arrow. The boy's shot flies high by several feet.

After the laughter of those watching dies down, Maid Marian, standing behind the boy, asks Robin, "Can you?"

Robin Hood raises his bow and takes aim. Just as he releases the arrow, Maid Marian leans beside him and flirtatiously blows into his face. The arrow misses the target, glances off the tree behind it, and scarcely misses a bystander.

Distractions come in all types, and whether they are painful or pleasant, the result is the same: We miss God's mark.

Penney F. Nichols

(Sin, Temptation)

Dates used:____________

Empathy

Mr. Alter's fifth-grade class at Lake Elementary School in Oceanside, California, included fourteen boys who had no hair. Only one, however, had no choice in the matter.

In an Associated Press story (March 1994), Ian O'Gorman, undergoing chemotherapy for lymphoma, faced the prospect of having his hair fall out in clumps. So he had his head shaved. But then thirteen of his classmates shaved their heads, so Ian wouldn't feel out of place.

Ten-year-old Kyle Hanslik started it all. He talked to some other boys, and before long they all trekked to the barbershop. "The last thing he would want is to not fit in," said Kyle. "We just wanted to make him feel better."

"Carry each other's burdens, and in this way you will fulfill the law of Christ" (Gal. 6:2).

Sherman L. Burford

(Caring, Compassion)

Dates used:____________

Encouragement

For years William Wilberforce pushed Britain's Parliament to abolish slavery. Discouraged, he was about to give up. His elderly friend, John Wesley, heard of it and from his deathbed called for pen and paper.

With trembling hand, Wesley wrote: "Unless God has raised you up for this very thing, you will be worn out by the opposition of men and devils. But if God be for you, who can be against you? Are all of them stronger than God?

"Oh be not weary of well-doing! Go on, in the name of God and in the power of his might, till even American slavery shall vanish away before it."

Wesley died six days later. But Wilberforce fought for forty-five more years and in 1833, three days before his own death, saw slavery abolished in Britain.

Even the greatest ones need encouragement.

Carol Porter

(Opposition, Perseverance)

Dates used:____________

Endurance

Portable camcorders have a battery pack for power. Instructions typically recommend that users allow the battery pack to completely discharge before recharging, especially the first few times. This actually increases the endurance of the battery.

In like manner, our trials "discharge" us, emptying us of our dependence on human strength and increasing our capacity to receive God's limitless power.

Philip Bourdon

(Dependence, God's Power)

Dates used:____________

Ethics

Nearly half (48 percent) of American workers admitted to taking unethical or illegal actions in the past year. *USA Today* (4/4/97) revealed the top five types of unethical/illegal behavior that workers say they have engaged in over the past year because of pressure:

- Cut corners on quality control
- Covered up incidents
- Abused or lied about sick days
- Lied to or deceived customers
- Put inappropriate pressure on others.

survey by Ethics Officers Association and the American Society of Chartered Life Underwriters and Chartered Financial Consultants

(Dishonesty, Lying)

Dates used:____________

Evangelism

The Oakland, California, police force recently unveiled its first "lowrider" police car. The vehicle has the standard logo, lights, and siren, but also includes chrome wheels, hydraulic lifts, and a 500-watt sound system. The car was put on the force to help officers build better relationships with inner-city kids.

Paul applied the same principle to evangelism in 1 Corinthians 9:22–23: "I have become all things to all men so that by all possible means I might save some."

Chip Johnston

(Relationships, Strategy)

Dates used:____________

Louis Pasteur, the pioneer of immunology, lived at a time when thousands of people died each year of rabies. Pasteur had worked for years on a vaccine. Just as he was about to begin experimenting on himself, a nine-year-old, Joseph Meister, was bitten by a rabid dog. The boy's mother begged Pasteur to experiment on her son. Pasteur injected Joseph for ten days—and the boy lived.

Decades later, of all the things Pasteur could have had etched on his headstone, he asked for three words: JOSEPH MEISTER LIVED.

Our greatest legacy will be those who live eternally because of our efforts.

R. Wayne Willis

(Legacy, Service)

Dates used:___________

In *Conspiracy of Kindness*, Steve Sjogren (pronounced Show-gren) tells the true story of Joe Delaney and his eight-year-old son, Jared, who were playing catch in their backyard.

Jared asked, "Dad, is there a God?"

Joe replied that he went to church only a few times when he was a kid; he really had no idea.

Jared ran into the house. "I'll be right back!" he yelled.

Moments later he returned with a helium balloon from the circus, a pen, and an index card. "I'm going to send God an airmail message," Jared explained. "Dear God," wrote Jared, "if you are real, and you are there, send people who know you to Dad and me."

God, I hope you're watching, Joe thought, as they watched the balloon and message sail away.

Two days later, Joe and Jared pulled into a car wash sponsored by Sjogren's church. When Joe asked, "How much?" Sjogren answered, "It's free. No strings attached. We just want to show God's love in a practical way."

"Are you guys Christians, the kind of Christians who believe in God?" Joe asked.

Sjogren said, "Yes, we're that kind of Christians."

From that encounter, Steve led Joe to faith in Christ.

Many people may be only one act of kindness from meeting a true Christian.

Tom Lundeen

(Kindness, Ministry)

Dates used:___________

Doug Nichols shares this story:

While serving with Operation Mobilization in India in 1967, tuberculosis forced me into a sanitarium for several months. I sensed many weren't happy about a rich American (to them all Americans were rich) being in a free, government-run sanitarium. I did not yet speak the language, but I tried to give Christian literature written in their language to the patients, doctors, and nurses. Everyone politely refused.

The first few nights I woke around 2 a.m., coughing. One morning during my coughing spell, I noticed one of the older and sicker patients across the aisle trying to get out of bed. He would sit up on the edge of the bed and try to stand, but in weakness would fall back into bed. I didn't understand what he was trying to do. He finally fell back into bed exhausted. I heard him crying softly.

The next morning I realized he had been trying to get up and walk to the bathroom! The stench in our ward was awful. Other patients yelled insults at the man. Angry nurses moved him roughly from side to side as they cleaned up the mess. One nurse even slapped him. The old man curled into a ball and wept.

The next night I again woke up coughing. I noticed the man across the aisle again try to stand. Like the night before, he fell back whimpering. I don't like bad smells, and I didn't want to become involved, but I got out of bed and went over to him. When I touched his shoulder, his eyes opened wide with fear. I smiled, put my arms under him, and picked him up.

He was very light due to old age and advanced TB. I carried him to the washroom, which was just a filthy, small room with a hole in the floor. I stood behind him with my arms under his armpits as he took care of himself. After he finished, I picked him up, and carried him back to his bed. As I laid him down, he kissed me on the cheek, smiled, and said something I couldn't understand.

The next morning another patient woke me and handed me a steaming cup of tea. He motioned with his hands that he wanted a tract.

As the sun rose, other patients approached and indicated they also wanted the booklets I had tried to distribute before. Throughout the day nurses, interns, and doctors asked for literature.

Weeks later an evangelist who spoke the language visited me, and discovered that several had put their trust in Christ as Savior as a result of reading the literature.

What did it take to reach these people with the gospel? It wasn't health, the ability to speak their language, or a persuasive talk. I simply took a trip to the bathroom.

(Compassion, Ministry)

Dates used:____________

In 1992, a Los Angeles County parking control officer came upon a brown El Dorado Cadillac illegally parked next to the curb on street-sweeping day.

The officer dutifully wrote out a ticket. Ignoring the man seated at the driver's wheel, the officer reached inside the open car window and placed the $30 citation on the dashboard.

The driver of the car made no excuses. No argument ensued—and with good reason. The driver of the car had been shot in the head ten to twelve hours before but was sitting up, stiff as a board, slumped slightly forward, with blood on his face. He was dead.

The officer, preoccupied with ticket-writing, was unaware of anything out of the ordinary. He got back in his car and drove away.

Many people around us are "dead in transgressions and sins." What should catch our attention most is their need, not their offenses. They don't need a citation; they need a Savior.

Greg Asimakoupoulos

(Attention, Neglect)

Dates used:____________

Andrew Meekens, an elder in the International Evangelical Church of Addis Ababa, was one of those who died on November 23, 1996, when a hijacked jet ran out of fuel and crashed near the Comoros Islands.

According to survivors of the crash, after the pilot announced he would attempt an emergency landing, Meekens stood up and spoke, calming passengers on the Ethiopian Airlines flight. Meekens then presented the gospel of Jesus Christ, and invited people to respond.

A surviving flight attendant said that about twenty people accepted salvation, including a flight attendant who did not survive the crash.

We preach as dying people to dying people.

Beacon *(1/97)*

(Courage, Salvation)

Dates used:____________

On his night job at Taco Bell, seventeen-year-old Nicholas Zenns was taking orders at the drive-up window. He heard a woman scream, turned, and saw a very pregnant Devorah Anderson standing in front of him. The high-school student pulled off his headset, called the paramedics, and tried to make the woman comfortable. But the baby wouldn't wait. "The baby's head just popped out into my hands," Nicholas said.

Paramedics finally arrived and took baby and parents to the hospital. Nicholas cleaned up, "sterilized my hands about a thousand times," and finished his shift.

Nicholas says this event changed his perspective. "Things have been pretty bad in my life lately, and then I got to do this. I'm really glad."

In the same way, nothing makes life more meaningful than leading someone to new birth in Christ.

San Diego Union-Tribune *(5/23/96)*

(Outreach, Salvation)

Dates used:____________

Example

According to the *Bergen* (NJ) *Record*, the zoo in Copenhagen, Denmark, recently put a human couple on display. Henrik Lehmann and Malene Botoft live in a see-through cage, in the primate display, next to the baboons and the monkeys.

Their 320-square-foot habitat has a living room with furniture, a computer, a television, and stereo. The kitchen and bedroom are part of the display. Only the bathroom is excluded from public view.

Unlike their neighbors, who aren't allowed out, the two humans occasionally leave their fishbowl existence to shop and water the flowers on their porch back home.

"We don't notice visitors anymore," said Lehmann. "If I want to pick my nose or my toes now, I do it."

We would do well to remember that people are watching the way we live. "In everything set them an example by doing what is good" (Titus 2:7).

Parade *(12/29/96)*

(Marriage, Privacy)

Dates used:____________

Expectations

A traveler nearing a great city asked an old man seated by the road, "What are the people like in this city?"

The man replied, "What were they like where you came from?"

"A terrible lot," the traveler reported. "Mean, untrustworthy, detestable in all respects."

"Ah," said the old man. "You will find them the same in the city ahead."

Scarcely had the first traveler gone on his way when another stopped to inquire about the people in the city before him. Again the old man asked about the people in the place the traveler had just left.

"They were fine people, honest, industrious, and generous to a fault. I was sorry to leave," declared the second traveler.

Responded the wise one, "So you will find them in the city ahead."

Boyd Seevers

(Attitude, Relationships)

Dates used:____________

"First day in the sixth grade, I'll never forget it," recalls Jesse Jackson, who ran for president of the United States in 1988. "My teacher was Miz Shelton, and she began writing these long words on the blackboard we couldn't understand, never even heard of before. We all looked around and started whispering to each other, 'She got the wrong class. She thinks we the eighth-grade class.'

"Somebody finally called out, 'Uh, Miz Shelton? Those are eighth-grade words. We only the sixth grade here.'

"She turned around. 'I know what grade you are. I work here. And you'll learn every one of these words, and a lot more like them, before this year is over. I will not teach down to you. One of you little brats just might be mayor or governor, or even president, some day, and I'm gonna make sure you'll be ready.'

"And she turned back and went right on writing." At that time, Jackson says, her proposition prompted no glow of possibility in him. "Aim to be governor? Even aim to be mayor, when in Greenville then there wasn't a single African-American on the Board of Education, in the police department, the fire department? And aim to be president?!"

Before any great accomplishment, someone must have a vision.

New Yorker *(2/10/92)*

(Hope, Vision)

Dates used:____________

Failure

Dani Tyler, third-base star for the U.S. women's Olympic softball team, hit a home run. Or so she thought. In her excitement rounding the bases, she accidentally stepped over home plate. The umpire disallowed the run. Because of that one misstep, the U.S. team lost in extra innings 2–1, only their second international loss in ten years.

The next evening, Tyler played well. *Sports Illustrated* writer Peter King (8/12/96) asked her why the mistake hadn't become a mental ball-and-chain.

"Well, I didn't want to get out of bed this morning," she admitted. "But this is sports. One play doesn't make a game, and one play won't define my life. I've never been the best athlete, but I try to have the best attitude and work the hardest. What happened was a freak thing. It's over. If I whine about it, or make excuses, or argue, what happens? I look like a jerk."

(Adversity, Excuses)

Dates used:____________

Faith

William Plummer and Bonnie Bell wrote in *People* magazine:

The Northwestern University Wildcats shocked the world of college football in 1995 by making it to the Rose Bowl Tournament. The man behind the team's turnaround was coach Gary Barnett. . . . [Barnett] was determined to prove that kids at the Big Ten's smallest and most academically demanding school could play football. He ordered a Tournament of Roses flag for the football building and kept a silk rose on his desk to remind everyone where they were headed.

"At the first meeting," says kicker Sam Valenzisi, "he told us we needed belief without evidence. He asked, 'Do you know what that is? That's faith.'"

Sherman L. Burford

(Achievement, Belief)

Dates used:____________

Ben Patterson, in *Waiting*, writes:

In 1988, three friends and I climbed Mount Lyell, the highest peak in Yosemite National Park. Our base camp was less than 2,000 feet from the peak, but the climb to the top and back was to take the better part of a day, due in large part to the difficulty of the glacier we had to cross to get to the top. The morning of the climb we started out chattering and cracking jokes.

As the hours passed, the two more experienced mountaineers opened up a wide gap between me and my less-experienced companion. Being competitive by nature, I began to look for shortcuts to beat them to the top. I thought I saw one to the right of an outcropping of rock—so I went, deaf to the protests of my companion.

Perhaps it was the effect of the high altitude, but the significance of the two experienced climbers not choosing this path did not register in my consciousness. It should have, for thirty minutes later I was trapped in a cul-de-sac of rock atop the Lyell Glacier, looking down several hundred feet of a sheer slope of ice, pitched at about a forty-five degree angle. . . . I was only about ten feet from the safety of a rock, but one little slip and I wouldn't stop sliding until I landed in the valley floor some fifty miles away! It was nearly noon, and the warm sun had the glacier glistening with slippery ice. I was stuck, and I was scared.

It took an hour for my experienced climbing friends to find me. Standing on the rock I wanted to reach, one of them leaned out and used an ice ax to chip two little footsteps in the glacier. Then he gave me the following instructions: "Ben, you must step out from where you are and put your foot where the first foothold is. When your foot touches it, without a moment's hesitation swing your other foot across and land it on the next step. When you do that, reach out and I will take your hand and pull you to safety."

That sounded real good to me. It was the next thing he said that made me more frightened than ever. "But listen carefully: As you step across, do not lean into the mountain! If anything,

NEXT PAGE

lean out a bit. Otherwise, your feet may fly out from under you, and you will start sliding down."

I don't like precipices. When I am on the edge of a cliff, my instincts are to lie down and hug the mountain, to become one with it, not to lean away from it! But that was what my good friend was telling me to do. For a moment, based solely on what I believed to be the good will and good sense of my friend, I decided to say no to what I felt, to stifle my impulse to cling to the security of the mountain, to lean out, step out, and traverse the ice to safety. It took less than two seconds to find out if my faith was well-founded.

To save us, God often tells us to do things that are the opposite of our natural inclination. Is God loving and faithful? Can we trust him?

He is. We can.

(Obedience, Trust)

Dates used:____________

The mighty Niagara River plummets some 180 feet at the American and Horseshoe Falls. Before the falls, there are violent, turbulent rapids. Farther upstream, however, where the river's current flows more gently, boats are able to navigate. Just before the Welland River empties into the Niagara, a pedestrian walkway spans the river. Posted on this bridge's pylons is a warning sign for all boaters: DO YOU HAVE AN ANCHOR? followed by, DO YOU KNOW HOW TO USE IT?

Faith, like an anchor, is something we need to have and use to avoid spiritual cataclysm.

Paul Adams

(Crisis, Preparation)

Dates used:____________

X

Faithfulness

While Eric Hulstrand of Binford, North Dakota, was preaching one Sunday, an elderly woman, Mary, fainted and struck her head on the end of the pew. Immediately, an EMT in the congregation called an ambulance.

As they strapped her to a stretcher and got ready to head out the door, Mary regained consciousness. She motioned for her daughter to come near. Everyone thought she was summoning her strength to convey what could be her final words. The daughter leaned over until her ear was at her mother's mouth.

"My offering is in my purse," she whispered.

(Generosity, Stewardship)

Dates used:____________

Newsweek (11/19/90) ran an article titled "Letters in the Sand," a compilation of letters written by military personnel to family and friends in the States during the Gulf War.

One was written by Marine Corporal Preston Coffer. He told a friend, "We are talking about Marines, not the Boy Scouts. We all joined the service knowing full well what might be expected of us." He signed off with the Marine motto, *Semper Fi,* Latin for "always faithful."

The Bible says, "Now it is required that those who have been given a trust must prove faithful" (1 Cor. 4:2).

Richie Lewis

(Dedication, Expectations)

Dates used:____________

Family of God

When she turned twenty-one, Tammy Harris from Roanoke, Virginia, began searching for her biological mother. After a year, she had not succeeded. What she didn't know was that her mother, Joyce Schultz, had been trying to locate her for twenty years.

According to a recent Associated Press story, there was one more thing Tammy didn't know: Her mother was one of her coworkers at the convenience store where she worked! One day Joyce overheard Tammy talking with another coworker about trying to find her mother. Soon they were comparing birth certificates.

When Tammy realized that the coworker she had known was, in fact, her mother, she fell into her arms. "We held on for the longest time," Tammy said. "It was the best day of my life."

Each week we rub shoulders with people whom we may barely notice. But if they share a birth in Christ, they are our dearest relatives. How precious is the family of God!

B. Paul Greene

(Church, Relationships)

Dates used:____________

Fatherhood

At a 1994 Promise Keepers' conference in Denton, Texas, pastor James Ryle told his story:

When he was two years old, his father was sent to prison. When he was seven, authorities placed him in an orphanage. At nineteen, he had a car wreck that killed a friend. He sold drugs to raise money for his legal fee, and the law caught up to him. He was arrested, charged with a felony, and sent to prison.

While in prison James accepted Christ, and after he served his time, he eventually went into the ministry. Years later he sought out his father to reconcile with him. When they got together, the conversation turned to prison life.

James's father asked, "Which prison were you in?"

James told him, and his father was taken aback. "I helped build that prison," he said. He had been a welder who went from place to place building penitentiaries.

Pastor Ryle concluded, "I was in the prison my father built."

A father's example builds a place to live for his children. Will it be a house, or a prison?

Larry Pillow

(Example, Legacy)

Dates used:____________

Greg Norman intimidates most other professional golfers with his ice-cold stoicism. He learned his hard-nosed tactics from his father. "I used to see my father, getting off a plane or something, and I'd want to hug him," he recalled once. "But he'd only shake my hand." Commenting on his aloofness going into the 1996 Masters golf tournament, Norman said, "Nobody really knows me out here."

After leading golf's most prestigious event from the start, Norman blew a six-shot lead in the last round, losing to rival Nick Faldo.

Rick Reilly writes, "Now, as Faldo made one last thrust into Norman's heart with a fifteen-foot birdie putt on the seventy-second hole, the two of them came toward each other, Norman trying to smile, looking for a handshake and finding himself in the warmest embrace instead.

"As they held that hug, held it even as both of them cried, Norman changed just a little. 'I wasn't crying because I'd lost,' Norman said the next day. 'I've lost a lot of golf tournaments before. I'll lose a lot more. I cried because I'd never felt that from another man before. I've never had a hug like that in my life.'"

Sports Illustrated *(12/30/96)*

(Brotherhood, Men)

Dates used:____________

Final Judgment

Steve Winger from Lubbock, Texas, writes about his last college test—a final in a logic class known for its difficult exams:

To help us on our test, the professor told us we could bring as much information to the exam as we could fit on a piece of notebook paper. Most students crammed as many facts as possible on their 8-1/2 x 11 inch sheet of paper.

But one student walked into class, put a piece of notebook paper on the floor, and had an advanced logic student stand on the paper. The advanced logic student told him everything he needed to know. He was the only student to receive an A.

The ultimate final exam will come when we stand before God and he asks, "Why should I let you in?" On our own we cannot pass that exam. But we have Someone who will stand in for us.

(Intercession, Reconciliation)

Dates used:____________

Finishing Well

At 7 p.m. on October 20, 1968, a few thousand spectators remained in the Mexico City Olympic Stadium. It was cool and dark. The last of the marathon runners, each exhausted, were being carried off to first-aid stations. More than an hour earlier, Mamo Wolde of Ethiopia—looking as fresh as when he started the race—crossed the finish line, the winner of the 26-mile, 385-yard event.

As the remaining spectators prepared to leave, those sitting near the marathon gates suddenly heard the sound of sirens and police whistles. All eyes turned to the gate. A lone figure wearing number 36 and the colors of Tanzania entered the stadium. His name was John Stephen Akhwari. He was the last man to finish the marathon. He had fallen during the race and injured his knee and ankle. Now, with his leg bloodied and bandaged, he grimaced with each hobbling step around the 400-meter track.

The spectators rose and applauded him. After crossing the finish line, Akhwari slowly walked off the field. Later, a reporter asked Akhwari the question on everyone's mind: "Why did you continue the race after you were so badly injured?"

He replied, "My country did not send me 7,000 miles to start the race. They sent me 7,000 miles to finish it."

"Let us run with perseverance the race marked out for us" (Heb. 12:1).

Wes Thompson

(Perseverance, Tenacity)

Dates used:____________

In a recent NCAA cross-country championship held in Riverside, California, 123 of the 128 runners missed a turn. One competitor, Mike Delcavo, stayed on the 10,000-meter course and began waving for fellow runners to follow him. Delcavo was able to convince only four other runners to go with him.

Asked what his competitors thought of his midrace decision not to follow the crowd, Delcavo responded, "They thought it was funny that I went the right way."

Delcavo ran correctly. In the same way, our goal is to run correctly—to finish the race marked out for us by Christ. We can rejoice over those who have courage to follow, ignoring the laughter of the crowd.

"I have fought the good fight, I have finished the race, I have kept the faith. Now there is in store for me the crown of righteousness" (2 Tim. 4:7–8).

Loren D. McBain

(Courage, Obedience)

Dates used:____________

Focus

On Day Six of the ill-fated mission of Apollo 13, the astronauts needed to make a critical course correction. If they failed, they might never return to Earth.

To conserve power, they shut down the onboard computer that steered the craft. Yet the astronauts needed to conduct a thirty-nine-second burn of the main engines. How to steer?

Astronaut Jim Lovell determined that if they could keep a fixed point in space in view through their tiny window, they could steer the craft manually. That focal point turned out to be their destination—Earth.

As shown in 1995's hit movie *Apollo 13*, for thirty-nine agonizing seconds, Lovell focused on keeping the earth in view. By not losing sight of that reference point, the three astronauts avoided disaster.

Scripture reminds us that to finish our life mission successfully, we must "Fix our eyes on Jesus, the author and perfecter of our faith" (Heb. 12:2).

Stephen Nordbye

(Completion, Success)

Dates used:____________

Warren Bennis, in *Why Leaders Can't Lead*, writes:

The flying Wallendas are perhaps the world's greatest family of aerialists and tightrope walkers. . . . I was struck with [Karl Wallenda's] capacity for concentration on the intention, the task, the decision. I was even more intrigued when, several months later, Wallenda fell to his death while walking a tightrope without a safety net between two high-rise buildings in San Juan, Puerto Rico. . . .

Later, Wallenda's wife said that before her husband had fallen, for the first time since she had known him, he had been concentrating on falling, instead of on walking the tightrope. He had personally supervised the attachment of the guide wires, which he had never done before.

Often the difference between success and failure, life and death, is the direction we're looking.

Rex Bonar

(Failure, Success)

Dates used:____________

Tom Friends of *The New York Times* asked coach Jimmy Johnson what he told his players before leading the Dallas Cowboys onto the field for the 1993 Super Bowl.

"I told them that if I laid a two-by-four across the floor, everybody there would walk across it and not fall, because our focus would be on walking the length of that board. But if I put that same board ten stories high between two buildings, only a few would make it, because the focus would be on falling."

Johnson told his players not to focus on the crowd, the media, or the possibility of falling, but to focus on each play of the game as if it were a good practice session. The Cowboys won the game 52–7.

A Christian must not focus on what people think, but only on what is "excellent or praiseworthy" (Phil. 4:8).

Steve Chandler
100 Ways to Motivate Yourself

(Target, Thoughts)

Dates used:____________

Forgiveness

The picture haunted him. Like many Americans, Rev. John Plummer, minister of Bethany United Methodist Church in Purcellville, Virginia, was moved by the Vietnam-era Pulitzer-Prize-winning photo of nine-year-old Phan Thi Kim Phuc, naked and horribly burned, running from a napalm attack.

But for Plummer, that picture had special significance. In 1972 he was responsible for setting up the air strike on the village of Trang Bang—a strike approved after he was twice assured there were no civilians in the area.

Plummer said that even though he knew he had done everything possible to make sure the area was clear of civilians, he experienced new pain each time he saw the picture. He wanted to tell Kim Phuc how sorry he was.

After becoming a Christian in 1990, Plummer felt called to the ministry and attended seminary. In June 1996 he learned that Kim Phuc was still alive and living in Toronto. The next month he attended a military reunion and met someone who knew both Kim Phuc and the photographer. Plummer learned that on that fateful day in 1972, Kim Phuc and her family were hiding in a pagoda in Trang Bang when a bomb hit the building. Kim Phuc and others ran into the street, where they were hit by napalm being dropped from another plane. She tore off her burning clothing as she fled. Two of her cousins were killed.

The photographer and other journalists poured water from canteens on her burns. She collapsed moments after the famous photo and was rushed by car to a hospital. The girl spent fourteen months in hospitals and was operated on by a San Francisco plastic surgeon.

Plummer learned that Kim Phuc was speaking at the Vietnam Veterans Memorial in Washington, D.C. He went and heard Kim Phuc say that if she ever met the pilot of the plane, she would tell him she forgives him and that they cannot change the past, but she hoped they could work together in the future.

Plummer was able to get word to Kim Phuc that the man she wanted to meet was there.

Next page →

"She saw my grief, my pain, my sorrow," Plummer wrote in an article in the *Virginia Advocate*. "She held out her arms to me and embraced me. All I could say was, 'I'm sorry; I'm so sorry; I'm sorry' over and over again. At the same time she was saying, 'It's all right; it's all right; I forgive; I forgive.'"

Plummer learned that although she was raised a Buddhist, Kim Phuc became a Christian in 1982.

Evangelical Press News Service

(Pardon, Restitution)

Dates used:____________

The story of "Wrong Way Riegels" is a familiar one, but it bears repeating.

On New Year's Day, 1929, Georgia Tech played University of California Berkeley in the Rose Bowl. In that game a young man named Roy Riegels recovered a fumble for California. Picking up the loose ball, he lost his direction and ran sixty-five yards toward the wrong goal line. One of his teammates, Benny Lom, ran him down and tackled him just before he scored for the opposing team. Several plays later, the Bruins had to punt. Tech blocked the kick and scored a safety, demoralizing the California team.

The strange play came in the first half. At half-time the California players filed off the field and into the dressing room. As others sat down on the benches and the floor, Riegels sat down in a corner, and put his face in his hands.

A football coach usually has a great deal to say to his team during halftime. That day Coach Price was quiet. No doubt he was trying to decide what to do with Riegels.

When the timekeeper came in and announced that there were three minutes before playing time, Coach Price looked at the team and said, "Men, the same team that played the first half will start the second." The players got up and started out, all but Riegels. He didn't budge. The coach looked back and called to him. Riegels didn't move. Coach Price went over to where Riegels sat and said, "Roy, didn't you hear me? The same team that played the first half will start the second."

Roy Riegels looked up, his cheeks wet with tears. "Coach," he said, "I can't do it. I've ruined you. I've ruined the university's reputation. I've ruined myself. I can't face that crowd out there."

Coach Price reached out, put his hand on Riegels's shoulder, and said, "Roy, get up and go on back. The game is only half over."

Riegels finally did get up. He went onto the field, and the fans saw him play hard and play well.

All of us have run a long way in the wrong direction. Because of God's mercy, however, the game is only half over.

Wayne Rouse

(Mistakes, Starting Over)

Dates used:____________

OK (51)

Ronald Reagan's attitude after the 1981 attempt on his life made an impression on his daughter, Patti Davis:

"The following day my father said he knew his physical healing was directly dependent on his ability to forgive John Hinckley. By showing me that forgiveness is the key to everything, including physical health and healing, he gave me an example of Christlike thinking."

Angels Don't Die

(Example, Healing)

Dates used:____________

Freedom

Freedom does not mean the absence of constraints or moral absolutes. Suppose a skydiver at 10,000 feet announces to the rest of the group, "I'm not using a parachute this time. I want freedom!"

The fact is that a skydiver is constrained by a greater law—the law of gravity. But when the skydiver chooses the "constraint" of the parachute, she is free to enjoy the exhilaration.

God's moral laws act the same way: They restrain, but they are absolutely necessary to enjoy the exhilaration of real freedom.

Colin Campbell

(Law, Obedience)

Dates used:____________

Eating lunch at a small cafe, Mark Reed of Camarillo, California, saw a sparrow hop through the open door and peck at the crumbs near his table. When the crumbs were gone, the sparrow hopped to the window ledge, spread its wings, and took flight. Brief flight. It crashed against the windowpane and fell to the floor.

The bird quickly recovered and tried again. Crash. And again. Crash.

Mark got up and attempted to shoo the sparrow out the door, but the closer he got, the harder it threw itself against the pane. He nudged it with his hand. That sent the sparrow fluttering along the ledge, hammering its beak at the glass.

Finally, Mark reached out and gently caught the bird, folding his fingers around its wings and body. It weighed almost nothing. He thought of how powerless and vulnerable the sparrow must have felt. At the door he released it, and the sparrow sailed away.

As Mark did with the sparrow, God takes us captive only to set us free.

(Captive, God's Love)

Dates used:____________

When you stand beside a 747 jet on the runway, its massive weight and size makes it seem incapable of breaking the holds of gravity.

But when the power of its engines combines with the laws of aerodynamics, the plane is able to lift itself to 35,000 feet and travel at 600 miles per hour. Gravity is still pulling on the plane, but as long as it obeys the laws of aerodynamics, it can break free from the bonds of earth.

"Through Christ Jesus the law of the Spirit of life set me free from the law of sin and death" (Rom. 8:2).

Bill Morris

(Law, Obedience)

Dates used:____________

Future

In an essay entitled "Good Guys Finish First (Sometimes)," Andrew Bagnato told the following story:

Following a rags-to-riches season that led them to the Rose Bowl—their first in decades—Northwestern University's Wildcats met with coach Gary Barnett for the opening of spring training.

As players found their seats, Barnett announced that he was going to hand out the awards that many Wildcats had earned in 1995. Some players exchanged glances. Barnett does not normally dwell on the past. But as the coach continued to call players forward and handed them placards proclaiming their achievements, they were cheered on by their teammates.

One of the other coaches gave Barnett a placard representing his seventeen national coach-of-the-year awards. Then, as the applause subsided, Barnett walked to a trash can marked "1995." He took an admiring glance at his placard, then dumped it in the can.

In the silence that followed, one by one, the team's stars dumped their placards on top of Barnett's. Barnett had shouted a message without uttering a word: "What you did in 1995 was terrific, lads. But look at the calendar: It's 1996."

It's great to celebrate the accomplishments of the past. But with God, our best days are always ahead.

Chicago Tribune Magazine *(9/1/96)*

(Achievement, Nostalgia)

Dates used:____________

Generosity

Anne Keegan's article "Blue Christmas" was a collection of Christmas stories told by Chicago police officers. One was the story of George White.

George lived in a rented room at the YMCA. He had one set of clothes, shoes wrapped with rubber bands to keep the soles from flopping, and a threadbare black overcoat. He spent his mornings napping in an old metal chair by the heater in the back of the 18th District office.

Two officers, Kitowski and Mitch, took an interest in the old man, occasionally slipping him a few bucks. They found out that Billy the Greek over at the G&W grill gave him a hot breakfast every morning, no charge.

The two policemen and their families decided to have George as their guest for Christmas dinner. They gave him presents, which he unwrapped carefully.

As they drove him back to the Y, George asked, "Are these presents really mine to keep?" They assured him they were. "Then we must stop at the G&W before I go home," he said. With that, George began rewrapping his presents.

When they walked into the restaurant, Billy the Greek was there as always. "You been good to me, Billy," said George. "Now I can be good to you. Merry Christmas." George gave all his presents away on the spot.

Generosity is natural when a grateful attitude prevails.

Chicago Tribune Magazine *(12/24/95)*

(Attitude, Selflessness)

Dates used:____________

Gentleness

Under the headline "Gear Blamed in Crash That Killed Senator," the April 29, 1992, issue of the *Chicago Tribune* reported:

A stripped gear in the propeller controls of a commuter plane caused it to nosedive into the Georgia woods last April, killing former U.S. Senator John Tower of Texas and twenty-two others, the government concluded Tuesday.

A gear that adjusted the pitch of the left engine's propellers was slowly worn away by an opposing part with a harder titanium coating, the National Transportation Safety Board said.

"It acted like a file, and over time it wore down the teeth that controlled the propeller," said acting board chairman Susan Coughlin.

Like the titanium-coated gear that wore away the softer gear engaged to it, so one abrasive, unkind spouse or friend can wear away the spirit of another.

(Relationships, Unkindness)

Dates used:____________

Giving

Fortune magazine reported that the nation's top twenty-five philanthropists gave away more than $1.5 billion in 1996. The most generous was George Soros, president of Soros Fund Management, who donated $350 million last year.

Of the top twenty-five philanthropists, only four inherited fortunes. Most attributed their generosity in part to religious backgrounds. And most were donors even before they became wealthy.

(Generosity, Stewardship)

Dates used:____________

In *Run with the Horses*, Eugene Peterson writes about seeing a family of birds teaching the young to fly. Three young swallows were perched on a dead branch that stretched out over a lake.

"One adult swallow got alongside the chicks and started shoving them out toward the end of the branch—pushing, pushing, pushing. The end one fell off. Somewhere between the branch and the water four feet below, the wings started working, and the fledgling was off on his own. Then the second one.

"The third was not to be bullied. At the last possible moment his grip on the branch loosened just enough so that he swung downward, then tightened again, bulldog tenacious. The parent was without sentiment. He pecked at the desperately clinging talons until it was more painful for the poor chick to hang on than risk the insecurities of flying. The grip was released, and the inexperienced wings began pumping. The mature swallow knew what the chick did not—that it would fly—that there was no danger in making it do what it was perfectly designed to do.

"Birds have feet and can walk. Birds have talons and can grasp a branch securely. They can walk; they can cling. But flying is their characteristic action, and not until they fly are they living at their best, gracefully and beautifully.

"Giving is what we do best. It is the air into which we were born. It is the action that was designed into us before our birth. . . . Some of us try desperately to hold on to ourselves, to live for ourselves. We look so bedraggled and pathetic doing it, hanging on to the dead branch of a bank account for dear life, afraid to risk ourselves on the untried wings of giving. We don't think we can live generously because we have never tried. But the sooner we start, the better, for we are going to have to give up our lives finally, and the longer we wait, the less time we have for the soaring and swooping life of grace."

David B. Jackson

(Adversity, Miserliness)

Dates used:____________

God's Glory

During construction of Emerson Hall at Harvard University, President Charles Eliot invited psychologist and philosopher William James to suggest a suitable inscription for the stone lintel over the doors of the new home of the philosophy department.

After some reflection, James sent Eliot a line from the Greek philosopher Protagoras: "Man is the measure of all things."

James never heard back from Eliot, so his curiosity was piqued when he spotted artisans working on a scaffold hidden by a canvas. One morning the scaffold and canvas were gone. The inscription? "What is man that thou art mindful of him?"

Eliot had replaced James's suggestion with words from the Psalmist. Between these two lines lies the great distance between the God-centered and the human-centered points of view.

Warren Bird

(God's Love, Humanism)

Dates used:____________

God's Greatness

Thomas Aquinas, the famous medieval theologian, created one of the greatest intellectual achievements of Western civilization in his *Summa Theologica*. It's a massive work: thirty-eight treatises, three thousand articles, ten thousand objections. Thomas tried to gather into one coherent whole all of truth. What an undertaking: anthropology, science, ethics, psychology, political theory, and theology, all under God.

On December 6, 1273, Thomas abruptly stopped his work. While celebrating Mass in the Chapel of St. Thomas, he caught a glimpse of eternity, and suddenly he knew that all his efforts to describe God fell so far short that he decided never to write again.

When his secretary, Reginald, tried to encourage him to do more writing, he said, "Reginald, I can do no more. Such things have been revealed to me that all I have written seems as so much straw."

Even the greatest human minds cannot fathom the greatness of God.

Don McCullough

(Human Limitations, Insignificance)

Dates used:____________

God's Nature

Recently, third- and fourth-graders at Wheaton (IL) Christian Grammar School were asked to complete the following sentence: "By faith, I know that God is . . .

- "forgiving, because he forgave in the Bible, and he forgave me when I went in the road on my bike without one of my parents" (Amanda)
- "providingful, because he dropped manna for Moses and the people, and he gave my dad a job" (Brandon)
- "caring, because he made the blind man see, and he made me catch a very fast line drive that could have hurt me. He probably sent an angel down" (Paul)
- "merciful, because my brother has been nice to me for a year" (Jeremy)
- "faithful, because the school bill came, and my mom didn't know how we were going to pay it. Two minutes later, my dad called, and he just got a bonus check. My mom was in tears" (anonymous)
- "sweet, because he gave me a dog. God tells me not to do things that are bad. I need someone like that" (Hannah).

Cornerstone newsletter

(Children, Insight)

Dates used:____________

God's Voice

In *Directions*, James Hamilton writes:

Before refrigerators, people used icehouses to preserve their food. Icehouses had thick walls, no windows, and a tightly fitted door. In winter, when streams and lakes were frozen, large blocks of ice were cut, hauled to the icehouses, and covered with sawdust. Often the ice would last well into the summer.

One man lost a valuable watch while working in an icehouse. He searched diligently for it, carefully raking through the sawdust, but didn't find it. His fellow workers also looked, but their efforts, too, proved futile. A small boy who heard about the fruitless search slipped into the icehouse during the noon hour and soon emerged with the watch.

Amazed, the men asked him how he found it.

"I closed the door," the boy replied, "lay down in the sawdust, and kept very still. Soon I heard the watch ticking."

Often the question is not whether God is speaking, but whether we are being still enough, and quiet enough, to hear.

Phillip Gunter

(Listening, Solitude)

Dates used:____________

Grace

David Seamands ends his book *Healing Grace* with this story:

For more than six hundred years the Hapsburgs exercised political power in Europe. When Emperor Franz-Josef I of Austria died in 1916, his was the last of the extravagant imperial funerals.

A processional of dignitaries and elegantly dressed court personages escorted the coffin, draped in the black-and-gold imperial colors. To the accompaniment of a military band's somber dirges and by the light of torches, the cortege descended the stairs of the Capuchin Monastery in Vienna. At the bottom was a great iron door leading to the Hapsburg family crypt. Behind the door was the Cardinal-Archbishop of Vienna.

The officer in charge followed the prescribed ceremony, established centuries before. "Open!" he cried.

"Who goes there?" responded the Cardinal.

"We bear the remains of his Imperial and Apostolic Majesty, Franz-Josef I, by the grace of God Emperor of Austria, King of Hungary, Defender of the Faith, Prince of Bohemia-Moravia, Grand Duke of Lombardy, Venezia, Styrgia . . ." The officer continued to list the Emperor's thirty-seven titles.

"We know him not," replied the Cardinal. "Who goes there?"

The officer spoke again, this time using a much-abbreviated and less-ostentatious title reserved for times of expediency.

"We know him not," the Cardinal said again. "Who goes there?"

The officer tried a third time, stripping the emperor of all but the humblest of titles: "We bear the body of Franz-Josef, our brother, a sinner like us all!"

At that, the doors swung open, and Franz-Josef was admitted.

In death, all are reduced to the same level. Neither wealth nor fame can open the way of salvation, but only God's grace, given to those who will humbly acknowledge their need.

Alan J. White

(Humility, Power)

Dates used:___________

Overseas Crusades International missionary Chuck Holsinger relates the following experience of one of his Wheaton College classmates:

It was 1944 and my friend, Bert Frizen, was an infantryman on the front lines in Europe. American forces had advanced in the face of intermittent shelling and small-arms fire throughout the morning hours, but now all was quiet. His patrol reached the edge of a wooded area with an open field before them. Unbeknownst to the Americans, a battery of Germans was ready and waiting in a hedgerow about two hundred yards across the field.

Bert was one of the two scouts who moved out into the clearing. Once he was half-way across the field, the remainder of his battalion followed. Suddenly the Germans opened fire and machine gun fire ripped into both of Bert's legs. The American battalion withdrew into the woods for protection, while a rapid exchange of fire continued.

Bert lay helplessly in a small stream as shots volleyed overhead from side to side. There seemed to be no way out of his dilemma. To make matters worse, he now noticed that a German soldier was crawling toward him. Death appeared imminent; he closed his eyes and waited. To his surprise, a considerable period passed without the expected attack, so he ventured opening his eyes again. He was startled to see the German kneeling at his side, smiling. He then noticed that the shooting had stopped. Troops from both sides of the battlefield watched anxiously. Without any verbal exchange, this mysterious German reached down to lift Bert in his strong arms, and proceeded to carry him to the safety of his own comrades.

Having accomplished his self-appointed mission, and still without speaking a word, the German soldier turned and walked back across the field to his own troop. No one dared break the silence of this sacred moment. Moments later the cease-fire ended, but not before all those present had witnessed the power of self-abdicating love, how one man risked everything for his enemy.

Bert's life was saved through the compassion of one man, his enemy. This courageous act pictures what Jesus risked for us: While we were still God's enemies, Christ died for us (Rom. 5:8).

Lynn McAdam

(Mercy, War)

Dates used:____________

Actor Kevin Bacon recounted when his six-year-old son saw *Footloose* for the first time:

He said, "Hey, Dad, you know that thing in the movie where you swing from the rafters of that building? That's really cool, how did you do that?"

I said, "Well, I didn't do that part . . . it was a stunt man."

"What's a stunt man?" he asked.

"That's someone who dresses like me and does things I can't do."

"Oh," he replied and walked out of the room looking a little confused.

A little later he said, "Hey, Dad, you know that thing in the movie where you spin around on that gym bar and land on your feet? How did you do that?"

I said, "Well, I didn't do that. It was a gymnastics double."

"What's a gymnastics double?" he asked.

"That's a guy who dresses in my clothes and does things I can't do."

There was silence from my son, then he asked in a concerned voice, "Dad, what *did* you do?"

"I got all the glory," I sheepishly replied.

That's the grace of God in our lives. Jesus took our sin upon himself and did what we couldn't do. We stand forgiven and bask sheepishly triumphant in Jesus' glory.

Joel Sarrault

(Credit, Glory)

Dates used:____________

An engagement ring that fell into the sea off the west coast of Sweden in 1994 miraculously found its way back to its owner. The ring was consumed by a mussel that turned up in a load of shellfish caught by fisherman Peder Carlsson.

Carlsson was able to return the ring to its owner because the woman, Agneta Wingstedt, had her name engraved on the inside.

If we bear Christ's name, we know we'll be returned to him one day.

Parade *(12/26/96)*

(Heaven, Marriage)

Dates used:____________

Reader's Digest told of the late Harvey Penick: In the 1920s Penick bought a red spiral notebook and began jotting down observations about golf. He never showed the book to anyone except his son until 1991, when he shared it with a local writer and asked if he thought it was worth publishing. The man read it and told him yes. He left word with Penick's wife the next evening that Simon & Schuster had agreed to an advance of $90,000.

When the writer saw Penick later, the old man seemed troubled. Finally, Penick came clean. With all his medical bills, he said, there was no way he could advance Simon & Schuster that much money. The writer had to explain that Penick would be the one to receive the $90,000.

His first golf book, *Harvey Penick's Little Red Book*, sold more than a million copies, one of the biggest in the history of sports books. His second book, *And If You Play Golf, You're My Friend*, sold nearly three-quarters of a million.

People often have Penick's reaction to the fabulous gift of salvation offered in Jesus Christ. We ask, "What must I do?"

God answers, "Just receive."

Eric Hulstrand

(Gift, Salvation)

Dates used:____________

Gratitude

Mother Teresa told this story in an address at the National Prayer Breakfast in 1994:

One evening we went out, and we picked up four people from the street. One of them was in a most terrible condition. I told the sisters, "You take care of the other three; I will take care of the one who looks the worst." So I did for her all that my love could do. I put her in bed, and there was such a beautiful smile on her face. She took hold of my hand as she said two words only: "Thank you." Then she died.

I could not help but examine my conscience before her. *What would I say if I were in her place?* My answer was very simple. I would have tried to draw a little attention to myself. I would have said, "I am hungry, I am dying, I am in pain," or something. But she gave me much more; she gave me her grateful love. And she died with a smile on her face.

Gratitude brings a smile and becomes a gift.

(Death, Ministry)

Dates used:____________

An article in the *National Geographic* (9/91) tells of a young man from Hanover, Pennsylvania, who was badly burned in a boiler explosion. To save his life, physicians covered him with 6,000 square centimeters of donor skin, as well as sheets of skin cultured from a stamp-sized piece of his own unburned skin.

A journalist asked him, "Do you ever think about the donor who saved you?"

The young man replied, "To be alive because of a dead donor is too big, too much, so I don't think about it."

Difficult to do, yes, but Christians have also received a similar gift—overwhelming, and worth thinking about.

Bob Kapler

(Recognition, Sacrifice)

Dates used:____________

Hardship

No professional football team that plays its home games in a domed stadium with artificial turf has ever won the Super Bowl.

While a climate-controlled stadium protects players (and fans) from the misery of sleet, snow, mud, heat, and wind, players who brave the elements on a regular basis are disciplined to handle hardship wherever it's found. The Green Bay Packers were the 1996 Super Bowl champions, in part, because of the discipline gained from regularly playing in some of the worst weather in the country.

"Endure hardship as discipline. . . . No discipline seems pleasant at the time, but painful. Later on, however, it produces a harvest of righteousness and peace for those who have been trained by it" (Heb. 12:7, 11).

Greg Asimakoupoulos

(Discipline, Training)

Dates used:____________

Harmony

The *Atlantic Monthly* (11/94) told about superstar tenors Jose Carreras, Placido Domingo, and Luciano Pavarotti performing together in Los Angeles. A reporter tried to press the issue of competitiveness between the three men.

"You have to put all of your concentration into opening your heart to the music," Domingo said. "You can't be rivals when you're together making music."

That's also true in the church.

(Rivalry, Teamwork)

Dates used:____________

When Charles V stepped down as the Holy Roman Emperor some four hundred years ago, he spent much of his time at his palace in Spain. He had six clocks there, and no matter how he tried, he could never get them to chime together on the hour.

In his memoirs he wrote, "How is it impossible for six different clocks to chime all at the same time? How is it even more impossible for the six nations of the Holy Roman Empire to live in harmony? It can't be done. It's impossible, even if they call themselves Christians."

Today, we know it's possible to have clocks in perfect harmony, when all are powered by the same source and all are calibrated to the same standard—Greenwich Mean Time. Likewise, unity in the church is possible, but only when all are calibrated to one standard—Christ.

Wayne Brouwer
Preaching Today

(Cooperation, Unity)

Dates used:____________

Heart

In September 1993, with the Major League Baseball season nearing its end, the first-place Philadelphia Phillies visited the second-place Montreal Expos.

In the first game of the series, the home team Expos came to bat one inning, trailing 7–4. Their first two batters reached base. The manager sent a pinch hitter to the plate, rookie Curtis Pride, who had never gotten a hit in the major leagues. Pride took his warm-up swings, walked to the plate, and on the first pitch placed a double, scoring two runners.

The stadium thundered as 45,757 fans screamed their approval. The Expos third-base coach called time, walked toward Pride, and told him to take off his batting helmet.

What's wrong with my helmet? wondered the rookie. Then, realizing what his coach meant, Pride tipped his cap to the appreciative fans.

After the game, someone asked Pride if he could hear the cheering. This person wasn't giving the rookie a hard time. Curtis Pride is 95 percent deaf.

"Here," Pride said, pointing to his heart. "I could hear it here."

Sometimes we hear things loudest in our hearts.

Harry J. Heintz

(Approval, Celebration)

Dates used:____________

Hidden Sins

Annie Dillard, in her book *Pilgrim at Tinker Creek*, writes:

At the end of the island I noticed a small green frog. He was exactly half in and half out of the water.

He was a very small frog with wide, dull eyes. And just as I looked at him, he slowly crumpled and began to sag. The spirit vanished from his eyes as if snuffed. His skin emptied and drooped; his very skull seemed to collapse and settle like a kicked tent. . . .

An oval shadow hung in the water behind the drained frog: Then the shadow glided away. The frog skin bag started to sink.

I had read about the water bug, but never seen one. "Giant water bug" is really the name of the creature, which is an enormous, heavy-bodied brown beetle. It eats insects, tadpoles, fish, and frogs. Its grasping forelegs are mighty and hooked inward. It seizes a victim with these legs, hugs it tight, and paralyzes it with enzymes injected during a vicious bite. Through the puncture shoots the poison that dissolves the victim's muscles and bones and organs—all but the skin—and through it the giant water bug sucks out the victim's body, reduced to juice.

Hidden sins can suck the life out of us.

Dave Goetz

(Satan, Sin's Penalty)

Dates used:____________

Holy Spirit

In the book *Healing the Masculine Soul,* Gordon Dalbey says that when Jesus refers to the Holy Spirit as the Helper, he uses a Greek word, *paraclete,* that was an ancient warrior's term.

"Greek soldiers went into battle in pairs," says Dalbey, "so when the enemy attacked, they could draw together back-to-back, covering each other's blind side. One's battle partner was the paraclete."

Our Lord does not send us to fight the good fight alone. The Holy Spirit is our battle partner who covers our blind side and fights for our well-being.

Tom Tripp

(Help, Support)

Dates used:____________

Pastor John B. McGarvey tells this story:

One day our church copier broke down. I'm not mechanically minded, but I called the repair shop to see if they could tell me what the problem was and if I could do anything about it. I quickly discovered, however, that I didn't even know how to describe what was broken. I didn't know the names of the parts or what was specifically wrong. I just knew the copy machine didn't work.

So the repair shop sent out a technician. While working on our machine, he also called the shop. Unlike me, he knew how to describe what was needed. He used words I didn't understand, but the person at the shop did, and soon the copier was repaired.

My need was met because someone came and communicated to headquarters in words I could not express. The apostle Paul teaches in Romans 8 that this is what the Holy Spirit does for us. When we don't know how to pray, the Holy Spirit knows precisely what we need and prays in a language the Father perfectly understands.

(Intercession, Prayer)

Dates used:____________

Honesty

Charles Swindoll, in *Growing Deep in the Christian Life*, tells about a man who bought fried chicken dinners for himself and his date late one afternoon. The attendant at the fast-food outlet, however, inadvertently gave him the proceeds from the day's business—a bucket of money (much of it cash) instead of fried chicken. Swindoll writes:

After driving to their picnic site, the two of them sat down to enjoy some chicken. They discovered a whole lot more than chicken—over $800! But he was unusual. He quickly put the money back in the bag. They got back into the car and drove all the way back. By then, the manager was frantic.

Mr. Clean got out, walked in, and became an instant hero. "I want you to know I came by to get a couple of chicken dinners and wound up with all this money here."

Well, the manager was thrilled to death. He said, "Let me call the newspaper. I'm gonna have your picture put in the local paper. You're one of the most honest men I've ever heard of."

To which the man quickly responded, "Oh, no. No, no, don't do that!" Then he leaned closer and whispered, "You see, the woman I'm with . . . she's, uh, somebody else's wife."

One can be honest and still not have integrity.

Phillip Gunter

(Infidelity, Integrity)

Dates used:____________

A little honesty paid handsome dividends for Herbert Tarvin, eleven, who drew praise for returning eighty-five cents that he picked up after an armored car crashed and spilled hundreds of thousands of dollars on a Miami street. For his honesty, Herbert, his family, and his sixth-grade class at St. Francis Xavier Catholic School spent the day at Walt Disney World in Orlando, Florida, on the tab of Disney and Southwest Airlines. Herbert said he had to "do the right thing and turn the money in because it doesn't belong to me."

Police say more than $500,000 is still missing. Only a single mother of six, who turned in about $20 in quarters and pennies, and Herbert returned the money, officials said.

USA Today *(2/14/97)*

(Integrity, Rewards)

Dates used:____________

Coming home from work, a woman stopped at the corner deli to buy a chicken for supper. The butcher reached into a barrel, grabbed the last chicken he had, flung it on the scales behind the counter, and told the woman its weight.

She thought for a moment. "I really need a bit more chicken than that," she said. "Do you have any larger ones?"

Without a word, the butcher put the chicken back into the barrel, groped around as though finding another, pulled the same chicken out, and placed it on the scales. "This chicken weighs one pound more," he announced.

The woman pondered her options and then said, "Okay. I'll take them both."

Deceit is detected sooner or later.

Clark Cothern

(Deceit, Guile)

Dates used:____________

Honor

In October 1864, word came to President Abraham Lincoln of a Mrs. Bixby, a Boston widow whose five sons had all been killed fighting in the Civil War. Lincoln later wrote his condolences:

Dear Madam,

I have been shown in the files of the War Department a statement of the Adjutant General of Massachusetts that you are the mother of five sons who have died gloriously on the field of battle.

I feel how weak and fruitless must be any word of mine which should attempt to beguile you from the grief of loss so overwhelming. But I cannot refrain from tendering you the consolation that may be found in the thanks of the republic they died to save.

I pray that our heavenly Father may assuage the anguish of your bereavement, and leave you only the cherished memory of the loved and lost, and the solemn pride that must be yours to have laid so costly a sacrifice upon the altar of freedom.

Yours very sincerely and respectfully,

Abraham Lincoln.

How beautiful the story would be if it ended here with the simple, literary elegance that was Lincoln's alone. But the story took an ironic turn just a few weeks after the letter was sent. No sooner had Mrs. Bixby received her letter when it was leaked to the press by someone in the White House. It was proclaimed a masterpiece for some weeks until a reporter went to the records of the Adjutant General and discovered that the president had been given bad information.

Mrs. Bixby had not lost all five of her sons in battle. One was killed in action at Fredericksburg. One was killed in action at Petersburg. One was taken prisoner at Gettysburg and later exchanged and returned to his mother in good health. One deserted to the enemy. One deserted his post and fled the country.

Word got out, and the press, as well as the rest of the Union, became divided in its support of the president. Some said he had been innocently duped. Others said his feelings were sincere if the cause was not.

Carl Sandburg, in his exhaustive biography of Lincoln, has the last word:

"Whether all five had died on the field of battle, or only two, four of her sons had been poured away into the river of war. The two who had deserted were as lost to her as though dead. The one who had returned had fought at Gettysburg. . . . She deserved some kind of token, some award approaching the language Lincoln had employed. Lincoln was not deceived."

How like the Bixby family is each one of us: a mixture of success and failure, honor and shame. Yet, knowing the whole story of our lives, Christ will honor those who serve him.

Dean Feldmeyer

(Deception, War)

Dates used:____________

Hope

As vice president, George Bush represented the United States at the funeral of former Soviet leader Leonid Brezhnev. Bush was deeply moved by a silent protest carried out by Brezhnev's widow. She stood motionless by the coffin until seconds before it was closed. Then, just as the soldiers touched the lid, Brezhnev's wife performed an act of great courage and hope, a gesture that must surely rank as one of the most profound acts of civil disobedience ever committed: She reached down and made the sign of the cross on her husband's chest.

There, in the citadel of secular, atheistic power, the wife of the man who had run it all hoped that her husband was wrong. She hoped that there was another life, and that that life was best represented by Jesus who died on the cross, and that the same Jesus might yet have mercy on her husband.

Gary Thomas
Christianity Today *(10/3/94)*

(Civil Disobedience, Faith)

Dates used:____________

When complimented on her homemade biscuits, the cook at a popular Christian conference center told Dr. Harry Ironside, "Just consider what goes into the making of these biscuits. The flour itself doesn't taste good, neither does the baking powder, nor the shortening, nor the other ingredients. However, when I mix them all together and put them in the oven, they come out just right."

Much of life seems tasteless, even bad, but God is able to combine these ingredients of our life in such a way that a banquet results.

Greg Asimakoupoulos

(Circumstance, Providence)

Dates used:____________

Humanity

In 1994, Thurman Thomas, head bowed with his hands covering his face, sat on the Buffalo Bills bench following his team's fourth straight Super Bowl loss. His three fumbles had helped seal their awful fate.

Suddenly, standing before him was the Dallas Cowboys' star running back, Emmitt Smith. Just named MVP for Super Bowl XXVIII, Smith was carrying his small goddaughter. Smith looked down at her and said, "I want you to meet the greatest running back in the NFL, Mr. Thurman Thomas."

Paul tells us, "In humility consider others better than yourselves" (Phil. 2:3).

Allen Mann

(Recognition, Reputation)

Dates used:____________

Identity

In the town of Stepanavan, Armenia, I met a woman whom everyone called "Palasan's Wife." She had her own name, of course, but townspeople called her by her husband's name to show her great honor.

When the devastating 1988 earthquake struck Armenia, it was nearly noon, and Palasan was at work. He rushed to the elementary school where his son was a student. The facade was already crumbling, but he entered the building and began pushing children outside to safety. After Palasan had managed to help twenty-eight children out, an aftershock hit that completely collapsed the school building and killed him.

So the people of Stepanavan honor his memory and his young widow by calling her Palasan's wife.

Sometimes a person's greatest honor is not who he or she is but to whom he or she is related. The highest honor of any believer is to be called a disciple of Jesus Christ, who laid down his life for all people.

L. Nishan Bakalian

(Discipleship, Sacrifice)

Dates used:____________

In 1990, center fielder Brett Butler left the San Francisco Giants as a free agent, joining the cross-state rivals, the Los Angeles Dodgers. When Butler returned to San Francisco for the first time as a Los Angeles Dodger, Giants fans greeted him with a mix of boos and cheers.

The cheers turned to boos, however, when Butler hugged Los Angeles manager Tommy Lasorda. "It turned a page in my career," said Butler. "I'm an L.A. Dodger now; I'm not a Giant. That just kind of solidified it. I wanted them to know, I'm a Dodger."

When people become Christians, in one way or another they need to identify with Jesus in the sight of all their family, friends, and acquaintances.

Richard C. Kauffman Jr.

(Baptism, Witness)

Dates used:____________

Incarnation

On March 5, 1994, Deputy Sheriff Lloyd Prescott was teaching a class for police officers in the Salt Lake City Library. As he stepped into the hallway he noticed a gunman herding eighteen hostages into the next room. Dressed in street clothes, Prescott joined the group as the nineteenth hostage, followed them into the room, and shut the door. When the gunman announced the order in which hostages would be executed, Prescott identified himself as a cop. In the scuffle that followed, Prescott, in self-defense, fatally shot the armed man. The hostages were released unharmed.

God dressed in street clothes and entered our world, joining those held hostage to sin. On the cross Jesus defeated Satan and set us free from the power of sin.

Greg Asimakoupoulos

(Sacrifice, Salvation)

Dates used:____________

Joe Torre had been a catcher and a broadcast announcer for the St. Louis Cardinals. Shortly after he was named manager, according to the *Pittsburgh Press,* New York Yankees' announcer Phil Rizzuto suggested that managing could be done better from high above the baseball field—from the level of the broadcasting booth.

Torre replied, "Upstairs, you can't look in their eyes."

In Jesus Christ, God also chose to come down on the field and look into our eyes.

David R. Martin

(Identification, Viewpoint)

Dates used:____________

Joseph Damien was a nineteenth-century missionary who ministered to people with leprosy on the island of Molokai, Hawaii. Those suffering grew to love him and revered the sacrificial life he lived out before them.

One morning before Damien was to lead daily worship, he was pouring some hot water into a cup when the water swirled out and fell onto his bare foot. It took him a moment to realize that he had not felt any sensation. Gripped by the sudden fear of what this could mean, he poured more hot water on the same spot. No feeling whatsoever.

Damien immediately knew what had happened. As he walked tearfully to deliver his sermon, no one at first noticed the difference in his opening line. He normally began every sermon with, "My fellow believers." But this morning he began with, "My fellow lepers."

In a greater measure Jesus came into this world knowing what it would cost him. He bore in his pure being the marks of evil, that we might be made pure. "For this I came into the world" (John 18:37).

Ravi Zacharias in Deliver Us From Evil

(Identification, Solidarity)

Dates used:____________

John Howard Griffin was a white man who believed he could never understand the plight of African-Americans unless he became like one. In 1959, he darkened his skin with medication, sun lamps, and stains, then traveled throughout the South. His book, *Black Like Me*, helped whites better understand the humiliation and discrimination faced daily by people of color.

Jesus Christ became like us; the Incarnation is evidence that God understands our plight. "He was despised and rejected by men, a man of sorrows, and familiar with suffering" (Isa. 53:3).

Tom Moorhouse

(Identity, Racial Reconciliation)

Dates used:____________

Indifference

An estimated 500,000 tons of water rush over Niagara Falls every minute. On March 29, 1948, the falls suddenly stopped. People living within the sound of the falls were awakened by the overwhelming silence. They believed it was a sign that the world was coming to an end. It was thirty hours before the rush of water resumed.

What happened? Heavy winds had set the ice fields of Lake Erie in motion. Tons of ice jammed the Niagara River entrance near Buffalo and stopped the flow of the river until the ice shifted again.

The flow of God's grace in our lives can be blocked by cold indifference.

Merle Mees

(Grace, Sin)

Dates used:____________

Individuality

Mezzo-soprano Susan Graham is one of opera's rising young stars. In a profile for *Texas Monthly* (12/96), writer Jamie Schilling Fields sought to compare Graham with one of opera's legendary mezzo-sopranos and asked if she could be the next Cecilia Bartoli.

Graham asserted, "I'm not sure I want to be the next *anyone*. I'd rather be the first Susan Graham."

(Comparison, Confidence)

Dates used:____________

Integrity

Scientists now say that a series of slits, not a giant gash, sank the *Titanic.*

The opulent, 900-foot cruise ship sank in 1912 on its first voyage from England to New York. Fifteen hundred people died in the worst maritime disaster of the time.

The most widely held theory is that the ship hit an iceberg, which opened a huge gash in the side of the liner. But an international team of divers and scientists recently used sound waves to probe through the wreckage, buried in mud two-and-a-half miles deep. Their discovery? The damage was surprisingly small. Instead of the huge gash, they found six relatively narrow slits across the six watertight holds. "Everything that could go wrong did," said William Garzke Jr., a naval architect who helped the team with their analysis.

Small damage, below the waterline and invisible to most, can sink a huge ship. In the same way, small compromises, unseen to others, can ultimately sink a person's character.

USA Today *(4/9/97)*

(Character, Reputation)

Dates used:____________

Joyful Giving

Don McCullough, president of San Francisco Seminary, told this story:

Scottish Presbyterians established churches in Ghana over a hundred years ago, and today their worship services still resemble a formal Scottish Presbyterian service. Recently, however, they have allowed traditional African expressions into the worship service.

Now the people dance as they bring their offerings forward. The music plays, and each individual joyfully dances down the aisle to the offering plate. According to the missionary to Ghana who told me this, the offering is the only time in the service when the people smile.

No doubt, God also smiles.

(Missions, Stewardship)

Dates used:_____________

Legacy

In his book *I Almost Missed the Sunset*, Bill Gaither writes: Gloria and I had been married a couple of years. We were teaching school in Alexandria, Indiana, where I had grown up, and we wanted a piece of land where we could build a house. I noticed the parcel south of town where cattle grazed, and I learned it belonged to a ninety-two-year-old retired banker named Mr. Yule. He owned a lot of land in the area, and he gave the same speech to everyone who inquired: "I promised the farmers they could use it for their cattle."

Gloria and I visited him at the bank. Although he was retired, he spent a couple of hours each morning in his office. He looked at us over the top of his bifocals.

I introduced myself and told him we were interested in a piece of his land. "Not selling," he said pleasantly. "Promised it to a farmer for grazing."

"I know, but we teach school here and thought maybe you'd be interested in selling it to someone planning to settle in the area."

He pursed his lips and stared at me. "What'd you say your name was?"

"Gaither. Bill Gaither."

"Hmmm. Any relation to Grover Gaither?"

"Yes, sir. He was my granddad."

Mr. Yule put down his paper and removed his glasses. "Interesting. Grover Gaither was the best worker I ever had on my farm. Full day's work for a day's pay. So honest. What'd you say you wanted?"

I told him again.

"Let me do some thinking on it, then come back and see me."

I came back within the week, and Mr. Yule told me he had had the property appraised. I held my breath. "How does $3,800 sound? Would that be okay?"

If that was per acre, I would have to come up with nearly $60,000! "$3,800?" I repeated.

"Yup. Fifteen acres for $3,800."

I knew it had to be worth at least three times that. I readily accepted.

Nearly three decades later, my son and I strolled that beautiful, lush property that had once been pasture land. "Benjy," I said, "you've had this wonderful place to grow up through nothing that you've done, but because of the good name of a great-granddad you never met."

"A good name is more desirable than great riches; to be esteemed is better than silver or gold" (Prov. 22:1).

(Character, Reputation)

Dates used:____________

Legalism

The following hand-lettered signs were prominently displayed around a drive-in restaurant in Pine Grove, California:

Do not back in

Restrooms are for customer use only

Not for diaper disposal or auto trash (on trash can)

Local checks for amount of purchase only

Vanilla frosties only dipped one size only

Please order by number

Observe all signs

"Christ is the end of the law so that there may be righteousness for everyone who believes" (Rom. 10:4).

Phillip W. Gunter

(Grace, Law)

Dates used:____________

Lifestyle

Lee Strobel, teaching pastor at Willow Creek Community Church in South Barrington, Illinois, offers a unique perspective on life in the '90s:

If you really are a person of the '90s . . .

You feel like life is whizzing past you at 90 miles an hour. You work 90 hours a week, and you've still got 90 items on your to-do list. You're on a 90-calorie-a-day diet because you look 90 pounds overweight in your swimming suit.

You've got 90 different bills to pay, and you're already $90 overdrawn—and that's just the interest. You're still paying $90 a month on your student loan, and you don't know where you're going to get $90,000 to send your kids to school.

You've got 90 channels of cable television, and there is still nothing worth watching. You drive your kids to 90 different activities and events a month. Your toddler just asked "Why?" for the 90th time today.

And you think everything would be fine, if you were just making 90 grand a year.

Wayne Rouse

(Perspective, Stress)

Dates used:____________

Listening

In his book *Stress Fractures*, Charles Swindoll writes:

I vividly remember some time back being caught in the undertow of too many commitments in too few days. It wasn't long before I was snapping at my wife and our children, choking down my food at mealtimes, and feeling irritated at those unexpected interruptions through the day. Before long, things around our home started reflecting the pattern of my hurry-up style. It was becoming unbearable.

I distinctly recall after supper one evening the words of our younger daughter, Colleen. She wanted to tell me about something important that had happened to her at school that day. She hurriedly began, "Daddy-I-wanna-tell-you-somethin'-and-I'll-tell-you-really-fast."

Suddenly realizing her frustration, I answered, "Honey, you can tell me . . . and you don't have to tell me really fast. Say it slowly."

I'll never forget her answer: "Then listen slowly."

Mike Schafer

(Hurry, Stress)

Dates used:____________

Loneliness

The German philosopher Schopenhauer compared the human race to a bunch of porcupines huddling together on a cold winter's night. He said, "The colder it gets outside, the more we huddle together for warmth; but the closer we get to one another, the more we hurt one another with our sharp quills. And in the lonely night of earth's winter eventually we begin to drift apart and wander out on our own and freeze to death in our loneliness."

Christ has given us an alternative: to forgive each other for the pokes we receive. That allows us to stay together and stay warm.

Wayne Brouwer
Preaching Today

(Forgiveness, Relationships)

Dates used:____________

Longevity

After winning the gold medal for the long jump in the 1996 Olympic games, Carl Lewis was asked by Bryant Gumbel on the *Today Show:* "You have competed for almost twenty years. To what do you attribute your longevity?"

Lewis, perhaps the greatest track and field athlete of all time, did not hesitate with his answer: "Remembering that you have both wins and losses along the way. Don't take either one too seriously."

Sherman L. Burford

(Failure, Success)

Dates used:____________

Love

Lee Iacocca once asked legendary football coach Vince Lombardi what it took to make a winning team. The book *Iacocca* records Lombardi's answer:

There are a lot of coaches with good ball clubs who know the fundamentals and have plenty of discipline but still don't win the game. Then you come to the third ingredient: If you're going to play together as a team, you've got to care for one another. You've got to love each other. Each player has to be thinking about the next guy and saying to himself: *If I don't block that man, Paul is going to get his legs broken. I have to do my job well in order that he can do his.*

"The difference between mediocrity and greatness," Lombardi said that night, "is the feeling these guys have for each other."

In the healthy church, each Christian learns to care for others. As we take seriously Jesus' command to love one another, we contribute to a winning team.

Christopher Stinnett

(Caregiving, Teamwork)

Dates used:____________

This story comes from a Sunday school ministry in the part of New York City that has been rated the "most likely place to get killed." Pastor Bill Wilson has been stabbed twice, shot at, and had a member of his team killed:

One Puerto Rican lady, after getting saved in church, came to me with an urgent request. She didn't speak a word of English, so she told me through an interpreter, "I want to do something for God, please."

"I don't know what you can do," I answered.

"Please, let me do something," she said in Spanish.

"Okay. I'll put you on a bus. Ride a different bus every week and just love the kids."

So every week she rode a different bus—we have fifty of them—and loved the children. She would find the worst-looking kid on the bus, put him on her lap, and whisper over and over the only words she had learned in English: "I love you. Jesus loves you."

After several months, she became attached to one little boy in particular. "I don't want to change buses anymore. I want to stay on this one bus," she said.

The boy didn't speak. He came to Sunday school every week with his sister and sat on the woman's lap, but he never made a sound. Each week she would tell him all the way to Sunday school and all the way home, "I love you and Jesus loves you."

One day, to her amazement, the little boy turned around and stammered, "I—I love you, too." Then he put his arms around her and gave her a big hug.

That was 2:30 on a Saturday afternoon. At 6:30 that night, the boy was found dead in a garbage bag under a fire escape. His mother had beaten him to death and thrown his body in the trash.

"I love you and Jesus loves you." Those were some of the last words he heard in his short life—from the lips of a Puerto Rican woman who could barely speak English.

Who among us is qualified to minister? Who among us even knows what to do? Not you; not me. But I ran to an altar once, and I got some fire and just went.

So did this woman who couldn't speak English. And so can you.

Bill Wilson
Charisma *(10/96)*
(Commitment, Service)

Dates used:____________

In the prologue to *Leadership Jazz,* Max DePree writes about his granddaughter, Zoe:

[Zoe] was born prematurely and weighed one pound, seven ounces, so small that my wedding ring could slide up her arm to her shoulder. The neonatologist who first examined her told us that she had a 5 to 10 percent chance of living three days. When Esther and I saw Zoe in her isolette in the neonatal intensive care unit, she had two IVs in her navel, one in her foot, a monitor on each side of her chest, and a respirator tube and a feeding tube in her mouth.

To complicate matters, Zoe's biological father had jumped ship the month before Zoe was born. Realizing this, a wise and caring nurse named Ruth gave me my instructions. "For the next several months, at least, you're the surrogate father. I want you to come to the hospital every day to visit Zoe, and when you come, I want you to rub her body and her legs and arms with the tip of your finger. While you're caressing her, you should tell her over and over how much you love her, because she has to be able to connect your voice to your touch."

God knew that we also needed both his voice and his touch. So he gave us the Word, his Son, and also his body, the church. God's voice and touch say, "I love you."

Ed Rotz

(Caregiving, Touch)

Dates used:____________

In *One Inch from the Fence,* Wes Seeliger writes:

I have spent long hours in the intensive care waiting room . . . watching with anguished people . . . listening to urgent questions: Will my husband make it? Will my child walk again? How do you live without your companion of thirty years?

The intensive care waiting room is different from any other place in the world. And the people who wait are different. They can't do enough for each other. No one is rude. The distinctions of race and class melt away. A person is a father first, a black man second. The garbage man loves his wife as much as the university professor loves his, and everyone understands this. Each person pulls for everyone else.

In the intensive care waiting room, the world changes. Vanity and pretense vanish. The universe is focused on the doctor's next report. If only it will show improvement. Everyone knows that loving someone else is what life is all about.

Could we learn to love like that if we realized that every day of life is a day in the waiting room?

Hugh Duncan

(Common Ground, Patience)

Dates used:____________

Lust

The Illinois Department of Natural Resources reports that more than 17,000 deer die each year after being struck by motorists on state highways. According to Paul Shelton, state wildlife director, the peak season for road kills is in late fall.

Why? The bucks are in rut in November. "They're concentrating almost exclusively on reproductive activities," he said, "and are a lot less wary than they normally would be."

Deer aren't the only creatures destroyed by preoccupation with sex.

Greg Asimakoupoulos

(Preoccupation, Sex)

Dates used:____________

Lying

In *Boardroom Reports* (7/5/93), Peter LeVine writes:

When the Port Authority of New York and New Jersey ran a help-wanted ad for electricians with expertise at using Sontag connectors, it got 170 responses—even though there is no such thing as a Sontag connector. The Authority ran the ad to find out how many applicants falsify resumes.

(Honesty, Work)

Dates used:____________

Marriage

The space shuttle *Discovery* was grounded recently—not by technical difficulties or lack of government funding, but by woodpeckers. Yellow-shafted flicker woodpeckers found the insulating foam on the shuttle's external fuel tank irresistible material for pecking.

The foam is critical to the shuttle's performance. Without it, ice forms on the tank when it's filled with the supercold fuel, ice that can break free during liftoff and damage the giant spacecraft. The shuttle was grounded until the damage was repaired.

Marriages are frequently damaged not only by big things—infidelity or abuse or abandonment—but by the little things. Criticism, lack of respect, and taking each other for granted peck away at the relationship and keep us from reaching the heights of love.

(Criticism, Relationships)

Dates used:____________

Materialism

Finns who can't get enough of winter swarmed to the northern town of Kemi for the opening of a sprawling ice castle that features a theater, a playground, an art gallery, and a chapel.

Thirty workers took three months to build this year's castle with 13-foot walls stretching for 1,650 feet.

"We reckon this must be the world's most popular construction site," castle spokesman Simeoni Sainio said.

An Orthodox Church chapel, hewn from ice, already has been booked for four weddings and a christening. The theater has a capacity of 3,000 and will feature rock and pop concerts, musicals, modern dance, opera recitals, and the popular opera *Amahl and the Night Visitors*.

Construction and upkeep costs are estimated to be $1.1 million, yet the castle will melt sometime in mid-April.

The melting ice castle is a reminder that all the material things in this world will one day pass away. Let's lay up our treasure in heaven, not on earth (Matt. 6:19–24).

Scott Wooddell

(Folly, Wealth)

Dates used:____________

Maturity

In *First Things First*, A. Roger Merrill tells of a business consultant who decided to landscape his grounds. He hired a woman with a doctorate in horticulture who was extremely knowledgeable.

Because the business consultant was very busy and traveled a lot, he kept emphasizing to her the need to create his garden in a way that would require little or no maintenance on his part. He insisted on automatic sprinklers and other labor-saving devices.

Finally she stopped and said, "There's one thing you need to deal with before we go any further. If there's no gardener, there's no garden!"

There are no labor-saving devices for growing a garden of spiritual virtue. Becoming a person of spiritual fruitfulness requires time, attention, and care.

Bill Norman

(Discipleship, Spiritual Growth)

Dates used:____________

Obedience

A TV news camera crew was on assignment in southern Florida filming the widespread destruction of Hurricane Andrew.

In one scene, amid the devastation and debris stood one house on its foundation. The owner was cleaning up the yard when a reporter approached him.

"Sir, why is your house the only one still standing?" asked the reporter. "How did you manage to escape the severe damage of the hurricane?"

"I built this house myself," the man replied. "I also built it according to the Florida state building code. When the code called for two-by-six roof trusses, I used two-by-six roof trusses. I was told that a house built according to code could withstand a hurricane. I did, and it did. I suppose no one else around here followed the code."

When the sun is shining and the skies are blue, building our lives on something other than the guidelines in God's Word can be tempting. But there's only one way to be ready for a storm.

David R. Culver

(Rules, Word of God)

Dates used:____________

Optimism

Craig Randall drives a garbage truck in Peabody, Massachusetts. In a garbage container one day, he noticed a Wendy's soft drink cup bearing a contest sticker. Having won a chicken sandwich the week before, Randall checked it, hoping for some french fries or a soft drink.

Instead, he peeled a sticker worth $200,000 toward the construction of a new home, reported *U.S. News & World Report* (11/6/95).

What we get out of life depends a lot on what we look for. Are we more likely to see each experience as trash or a potential treasure?

Bob Weniger

(Expectations, Hope)

Dates used:____________

Outreach

Jerry Rice, who plays for football's San Francisco 49ers, is considered by many experts the best receiver in the NFL. Interviewers from Black Entertainment Television once asked Rice, "Why did you attend a small, obscure university like Mississippi Valley State University in Itta Bena, Mississippi?"

Rice responded, "Out of all the big-time schools (such as UCLA) to recruit me, MVSU was the only school to come to my house and give me a personal visit."

The big-time schools sent cards, letters, and advertisements, but only one showed Rice personal attention.

If we want to share our faith, there's still nothing like a personal touch.

Edward J. Robinson

(Evangelism, Friendship)

Dates used:____________

Past Events

Two Buddhist monks were walking just after a thunderstorm. They came to a swollen stream. A beautiful, young Japanese woman in a kimono stood there wanting to cross to the other side, but she was afraid of the currents.

One of the monks said, "Can I help you?"

"I need to cross this stream," replied the woman.

The monk picked her up, put her on his shoulder, carried her through the swirling waters, and put her down on the other side. He and his companion then went on to the monastery.

That night his companion said to him, "I have a bone to pick with you. As Buddhist monks, we have taken vows not to look on a woman, much less touch her body. Back there by the river you did both."

"My brother," answered the other monk, "I put that woman down on the other side of the river. You're still carrying her in your mind."

How easy it is to be obsessed with the past at the expense of the future.

John Claypool

(Lust, Temptation)

Dates used:____________

Author John Claypool shares this story:

Years ago a thunderstorm swept through southern Kentucky at the farm where my Claypool forebears have lived for six generations. In the orchard, the wind blew over an old pear tree that had been there as long as anybody could remember. My grandfather was grieved to lose the tree on which he had climbed as a boy and whose fruit he had eaten all his life.

A neighbor came by and said, "Doc, I'm really sorry to see your pear tree blown down."

"I'm sorry too," said my grandfather. "It was a real part of my past."

"What are you going to do?" the neighbor asked.

My grandfather paused for a moment and then said, "I'm going to pick the fruit and burn what's left."

That is the wise way to deal with many things in our past. We need to learn their lessons, enjoy their pleasures, and then go on with the present and the future.

(Memories, Regret)

Dates used:____________

Perfectionism

In a full-page ad in *USA Today*, sports shoe manufacturer Fila honored its NBA all-star spokesman Grant Hill and, at the same time, took a wry swipe at the pressure young people feel to be perfect. The ad pictures Hill surrounded by this copy:

This year Grant Hill led his team in scoring, rebounding, assists, and steals, led his team back into the playoffs, led the league in triple doubles, led the league in All-Star balloting, earned a place [on the Olympic team] in Atlanta, didn't punch an official, didn't demand a contract extension, was never tardy, was always cordial, didn't dump his high school friends, listened to his mother, remembered the doorman at Christmas, made his bed daily, threw a successful party, . . . promised to take shorter showers in an effort to conserve water, got plenty of sleep, finally fixed that loose brick in the walkway so the mailman wouldn't trip, got to the bottom of it all, didn't hurt a fly, organized his thoughts, chose paper over plastic, appeared fully clothed in most interviews, improved his vocabulary, counted his blessings, rewound tapes before returning them, said nice things about his teammates, fed coins into other people's meters, kept his thermostat at 68, practiced what he preached, actually paid attention to the stewardess's emergency flight instructions, donated a kidney, and vowed to do better next year.

(Fantasy, Overachievement)

Dates used:____________

Perseverance

Jean-Dominique Bauby, forty-five, a French journalist who had been editor-in-chief of the fashion magazine *Elle*, suffered a stroke in December of 1995. It left him unable to either speak or move, although his mind was unaffected. The only part of his body still left under voluntary control was his left eyelid.

Bauby learned to communicate with that eyelid. First, he learned a signal for "yes" and another for "no." Then when a therapist recited or pointed to the letters in the French alphabet, he would blink when she reached the letter he wanted. In this way, he formed words, then sentences. Difficult though it was, he composed an entire book, *The Diving Suit and the Butterfly*, prior to his death on March 9, 1997. In its first week of publication, it sold 146,000 copies.

Bauby did what he could with what he had. To each of us the Lord has given some ability and some opportunity for service.

Harry Adams

(Achievement, Determination)

Dates used:____________

Mario Cuomo, former governor of New York, wrote in *Life* about a time when he was especially discouraged during a political campaign:

I couldn't help wondering what Poppa would have said if I told him I was tired or—God forbid—discouraged. A thousand pictures flashed through my mind, but one scene came sharply into view.

We had just moved to Holliswood, New York, from our apartment behind the store. We had our own house for the first time; it had some land around it, even trees. One in particular was a great blue spruce that must have been forty feet tall.

Less than a week after we moved in, there was a terrible storm. We came home from the store that night to find the spruce pulled almost totally from the ground and flung forward, its mighty nose bent in the asphalt of the street. My brother Frankie and I could climb poles all day; we were great at fire escapes; we could scale fences with barbed wire—but we knew nothing about trees. When we saw our spruce, defeated, its cheek on the canvas, our hearts sank. But not Poppa's.

Maybe he was five feet six if his heels were not worn. Maybe he weighed 155 pounds if he had a good meal. Maybe he could see a block away if his glasses were clean. But he was stronger than Frankie and me and Marie and Momma all together. We stood in the street, looking down at the tree.

"Okay, we gonna push 'im up!"

"What are you talking about, Poppa? The roots are out of the ground!"

"Shut up, we gonna push 'im up, he's gonna grow again." You couldn't say no to him. So we followed him into the house and we got what rope there was and we tied the rope around the tip of the tree that lay in the asphalt, and he stood up by the house, with me pulling on the rope and Frankie in the street in the rain, helping to push up the great blue spruce. In no time at all, we had it standing up straight again!

With the rain still falling, Poppa dug away at the place where the roots were, making a muddy hole wider and wider as the tree sank lower and lower toward security. Then we shoveled mud over the roots and moved boulders to the base to keep the tree in place. Poppa drove stakes in the ground, tied rope from the trunk to the stakes, and maybe two hours later looked at the spruce, the crippled spruce made straight by ropes, and said, "Don't worry, he's gonna grow again. . . ."

If you were to drive past that house today, you would see the great, straight blue spruce, maybe sixty-five feet tall, pointing up to the heavens, pretending it never had its nose in the asphalt.

Remembering that night in Holliswood, I now couldn't wait to get back into the campaign.

(Determination, Discouragement)

Dates used:__________

Runner's World (8/91) told the story of Beth Anne DeCiantis's attempt to qualify for the 1992 Olympic Trials marathon. A female runner must complete the 26-mile, 385-yard race in less than two hours, forty-five minutes to compete at the Olympic Trials.

Beth started strong but began having trouble around mile 23. She reached the final straightaway at 2:43, with just two minutes left to qualify. Two hundred yards from the finish, she stumbled and fell. Dazed, she stayed down for twenty seconds. The crowd yelled, "Get up!" The clock was ticking—2:44, less than a minute to go.

Beth Anne staggered to her feet and began walking. Five yards short of the finish, with ten seconds to go, she fell again. She began to crawl, the crowd cheering her on, and crossed the finish line on her hands and knees. Her time? Two hours, forty-four minutes, fifty-seven seconds.

Hebrews 12:1 reminds us to run our race with perseverance and never give up.

Terry Fisher

(Courage, Faithfulness)

Dates used:____________

Perspective

Gary Thomas writes in *Christianity Today*:

Thinking about eternity helps us retrieve [perspective]. I'm reminded of this every year when I figure my taxes. During the year, I rejoice at the paychecks and extra income, and sometimes I flinch when I write out the tithe and offering. I do my best to be a joyful giver, but I confess it is not always easy, especially when there are other perceived needs and wants.

At the end of the year, however, all of that changes. As I'm figuring my tax liability, I wince at every source of income and rejoice with every tithe and offering check—more income means more tax, but every offering and tithe means less tax. Everything is turned upside down, or perhaps, more appropriately, right-side up.

I suspect judgment day will be like that.

(Judgment Day, Stewardship)

Dates used:____________

Power

First, huge shovels dig house-sized scoops of lignite coal. Pulverized and loaded onto railroad boxcars, the coal travels to a generating plant in east Texas, where it is further crushed into powder. Superheated, this powder ignites like gasoline when blown into the huge furnaces that crank three turbines.

Whirring at 3,600 revolutions per minute, these turbines are housed in concrete-and-steel casings 100 feet long, 10 feet tall, and 10 feet across. They generate enough electricity for entire cities.

A visitor to this plant once asked the chief engineer, "Where do you store the electricity?"

"We don't store it," the engineer replied. "We just make it."

When a light switch is flipped on in Dallas one hundred miles west, it literally places a demand on the system; it registers at the generating plant and prompts greater output.

God's grace and power likewise cannot be stored. Though inexhaustible, they come in the measure required, at the moment of need.

Reggie McNeal

(God's Power, Intercession)

Dates used:____________

Major Osipovich, an air force pilot for the former USSR, planned to give a talk at his children's school about peace. He would need time off during the day to give his talk, so he volunteered for night duty. That's how Major Osipovich found himself patrolling the skies over the eastern regions of the Soviet Union on September 1, 1983—the night Korean Airlines Flight KE007 strayed into Soviet air space.

Soon the Soviet pilot was caught in a series of blunders and misinformation. In the end, Major Osipovich followed orders and shot down the unidentified aircraft. The actions of an air force major preparing to talk about peace plunged 240 passengers to their deaths and sparked an international incident that pushed world powers to a stand-off.

Our talk is important. But our actions carry far more weight.

(Actions, Consequences)

Dates used:____________

Praise

Dana Keeton told this story in *The Democratic Union* of Lawrenceburg, Tennessee:

The sun had just risen on a hot August day in 1944 in the small village of Plelo, in German–occupied France. The fifteen-year-old boy did not know why he and the other citizens of Plelo had been lined up before a firing squad in the middle of the town square. Perhaps they were being punished for harboring a unit of Marquisards, the French underground freedom fighters. Perhaps they were merely to satisfy the bloodlust of the German commanding officer who, the evening before, had routed the small group of Marquisard scouts. All the boy knew was that he was about to die.

As he stood before the firing squad, he remembered the carefree days of his early childhood, before the war, spent roaming the green of the French countryside. He thought about all he would miss by never growing up. Most of all he was terrified of dying. *How will the bullets feel ripping through my body?* he wondered. He hoped no one could hear the whimperings coming from deep in his throat every time he exhaled.

Suddenly, the boy heard the sound of exploding mortar shells beyond the limits of his little village. The Germans were forced to abandon the firing squad and face a small unit of U.S. tanks with twenty GIs led by Bob Hamsley, a corporal in Patton's Third Army. A Marquisard captain had asked Hamsley for help. After three hours, fifty Nazis were dead, and the other fifty were taken prisoner.

In 1990, the town of Plelo honored Bob Hamsley on the very spot where dozens of the town's citizens would have died if not for him. The man who initiated the search for Hamsley and the ceremony honoring him was the former mayor of Plelo, that same fifteen-year-old boy. He had determined to find the man who saved his life and honor him.

It's hard to forget your savior.

Tim Stafford

(Freedom, Salvation)

Dates used:____________

Prayer

Jean Giono tells the story of Elzeard Bouffier, a shepherd he met in 1913 in the French Alps.

At that time, because of careless deforestation, the mountains around Provence, France, were barren. Former villages were deserted because their springs and brooks had run dry. The wind blew furiously, unimpeded by foliage.

While mountain climbing, Giono came to a shepherd's hut, where he was invited to spend the night.

After dinner Giono watched the shepherd meticulously sort through a pile of acorns, discarding those that were cracked or undersized. When the shepherd had counted out 100 perfect acorns, he stopped for the night and went to bed.

Giono learned that the fifty-five-year-old shepherd had been planting trees on the wild hillsides for over three years. He had planted 100,000 trees, 20,000 of which had sprouted. Of those, he expected half to be eaten by rodents or die due to the elements, and the other half to live.

After World War I, Giono returned to the mountainside and discovered incredible rehabilitation: There was a veritable forest, accompanied by a chain reaction in nature. Water flowed in the once-empty brooks. The ecology, sheltered by a leafy roof and bonded to the earth by a mat of spreading roots, became hospitable. Willows, rushes, meadows, gardens, and flowers were birthed.

Giono returned again after World War II. Twenty miles from the lines, the shepherd had continued his work, ignoring the war of 1939 just as he had ignored that of 1914. The reformation of the land continued. Whole regions glowed with health and prosperity.

Giono writes: "On the site of the ruins I had seen in 1913 now stand neat farms. . . . The old streams, fed by the rains and snows that the forest conserves, are flowing again. . . . Little by little, the villages have been rebuilt. People from the plains, where land is costly, have settled here, bringing youth, motion, the spirit of adventure."

Those who pray are like spiritual reforesters, digging holes in barren land and planting the seeds of life. Through these seeds, dry spiritual wastelands are transformed into harvestable fields, and life-giving water is brought to parched and barren souls.

Hal Seed

(Healing, Hope)

Dates used:____________

According to the *Associated Press*, in September 1994 Cindy Hartman of Conway, Arkansas, walked into her house to answer the phone and was confronted by a burglar. He ripped the phone cord out of the wall and ordered her into a closet.

Hartman dropped to her knees and asked the burglar if she could pray for him. "I want you to know that God loves you and I forgive you," she said.

The burglar apologized for what he had done. Then he yelled out the door to a woman in a pickup truck: "We've got to unload all of this. This is a Christian home and a Christian family. We can't do this to them."

As Hartman remained on her knees, the burglar returned furniture he had taken from her home. Then he took the bullets out of his gun, handed the gun to Hartman, and walked out the door.

Praying for our enemies is incredibly disarming.

Scott Harrison

(Courage, Intercession)

Dates used:____________

In *Point Man,* Steve Farrar tells the story of George McCluskey:

When McCluskey married and started a family, he decided to invest one hour a day in prayer, because he wanted his kids to follow Christ. After a time, he expanded his prayers to include his grandchildren and great-grandchildren. Every day between 11 a.m. and noon, he prayed for the next three generations.

As the years went by, his two daughters committed their lives to Christ and married men who went into full-time ministry. The two couples produced four girls and one boy. Each of the girls married a minister, and the boy became a pastor.

The first two children born to this generation were both boys. Upon graduation from high school, the two cousins chose the same college and became roommates. During their sophomore year, one boy decided to go into the ministry. The other didn't. He undoubtedly felt some pressure to continue the family legacy, but he chose instead to pursue his interest in psychology.

He earned his doctorate and eventually wrote books for parents that became bestsellers. He started a radio program heard on more than a thousand stations each day. The man's name—James Dobson.

Through his prayers, George McCluskey affected far more than one family.

Loyal J. Martin

(Fathers, Persistency)

Dates used:____________

Presumption

The *Associated Press* ran the story of Andre-Francois Raffray. Thirty years ago, at the age of 47, he worked out a real estate deal with Jeanne Calment, then age 90. He would pay *her* $500 each month until her death, in order to secure ownership of her apartment in Arles, France. This is a common practice in France, benefiting both buyers and seniors on a fixed income.

Unfortunately for Raffray, Jeanne Calment has become the world's oldest living person. Still alive at 122, she outlived Raffray, who died in December 1995 at the age of 77. He paid $184,000 for an apartment he never lived in. According to the contract, Raffray's survivors must continue payment until Mrs. Calment dies.

James 4:13, 15 warns us of presuming to know what the future holds: "Now listen, you who say, 'Today or tomorrow we will go to this or that city, spend a year there, carry on business and make money. . . .' Instead, you ought to say, 'If it is the Lord's will, we will live and do this or that.'"

Steve Abbott

(Aging, Uncertainty)

Dates used:____________

Pride

Homiletics (Jan–Mar/96) told of a turtle who wanted to spend the winter in Florida, but he knew he could never walk that far. He convinced a couple of geese to help him, each taking one end of a piece of rope, while he clamped his viselike jaws in the center.

The flight went fine until someone on the ground looked up in admiration and asked, "Who in the world thought of that?"

Unable to resist the chance to take credit, the turtle opened his mouth to shout, "I did—"

(Bragging, Cooperation)

Dates used:____________

Priorities

In 1992, Kerrin-Lee Gartner of Calgary, Alberta, became the first Canadian in history to win Olympic gold in the women's downhill. In Canada she was an immediate sensation.

Shortly after her victory, an announcer interviewing her commented that this must surely be the most significant day of her life.

"No," she replied. "The most significant day was the day of my marriage—but this ranks pretty high."

Even great achievements cannot compare with great relationships.

Gerald Cameron

(Achievement, Marriage)

Dates used:____________

Providence

The only survivor of a shipwreck washed up on a small uninhabited island. He cried out to God to save him, and every day he scanned the horizon for help, but none seemed forthcoming.

Exhausted, he eventually managed to build a rough hut and put his few possessions in it. But then one day, after hunting for food, he arrived home to find his little hut in flames, the smoke rolling up to the sky. The worst had happened; he was stung with grief.

Early the next day, though, a ship drew near the island and rescued him.

"How did you know I was here?" he asked the crew.

"We saw your smoke signal," they replied.

Though it may not seem so now, your present difficulty may be instrumental to your future happiness.

John Yates

(Difficulties, God's Sovereignty)

Dates used:____________

Racial Reconciliation

In 1963, George C. Wallace, governor of Alabama, literally stood in the door of the University of Alabama, preventing Vivian Malone Jones, a young African-American woman, from enrolling as a student. Thirty-three years later, Wallace awarded Jones the first Lurleen B. Wallace Award of Courage. (The award, named in honor of Wallace's wife, recognizes women who have made outstanding contributions to the state of Alabama.) Wallace publicly apologized to Jones for the 1963 controversy; Jones in turn forgave Wallace.

Robert F. Kennedy Jr. on hand for the event, said, "This event really is a moment of reconciliation and redemption."

Edward J. Robinson

(Forgiveness, Restitution)

Dates used:____________

Redemption

A gem dealer was strolling the aisles at the Tucson Gem and Mineral Show when he noticed a blue-violet stone the size and shape of a potato. He looked it over, then as calmly as possible, asked the vendor, "You want $15 for *this*?" The seller, realizing the rock wasn't as pretty as others in the bin, lowered the price to $10.

The stone has since been certified as a 1,905-carat natural star sapphire, about 800 carats larger than the largest stone of its kind. It was appraised at $2.28 million.

It took a lover of stones to recognize the sapphire's worth. It took the Lover of Souls to recognize the true value of ordinary-looking people like us.

Wanda Vassallo

(Value, Wealth)

Dates used:____________

Rejoicing

On a balmy October afternoon in 1982, Badger Stadium in Madison, Wisconsin, was packed. More than sixty thousand die-hard University of Wisconsin supporters were watching their football team take on the Michigan State Spartans.

MSU had the better team. What seemed odd, however, as the score became more lopsided, were the bursts of applause and shouts of joy from the Wisconsin fans. How could they cheer when their team was losing?

It turned out that seventy miles away the Milwaukee Brewers were beating the St. Louis Cardinals in game three of the 1982 World Series. Many of the fans in the stands were listening to portable radios and responding to something other than their immediate circumstances.

Paul encourages us to fix our eyes not on what is seen but what is unseen (2 Cor. 4:18). When we do, we can rejoice even in hardships because we see Christ's larger victory.

Greg Asimakoupoulos

(Perspective, Victory)

Dates used:____________

Relationships

In March 1995, The New England Pipe Cleaning Company of Watertown, Connecticut, was digging twenty-five feet beneath the streets of Revere, Massachusetts, in order to clean a clogged ten-inch sewer line.

In addition to the usual materials one might expect to find in a clogged sewer line, the three-man team found sixty-one rings, vintage coins, eyeglasses, and silverware, all of which they were allowed to keep.

Whether it's pipes or people, if you put up with some mess, sometimes you find real treasure.

Stanley Carvell

(Hardship, Treasure)

Dates used:___________

Respect

In his book with Ken Blanchard, *Everyone's a Coach*, Don Shula tells of losing his temper near an open microphone during a televised game with the Los Angeles Rams. Millions of viewers were surprised and shocked by Shula's explicit profanity. Letters soon arrived from all over the country, voicing the disappointment of many who had respected the coach for his integrity.

Shula could have given excuses, but he didn't. Everyone who included a return address received a personal apology. He closed each letter by stating, "I value your respect and will do my best to earn it again."

There are two ways to gain respect. One is to act nobly. The other is, when you fail to do so, make no excuses.

(Apologizing, Excuses)

Dates used:____________

Sacrifice

Judy Anderson grew up as the daughter of missionaries in Zaire. As a little girl, she went to a day-long rally celebrating the one-hundredth anniversary of Christian missionaries coming to that part of Zaire.

After a full day of long speeches and music, an old man came before the crowd and insisted that he be allowed to speak. He said he soon would die, and that he alone had some important information. If he did not speak, that information would go with him to his grave.

He explained that when Christian missionaries came a hundred years before, his people thought the missionaries were strange and their message unusual. The tribal leaders decided to test the missionaries by slowly poisoning them to death. Over a period of months and years, missionary children died one by one. Then the old man said, "It was as we watched how they died that we decided we wanted to live as Christians."

That story had gone untold for one hundred years. Those who died painful, strange deaths never knew why they were dying or what the impact of their lives and deaths would be. They stayed because they trusted Jesus Christ.

Leith Anderson

(Courage, Trust)

Dates used:____________

In *From Jerusalem to Irian Jaya,* Ruth Tucker writes about Dr. Eleanor Chestnut. After arriving in China in 1893 under the American Presbyterian missions board, Dr. Chestnut built a hospital, using her own money to buy bricks and mortar. The need for her services was so great, she performed surgery in her bathroom until the building was completed.

One operation involved the amputation of a common laborer's leg. Complications arose, and skin grafts were needed. A few days later, another doctor asked Chestnut why she was limping. "Oh, it's nothing," was her terse reply.

Finally, a nurse revealed that the skin graft for the patient, a coolie, came from Dr. Chestnut's own leg, taken with only local anesthetic.

During the Boxer Rebellion of 1905, Dr. Chestnut and four other missionaries were killed by a mob that stormed the hospital.

(Devotion, Martyrdom)

Dates used:____________

Salvation

In *Executive Edge*, management-consultant Ken Blanchard retells the story of a little girl named Schia, which first appeared in *Chicken Soup for the Soul.* When Schia was four years old, her baby brother was born.

"Little Schia began to ask her parents to leave her alone with the new baby. They worried that, like most four-year-olds, she might want to hit or shake him, so they said no."

Over time, though, since Schia wasn't showing signs of jealousy, they changed their minds and decided to let Schia have her private conference with the baby. "Elated, Schia went into the baby's room and shut the door, but it opened a crack—enough for her curious parents to peek in and listen. They saw little Schia walk quietly up to her baby brother, put her face close to his, and say, 'Baby, tell me what God feels like. I'm starting to forget.'"

Jesus taught that to enter the kingdom of God, we must receive it like a little child (Mark 10:15).

(Innocence, Wonder)

Dates used:____________

Sanctity of Life

Susan Shelley writes in *Marriage Partnership*:

In the fifth month of my pregnancy, our doctor recommended a Level II ultrasound. As I lay on the examining table, Dr. Silver manipulated the ultrasound, measuring the cranium and the femur and viewing the internal organs. We all watched the embryonic motions.

"Is everything okay?" Marshall [her husband] asked. . . .

Moments later, Dr. Silver announced his observations in a matter-of-fact voice. "We have some problems. The fetus has a malformed heart—the aorta is attached incorrectly. There are missing portions of the cerebellum. A club foot. A cleft palate and perhaps a cleft lip. Possibly spina bifida. This is probably a case of Trisomy 13 or Trisomy 18. In either case, it is a condition incompatible with life."

Neither Marshall nor I could say anything. So Dr. Silver continued.

"It's likely the fetus will spontaneously miscarry. If the child is born, it will not survive long outside the womb. You need to decide if you want to try and carry this pregnancy to term."

We both knew what he was asking. My soul was shaken by the news, but I knew clearly what I was to do.

"God is the giver and taker of life," I said. "If the only opportunity I have to know this child is in my womb, I don't want to cut that time short. If the only world he is to know is the womb, I want that world to be as safe as I can make it."

(Courage, Motherhood)

Dates used:____________

Scripture

The Winter 1991 issue of the *University of Pacific Review* offers a chilling description of the 1986 Chernobyl nuclear disaster:

There were two electrical engineers in the control room that night, and the best thing that could be said for what they were doing is they were "playing around" with the machine. They were performing what the Soviets later described as an unauthorized experiment. They were trying to see how long a turbine would "freewheel" when they took the power off it.

Now, taking the power off that kind of a nuclear reactor is a difficult, dangerous thing to do, because these reactors are very unstable in their lower ranges. In order to get the reactor down to that kind of power, where they could perform the test they were interested in performing, they had to override manually six separate computer-driven alarm systems. One by one the computers would come up and say, "Stop! Dangerous! Go no further!" And one by one, rather than shutting off the experiment, they shut off the alarms and kept going. You know the results: nuclear fallout that was recorded all around the world, from the largest industrial accident ever to occur in the world.

The instructions and warnings in Scripture are just as clear. We ignore them at our own peril, and tragically, at the peril of innocent others.

Tom Tripp

(Consequences, Recklessness)

Dates used:____________

Second Coming

Ray Bakke shares this story:

I knew an old Glasgow professor named MacDonald who, along with a Scottish chaplain, was put in a prison camp. A high wire fence separated the Americans from the British. MacDonald was put in the American barracks, the chaplain with the Brits.

Unknown to the guards, the Americans had a little homemade radio and were able to get news from the outside. Every day, MacDonald would take a headline or two to the fence and share it with the chaplain in the ancient Gaelic language, indecipherable to the Germans.

One day, news came over the little radio that the German high command had surrendered and the war was over. MacDonald took the news to his friend, then watched him disappear into the barracks. A moment later, a roar of celebration came from the barracks.

Life in that camp was transformed. Men walked around singing and shouting, waving at the guards, even laughing at the dogs. When the German guards finally heard the news three nights later, they fled into the dark, leaving the gates unlocked. The next morning, Brits and Americans walked out as free men. Yet they had truly been set free three days earlier by the news that the war was over.

While Christ's kingdom is not fully achieved, we know the outcome of the battle. We too have been set free.

(Good News, Hope)

Dates used:____________

Self-evaluation

When Harry Truman was thrust into the presidency by the death of Franklin Delano Roosevelt, Sam Rayburn took him aside.

"From here on out, you're going to have lots of people around you. They'll try to put up a wall around you and cut you off from any ideas but theirs. They'll tell you what a great man you are, Harry. But you and I both know you ain't."

(Candor, Wisdom)

Dates used:____________

Executive consultant Richard Hagberg told this story:

The head of one large company recently told me about an incident that occurred as he and his wife waited in line to get his driver's license renewed. He was frustrated at how long it was taking and grumbled to his wife, "Don't they know who I am?"

She replied, "Yeah, you're a plumber's son who got lucky."

Fortune *(6/26/96)*

(Impatience, Pride)

Dates used:____________

Selflessness

In *The Trivialization of God,* Donald McCullough quotes Freeman Patterson, noted Canadian photographer, describing barriers that prevented him from seeing the best photo possibilities:

Letting go of the self is an essential precondition to real seeing. When you let go of yourself, you abandon any preconceptions about the subject matter which might cramp you into photographing in a certain, predetermined way. . . .

When you let go, new conceptions arise from your direct experience of the subject matter, and new ideas and feelings will guide you as you make pictures.

In the spiritual life, just as in photography, being preoccupied with self is the greatest barrier to seeing. But when we get past it, we catch glimpses of extraordinary beauty.

Merle Mees

(Perspective, Selfishness)

Dates used:____________

Self-worth

Perhaps no composer has captured the musical heart and soul of America as did Irving Berlin. In addition to familiar favorites such as "God Bless America" and "Easter Parade," he wrote, "I'm Dreaming of a White Christmas," which still ranks as the all-time bestselling musical score.

In an interview for the *San Diego Union*, Don Freeman asked Berlin, "Is there any question you've never been asked that you would like someone to ask you?"

"Well, yes, there is one," he replied. "'What do you think of the many songs you've written that didn't become hits?' My reply would be that I still think they are wonderful."

God, too, has an unshakable delight in what—and whom—he has made. He thinks each of his children is wonderful. Whether they're a "hit" in the eyes of others or not, he will always think they're wonderful.

Jim Adams

(Creation, God's Love)

Dates used:____________

Charles Colson and several other Christian leaders once met with President Borja of Ecuador to discuss Prison Fellowship International's ministry in Ecuadorian penitentiaries. They had no sooner been seated in luxurious leather chairs when the president interrupted the conversation with the story of his own imprisonment years before being elected to the presidency.

He had been involved in the struggle for democracy in Ecuador. The military cracked down, and he was arrested. Without trial, they threw him into a cold dungeon with no light and no window. For three days he endured the solitary fear and darkness that can drive a person mad.

Just when the situation seemed unbearable, the huge steel door opened, and someone crept into the darkness. Borja heard the person working on something in the opposite corner. Then the figure crept out, closed the door, and disappeared.

Minutes later the room suddenly blazed with light. Someone, perhaps taking his life into his hands, had connected electricity to the broken light fixture. "From that moment," explained President Borja, "my imprisonment had meaning because at least I could see."

Even more important than the light we see with our eyes is the light that Christ brings to our hearts, giving our lives the understanding and meaning only he can give.

Ronald W. Nikkel

(Light, Understanding)

Dates used:____________

Sharing

The *Los Angeles Times* (12/15/96) reported that David Suna and John Tu sold 80 percent of their company, Kingston Technology Corp., the world's largest manufacturer of computer memory products, for $1.5 billion dollars.

The two men decided to share their windfall with their employees. The average bonus payment their workers received was just over $75,000. Suna summarized their decision: "To share our success with everybody is the most joy we can have."

Scot Snyder

(Joy, Success)

Dates used:____________

Significance

Frank Capra, who directed *It's a Wonderful Life*, was asked years ago about the central message of his classic film. After thinking a few moments, Capra responded, "I believe the real message of *It's a Wonderful Life* is this: that under the sun, nothing is insignificant to God." Now, when you watch the movie again, you know that everything that happens has intended and unintended consequences. Everything, because it happened, causes something else to happen. Everybody in that story is important, because he or she relates to everyone else. Nothing is insignificant under the sun to God.

Perhaps you need to be reminded, not only that you are important to God, but also that everyone around you is significant to him, too.

Jay Akkerman

(God's Love, Hope)

Dates used:____________

Sin

In his book *Fuzzy Memories*, Jack Handey writes:

There used to be this bully who would demand my lunch money every day. Since I was smaller, I would give it to him. Then I decided to fight back. I started taking karate lessons. But then the karate lesson guy said I had to start paying him five dollars a lesson. So I just went back to paying the bully.

Too many people feel it is easier just to pay the bully than it is to learn how to defeat him.

Sherman L. Burford

(Capitulation, Self-defense)

Dates used:____________

For eight years Sally had been the Romero family pet. When they got her, she was only one foot long. But Sally grew until eventually she reached eleven-and-a-half feet and weighed eighty pounds.

On July 20, 1993, Sally, a Burmese python, turned on fifteen-year-old Derek, strangling the teenager until he died of suffocation. *Associated Press Online* (7/22/93) quoted the police as saying that the snake was "quite aggressive, hissing, and reacting" when they arrived to investigate.

Sins that seem little and harmless will grow. Tolerate or ignore sin, and it will eventually lead to death (James 1:15).

Bruce E. Truman

(Consequences, Death)

Dates used:___________

In 1991, a judge fined brothers Geno and Russell Capozziello, owners of a Bridgeport, Connecticut, wrecking company, nearly $900,000 for operating an illegal dump. In 1986, on the empty lots surrounding their facility, the brothers began dumping debris from buildings. Eventually the mound of rubble and muck covered two acres and reached a height of thirty-five feet, the equivalent of a three-story building.

The state ordered them to clean it up, but the brothers claimed there was no place to dump it legally in Bridgeport, and they could not afford to have it hauled away. While spending more than $330,000 the previous year to have debris hauled away, they barely dented the pile. According to Geno, "It was never supposed to get this high."

Like garbage, the effects of sinful habits have a way of accumulating beyond our plans and beyond our control.

Michael E. Hardin

(Accumulation, Consequences of Sin)

Dates used:____________

Sinful Nature

Scores of people lost their lives. The world's mightiest army was forced to abandon a strategic base. Property damage approached a billion dollars. All because the sleeping giant, Mount Pinatube in the Philippines, roared back to life after six hundred years of quiet slumber.

When asked to account for the incredible destruction caused by this volcano, a research scientist from the Philippines Department of Volcanology observed, "When a volcano is silent for many years, our people forget that it's a volcano and begin to treat it like a mountain."

Like Mount Pinatube, our sinful nature always has the potential to erupt, bringing great harm both to ourselves and to others. The biggest mistake we can make is to ignore the volcano and move back onto what seems like a dormant "mountain."

Stephen Schertzinger

(Destruction, Watchfulness)

Dates used:____________

The famous cuckoo bird never builds its own nest. It flies around until it sees another nest with eggs in it and no mother bird around. The cuckoo quickly lands, lays its eggs there, and flies away.

The thrush, whose nest has been invaded, comes back. Not being very good at arithmetic, she gets to work hatching the eggs. What happens? Four little thrushes hatch, but one large cuckoo hatches. The cuckoo is two or three times the size of the thrushes.

When Mrs. Thrush brings to the nest one large, juicy worm, she finds four petite thrush mouths, one cavernous cuckoo mouth. Guess who gets the worm? A full-sized thrush ends up feeding a baby cuckoo that is three times as big as it is.

Over time, the bigger cuckoo gets bigger and bigger, and the little thrushes get smaller and smaller. You can always find a baby cuckoo's nest. You walk along a hedgerow until you find dead little thrushes, which the cuckoo throws out one at a time.

Paul teaches in Romans 8:5–8 that spiritually speaking, you've got two natures in one nest. The nature that you go on feeding will grow, and the nature that you go on starving will diminish.

Stuart Briscoe

(New Birth, Spiritual Growth)

Dates used:____________

Spiritual Armor

In *The Encourager*, Charles Mylander writes:

Los Angeles motorcycle police officer Bob Vernon saw a red pickup truck speed through a stop sign. *This guy must be late to work,* he thought to himself. He turned on his emergency lights and radioed that he was in pursuit. The pickup pulled over, and the officer approached.

Meanwhile, the driver thought, *The cops already know!* He rested his hand on the same gun he had used a few moments before to rob a 24-hour market. The sack of stolen money was beside him.

The officer said, "May I see your—"

He never finished the sentence. The driver shoved his gun toward the policeman's chest and fired. The cop was knocked flat seven feet away.

A few seconds later, to the shock of the criminal, the officer stood up, pulled his service revolver, and fired twice. The first bullet went through the open window and smashed the windshield. The second tore through the door and ripped into the driver's left leg.

"Don't shoot!" the thief screamed, throwing the gun and sack of money out the pickup window.

What saved the policeman's life was Kevlar™, the superstrong fabric used for bulletproof vests. Only three-eighths of an inch thick, Kevlar can stop bullets cold.

In Ephesians 6, the Bible instructs every Christian to put on the full armor of God.

Mike Neifert

(Righteousness, Satan's Attack)

Dates used:____________

Spiritual Discipline

In the movie *Karate Kid*, young Daniel asks Mister Miagi to teach him karate. Miagi agrees under one condition: Daniel must submit totally to his instruction and never question his methods.

Daniel shows up the next day eager to learn. To his chagrin, Miagi has him paint a fence. Miagi demonstrates the precise motion for the job: up and down, up and down. Next, Miagi has him scrub the deck using a prescribed stroke. Daniel wonders, *What does this have to do with karate?* but says nothing.

Next, Miagi tells Daniel to wash and wax three weather-beaten cars and again prescribes the motion. Finally, Daniel reaches his limit: "I thought you were going to teach me karate, but all you have done is have me do your unwanted chores!"

Daniel has broken Miagi's one condition, and the old man's face pulses with anger. "I have been teaching you karate! Defend yourself!"

Miagi thrusts his arm at Daniel, who instinctively defends himself with an arm motion exactly like that used in one of his chores. Miagi unleashes a vicious kick, and again Daniel averts the blow with a motion used in his chores. After Daniel successfully defends himself from several more blows, Miagi simply walks away, leaving Daniel to discover what the master had known all along: Skill comes from repeating the correct but seemingly mundane actions.

The same is true of godliness.

Duke Winser

(Repetition, Submission)

Dates used:____________

Spiritual Dryness

In 1986 two brothers who live in a kibbutz near the Sea of Galilee made an incredible discovery. As these two Israeli fishermen monitored their equipment on the beaches of Gennesaret, they noticed something they'd not seen before. Something covered with mud glistened in the sun. Upon examination, archaeologists determined that what the brothers had discovered was a fishing boat dating from the time of Jesus.

The only reason the artifact was discovered was because of a three-year drought, resulting in unusually low water in the lake.

The Bible tells us that in times of spiritual dryness, God may uncover something of fabulous value within—his presence (2 Cor. 4:7–18).

Greg Asimakoupoulos

(Archaeology, God's Presence)

Dates used:____________

Spiritual Gifts

He wanted to conduct. His conducting style, however, was idiosyncratic. During soft passages he'd crouch extremely low. For loud sections, he'd often leap into the air, even shouting to the orchestra.

His memory was poor. Once he forgot that he had instructed the orchestra not to repeat a section of music. During the performance, when he went back to repeat that section, they went forward, so he stopped the piece, hollering, "Stop! Wrong! That will not do! Again! Again!"

For his own piano concerto, he tried conducting from the piano. At one point he jumped from the bench, bumping the candles off the piano. At another concert he knocked over a choir boy.

During one long, delicate passage, he jumped high to cue a loud entrance, but nothing happened because he had lost count and signaled the orchestra too soon.

As his hearing worsened, musicians tried to ignore his conducting and get their cues from the first violinist.

Finally the musicians pled with him to go home and give up conducting, which he did.

He was Ludwig van Beethoven.

As the man whom many consider to be the greatest composer of all time learned, no one is a genius of all trades.

David Sacks

(Example, Leadership)

Dates used:____________

Spiritual Warfare

Aqaba in 1917 seemed impregnable. Any enemy vessel approaching the port would have to face the battery of huge naval guns above the town. Behind Aqaba in every direction lay barren, waterless, inhospitable desert. To the east lay the deadly "anvil of the sun." The Turks believed Aqaba to be safe from any attack. But they were wrong.

Lawrence of Arabia led a force of irregular Arab cavalry across the "anvil of the sun." Together, they rallied support among the local people. On July 6, 1917, the Arab forces swept into Aqaba from the north, from the blind side. A climactic moment of the magnificent film *Lawrence of Arabia* is the long, panning shot of the Arabs on their camels and horses, with Lawrence at their head, galloping past the gigantic naval guns that are completely powerless to stop them. The guns were facing in the wrong direction. Aqaba fell, and the Turkish hold on Palestine was broken, to be replaced by the British mandate and eventually by the State of Israel.

The Turks failed to defend Aqaba because they made two mistakes. They did not know their enemy, and they did not have the right weapons.

We must be careful not to make the same mistakes. Ephesians 6:12 makes it very clear who our enemy is: "Our struggle is not against flesh and blood, but against the rulers, against the authorities, against the powers of this dark world."

Michael Boyland

(Spiritual Armor, Wisdom)

Dates used:____________

During Operation Desert Storm, the Iraqi war machine was overwhelmed by the Coalition Forces' ability to strike strategic targets with never-seen-before accuracy. Unknown to the Iraqis, the Allied Supreme Command had dropped Special Operations Forces (SOF) deep behind enemy lines. These men provided bombing coordinates for military targets and firsthand reports on the effectiveness of subsequent bombing missions.

To avoid unintended targets, pinpoint bombing was often required. A soldier from an SOF unit standing on the ground would request an aircraft high overhead to drop a laser-guided missile. Using a handheld laser, the soldier would point at the target. The missile would hone in on the soldier's target for the hit.

In much the same way, the prayers of Christians focus the attention of the spiritual powers on high.

Steve Schertzinger

(Intercession, Prayer)

Dates used:____________

Stewardship

Osceola McCarty, eighty-seven, did one thing all her life: laundry. Now she's famous for it—or at least for what she did with her profits.

For decades, Miss McCarty earned fifty cents per load doing laundry for the well-to-do families of Hattiesburg, Mississippi, preferring a washboard over an electric washing machine. Every week, she put a little bit in a savings account. When she finally retired, she asked her banker how much money she had socked away.

"$250,000," was his reply. She was in shock. "I had more than I could use in the bank," she explained. "I can't carry anything away from here with me, so I thought it was best to give it to some child to get an education."

This shy, never-married laundry woman gave $150,000 to nearby University of Southern Mississippi to help African-American young people attend college. "It's more blessed to give than to receive," she tells reporters. "I've tried it."

Christian Reader

(Frugality, Generosity)

Dates used:____________

Strength

Richard Mylander shares the following story:

On my way to a conference in Colorado, I was driving uphill along a major interstate when I overtook a freight train going the same direction at a slower speed. The train was being pushed uphill by two locomotives that sounded as if they were straining at full power. I'm a flatlander from the Midwest. *Is this how trains move in mountainous terrain?* I wondered.

A few minutes later, I gradually came alongside the front of the nearly mile-long string of cars. There I found five more locomotives pulling the train. Seven engines in all! Where I come from, I rarely see more than three.

That train was a lesson for me. I had been under serious strain for some time. I was feeling tired and was wondering whether I could persevere under the pressure.

How like God, I thought. When I am pushing a load uphill with all the strength I have and feel like my energy level is depleted, he wants me to know that he is in the lead pulling with power far greater than mine.

(God's Power, Perseverance)

Dates used:____________

Stress

For two years, scientists sequestered themselves in an artificial environment called *Biosphere 2*. Inside their self-sustaining community, the Biospherians created a number of mini-environments, including a desert, rain forest, even an ocean. Nearly every weather condition could be simulated except one, wind.

Over time, the effects of their windless environment became apparent. A number of acacia trees bent over and even snapped. Without the stress of wind to strengthen the wood, the trunks grew weak and could not hold up their own weight.

Though our culture shuns hardship, we would do well to remember that God uses it "for our good, that we may share in his holiness" (Heb. 12:10).

Jay Akkerman

(Hardship, Strength)

Dates used:____________

Stubbornness

Between two farms near Valleyview, Alberta, you can find two parallel fences, only two feet apart, running for a half mile. Why are there two fences when one would do?

Two farmers, Paul and Oscar, had a disagreement that erupted into a feud. Paul wanted to build a fence between their land and split the cost, but Oscar was unwilling to contribute. Since he wanted to keep cattle on his land, Paul went ahead and built the fence anyway.

After the fence was completed, Oscar said to Paul, "I see we have a fence."

"What do you mean 'we'?" Paul replied. "I got the property line surveyed and built the fence two feet into my land. That means some of my land is outside the fence. And if any of your cows sets foot on my land, I'll shoot it."

Oscar knew Paul wasn't joking, so when he eventually decided to use the land adjoining Paul's for pasture, he was forced to build another fence, two feet away.

Oscar and Paul are both gone now, but their double fence stands as a monument to the high price we pay for stubbornness.

Daren Wride

(Conflict, Neighbors)

Dates used:____________

Sunday School

Chuck Colson writes:

When I was at Buckingham Palace last year, Prince Philip asked me, "What can we do about crime here in England?"

I replied, "Send more children to Sunday school." He thought I was joking. But I pointed out a study by sociologist Christie Davies, which found that in the first half of the 1800s British society was marked by high levels of crime and violence, which dropped dramatically in the late 1800s and early 1900s. What changed an entire nation's national character? Throughout that period, attendance at Sunday schools rose steadily until, by 1888, a full 75 percent of children in England were enrolled. Since then, attendance has fallen off to one-third its peak level, with a corresponding increase in crime and disorder. If we fill the Sunday schools, we can change hearts and restore society.

Jubilee *(October 1995)*

(Children, Crime)

Dates used:____________

Support

In the summer of 1989, Mark Wellman, a paraplegic, gained national recognition by climbing the sheer granite face of El Capitan in Yosemite National Park. On the seventh and final day of his climb, the headlines of The *Fresno Bee* read, "Showing a Will of Granite." Accompanying the headline was a photo of Wellman being carried on the shoulders of his climbing companion Mike Corbett. A subtitle said, "Paraplegic and partner prove no wall is too high to scale."

What many people did not know is that Mike Corbett scaled the face of El Capitan three times in order to help Mark Wellman pull himself up once.

Greg Asimakoupoulos

(Friendship, Teamwork)

Dates used:____________

Suspicion

The *San Francisco Examiner* (7/7/93) reported that the California State Automobile Association claims office received a package by Federal Express. The unknown contents were bundled in a Fruit Loops cereal box.

Workers quickly became suspicious. The FBI had only days before uncovered a terrorist bombing ring in New York, and the media had been crackling with stories of terrorist bombings.

Security guards called the police, and about four hundred office workers were evacuated from the building. The bomb squad soon arrived on the scene. The Fruit Loops cereal box was "neutralized" with a small cannon, and its contents were blasted into the air. The bomb squad, however, found no explosives. Inside the suspicious package had been $24,000 in cash. The box contained bundles of $20 bills, $1,000 of which were destroyed in the blast.

"This was a first, finding money," said platoon leader Jim Seim. The package "arrived in such a way that it aroused our suspicions," he said. "We were able to render it neutral. We always err on the side of caution."

In our world it is prudent to use caution, but blanket suspicion can destroy things more valuable than money. Perhaps that is why Christ told us to be shrewd as snakes, and innocent as doves.

Craig Brian Larson

(Caution, Innocence)

Dates used:____________

Teamwork

Herman Ostry's barn floor was under twenty-nine inches of water because of a rising creek. The Bruno, Nebraska, farmer invited a few friends to a barn raising. He needed to move his entire 17,000-pound barn to a new foundation more than 143 feet away. His son Mike devised a latticework of steel tubing and nailed, bolted, and welded it on the inside and the outside of the barn. Hundreds of handles were attached.

After one practice lift, 344 volunteers slowly walked the barn up a slight incline, each supporting less than 50 pounds. In just 3 minutes, the barn was on its new foundation.

The body of Christ can accomplish great things when we work together.

Joseph F. Mlaker

(Accomplishments, Cooperation)

Dates used:____________

Thanksgiving

The Masai tribe in West Africa has an unusual way of saying thank-you. Translators tell us that when the Masai express thanks, they bow, put their foreheads on the ground, and say, "My head is in the dirt."

When members of another African tribe want to express gratitude, they sit for a long time in front of the hut of the person who did the favor and literally say, "I sit on the ground before you."

These Africans understand well what thanksgiving is and why it's difficult for us: At its core, thanksgiving is an act of humility.

Joel Gregory

(Gratitude, Humility)

Dates used:____________

While on a short-term missions trip, Pastor Jack Hinton was leading worship at a leper colony on the island of Tobago. A woman who had been facing away from the pulpit turned around.

"It was the most hideous face I had ever seen," Hinton said. "The woman's nose and ears were entirely gone. She lifted a fingerless hand in the air and asked, 'Can we sing "Count Your Many Blessings"?'"

Overcome with emotion, Hinton left the service. He was followed by a team member who said, "I guess you'll never be able to sing that song again."

"Yes I will," he replied, "but I'll never sing it the same way."

Pastor's Update *(5/96)*

(Gratitude, Joy)

Dates used:____________

Tongue

On September 11, 1995, a squirrel climbed on the Metro-North Railroad power lines near New York City. This set off an electrical surge, which weakened an overhead bracket, which let a wire dangle toward the tracks, which tangled in a train, which tore down all the lines. As a result, 47,000 commuters were stuck in Manhattan for hours that evening.

As James 3:5–6 teaches us, even something as small as the tongue can cause a lot of damage.

Sherman L. Burford

(Consequences, Gossip)

Dates used:____________

Trust

In May 1995, Randy Reid, a thirty-four-year-old construction worker, was welding on top of a nearly completed water tower outside Chicago. According to writer Melissa Ramsdell, Reid unhooked his safety gear to reach for some pipes when a metal cage slipped and bumped the scaffolding on which he stood. The scaffolding tipped, and Reid lost his balance. He fell 110 feet, landing facedown on a pile of dirt, just missing rocks and construction debris.

A fellow worker called 911. When paramedics arrived, they found Reid conscious, moving, and complaining of a sore back.

Apparently the fall didn't cost Reid his sense of humor. As paramedics carried him on a backboard to the ambulance, Reid had one request: "Don't drop me." (Doctors later said Reid came away from the accident with just a bruised lung.)

Sometimes we resemble that construction worker. God protects us from harm in a 110-foot fall, but we're still nervous about 3-foot heights. The God who saved us from hell and death can protect us from the smaller dangers we face this week.

Greg Asimakoupoulos

(Protection, Worry)

Dates used:____________

The Department of Transportation has set aside 200 million dollars for research and testing of an Automated Highway System. This system would purportedly relieve traffic woes with "super cruise control" in heavily congested cities.

Special magnets imbedded in the asphalt every four feet would transfer signals between vehicle and main computer system. Steering, acceleration, and braking would be controlled by sensors, computer navigation systems, and cameras along the side of the road. Control would be returned to drivers at their specified exit.

Researchers and government officials claim they have the technological capability to address any potential problem. The one challenge they have yet to address?

Says Mike Doble, Buick's technology manager, "The only thing we can't do yet is get people to comfortably trust the system. It's not a technology issue. Would *you* drive, closely spaced, at high speeds, through San Diego?"

Trust is always the question. "Trust in the LORD with all your heart and lean not on your own understanding; in all your ways acknowledge him, and he will make your paths straight" (Prov. 3:5–6).

USA Today *(4/9/97)*

(Faith, Obedience)

Dates used:____________

Gladys Aylward, missionary to China more than fifty years ago, was forced to flee when the Japanese invaded Yangcheng. But she could not leave her work behind. With only one assistant, she led more than a hundred orphans over the mountains toward Free China.

In their book *The Hidden Price of Greatness*, Ray Besson and Ranelda Mack Hunsicker tell what happened:

During Gladys's harrowing journey out of war-torn Yangcheng . . . she grappled with despair as never before. After passing a sleepless night, she faced the morning with no hope of reaching safety. A thirteen-year-old girl in the group reminded her of their much-loved story of Moses and the Israelites crossing the Red Sea.

"But I am not Moses," Gladys cried in desperation.

"Of course you aren't," the girl said, "but Jehovah is still God!"

When Gladys and the orphans made it through, they proved once again that no matter how inadequate we feel, God is still God, and we can trust in him.

Jonathan G. Yandell

(God's Care, Inadequacy)

Dates used:____________

In *The New Doublespeak: Why No One Knows What Anyone's Saying Anymore,* author William Lutz defines a few of the more creative doublespeak terms currently in vogue:

- *Meaningful downturn in aggregate output* (recession)
- *After-sales service* (kickback)
- *Resource development park* (trash dump)
- *Temporarily displaced inventory* (stolen goods)
- *Strategic misrepresentation* (lie)
- *Reality augmentation* (lie)
- *Terminological inexactitude* (lie)

Copy Editor *(Oct/Nov 1996)*

(Deceit, Lying)

Dates used:____________

In the classroom setting of one *Peanuts* comic strip, on the first day of the new school year, the students were told to write an essay about returning to class. In her essay Lucy wrote, "Vacations are nice, but it's good to get back to school. There is nothing more satisfying or challenging than education, and I look forward to a year of expanding knowledge."

Needless to say, the teacher was pleased with Lucy and complimented her fine essay. In the final frame, Lucy leans over and whispers to Charlie Brown, "After a while, you learn what sells."

The temptation to say "what sells," what others want to hear whether it is true or not, is always with us.

William M. Nieporte

(Deceit, Guile)

Dates used:___________

Unequal Yoke

Time (1/22/95) reported that the earthquake in Kobe, Japan, occurred when two plates on a fault line fifteen miles offshore suddenly shifted against each other, violently lurching six to ten feet in opposite directions. The result was the worst Japanese earthquake since 1923. Thousands died. More than 46,000 buildings lay in ruins. One-fifth of the city's population was left instantly homeless.

The destruction unleashed by those two tectonic plates depicts what happens when a Christian bonds unequally with a non-Christian. Two people committed to each other but going in different directions can lead only to trouble.

David Farnum

(Marriage, Relationships)

Dates used:____________

Ungratefulness

A man writing at the post office desk was approached by an older fellow with a postcard in his hand. The old man said, "Sir, could you please address this postcard for me?"

The man gladly did so, then agreed to write a short message and sign the card for the man. Finally the younger man asked, "Is there anything else I can do for you?"

The old fellow thought about it for a moment and said, "Yes, at the end could you put, 'P.S. Please excuse the sloppy handwriting.'"

Why is it that we often complain against those who do the most for us?

John Yates

(Complaining, Criticism)

Dates used:____________

Unity

Comedian Emo Philips used to tell this story:

In conversation with a person I had recently met, I asked, "Are you Protestant or Catholic?"

My new acquaintance replied, "Protestant."

I said, "Me too! What franchise?"

He answered, "Baptist."

"Me too!" I said. "Northern Baptist or Southern Baptist?"

"Northern Baptist," he replied.

"Me too!" I shouted.

We continued to go back and forth. Finally I asked, "Northern conservative fundamentalist Baptist, Great Lakes Region, Council of 1879 or Northern conservative fundamentalist Baptist, Great Lakes Region, Council of 1912?"

He replied, "Northern conservative fundamentalist Baptist, Great Lakes Region, Council of 1912."

I said, "Die, heretic!"

New Republic

(Denominations, Dissension)

Dates used:____________

The Unknown

An Arab chief tells the story of a spy captured and sentenced to death by a general in the Persian army. This general had the strange custom of giving condemned criminals a choice between the firing squad and "the big, black door."

The moment for execution drew near, and guards brought the spy to the Persian general. "What will it be," asked the general, "the firing squad or 'the big, black door'?"

The spy hesitated for a long time. Finally he chose the firing squad.

A few minutes later, hearing the shots ring out confirming the spy's execution, the general turned to his aide and said, "They always prefer the known to the unknown. People fear what they don't know. Yet, we gave him a choice."

"What lies beyond the big door?" asked the aide.

"Freedom," replied the general. "I've known only a few brave enough to take that door."

The best opportunities in our lives stand behind the forbidding door of the great unknown.

Don McCullough

(Courage, Freedom)

Dates used:____________

Victory

Lyle Arakaki shares this insight:

In Hawaii, because of the time difference with the continental U.S., the NFL Monday Night Football game is played in midafternoon, so the local TV station delays its telecast until 6:30 in the evening.

When my favorite team plays, I'm too excited to wait for television, so I'll listen to the game on the radio, which broadcasts it live. Then, because they're my favorite team, I'll watch the game on television, too.

If I know my team has won the game, it influences how I watch it on television. If my team fumbles the ball or throws an interception, it's not a problem. I think, *That's bad, but it's okay. In the end, we'll win!*

"In this world you will have trouble," said Jesus. "But take heart! I have overcome the world" (John 16:33).

When going through trouble, knowing the final outcome makes all the difference.

(Perspective, Trouble)

Dates used:____________

Vigilance

The January 13, 1992, issue of *Fortune* featured the "Biggest Business Goofs of 1991."

In an act of corporate cooperation, AT&T reached an agreement with the power company in New York City, ConEd. The contract stated that whenever power demands exceeded the utility's grid, AT&T would lessen their demands on the electric utility by throwing a switch, unplugging some of its facilities, and drawing power from internal generators at its 33 Thomas Street station in lower Manhattan.

On September 17, AT&T acted in accordance with its agreement. But when AT&T's own generators kicked in, the power surge kicked out some of their vital rectifiers, which handled 4.5 million domestic calls, 470,000 international calls, 1,174 flights across the nation carrying 85,000 passengers, and the total communications systems linking air traffic controllers at La Guardia, Kennedy, and Newark airports.

The alarm bells at the 33 Thomas Street station rang unheeded for six hours. The AT&T personnel in charge of the rectifiers were away attending a one-day seminar on how to handle emergencies.

Phillip W. Gunter

(Emergencies, Preparation)

Dates used:____________

Vision

In *More than You and Me,* Kevin and Karen Miller write of the power of a God-given vision:

One couple lived in London 130 years ago. For the first 10 years of their marriage, William Booth, especially, was in a quandary: What was God calling him to do?

Then his wife, Catherine, a skillful Bible teacher, was invited to preach in London. While they were there, William took a late-night walk through the slums of London's East End. Every fifth building was a pub. Most had steps at the counter so little children could climb up and order gin. That night he told Catherine, "I seemed to hear a voice sounding in my ears, 'Where can you go and find such heathen as these, and where is there so great a need for your labors?' Darling, I have found my destiny!"

Later that year, 1865, the couple opened the "Christian Mission" in London's slums. Their life vision: to reach the "down-and-outers" that other Christians ignored. That simple vision of two people grew into the Salvation Army, which now ministers through three million members in ninety-one countries.

(Ministry, Mission)

Dates used:____________

Wants and Needs

In his book *Maverick,* Ricardo Semler tells of a lesson he learned working at Semco:

We were in yet another meeting . . . when we came to the purchase of $50,000 worth of file cabinets. Several departments had been waiting months for the cabinets and in desperation had decided to pool their requests. . . .

We didn't buy a single new file cabinet that day. Instead, we decided to stop the company for half a day and hold the First Biannual Semco File Inspection and Clean-out. . . .

Our instructions were simple: We told everyone to look inside every file folder and purge every nonessential piece of paper. . . .

I was one of Semco's biggest file hogs, with four large cabinets and a request for two more. After our cleanup, I trimmed down to a single cabinet, and that was pretty much how it went throughout the company. . . . The cleanup went so well that when everyone had finished, Semco auctioned off dozens of unneeded file cabinets.

Sometimes what we think we need isn't what we really need. When we pray, we learn to distinguish between needs and wants.

Terry Fisher

(Excess, Greed)

Dates used:____________

Wealth

The *Chicago Tribune* (9/1/96) ran the story of Buddy Post, "living proof that money can't buy happiness." In 1988, he won $16.2 million in the Pennsylvania Lottery. Since then, he was convicted "of assault, his sixth wife left him, his brother was convicted of trying to kill him, and his landlady successfully sued him for one-third of the jackpot."

"Money didn't change me," insists Post, a fifty-eight-year-old former carnival worker and cook. "It changed people around me that I knew, that I thought cared a little bit about me. But they only cared about the money."

Post is trying to auction off seventeen future payments, valued at nearly $5 million, in order to pay off taxes, legal fees, and a number of failed business ventures.

He plans to spend his life as an ex-winner pursuing lawsuits he has filed against police, judges, and lawyers who he says conspired to take his money. "I'm just going to stay at home and mind my p's and q's," he said. "Money draws flies."

(Gambling, Money)

Dates used:____________

Jeff Ferrera of Waukegan, Illinois, was reconciling his checkbook and called First National Bank of Chicago to get his current balance.

"Your primary checking account currently has a balance of $924,844,204.32," droned the electronic voice. Ferrera was one of 826 customers who were almost billionaires for a day because of the biggest error in the history of U.S. banking. The goof amounted to almost $764 billion, more than six times the total assets of First Chicago NBD Corporation.

"I had a lot of people saying in jest to transfer it to the Cayman Islands and run for it," Ferrera said. But, like most of the others, he simply reported the error to bank officials, who could say only that it was a "computer programming error."

It pays to remember that all earthly wealth is just as temporal.

Chicago Tribune *(5/18/96)*

(Heaven, Honesty)

Dates used:____________

Wonder

In Bill Moyers's book *A World of Ideas II*, Jacob Needleman remembers:

I was an observer at the launch of *Apollo 17* in 1975. It was a night launch, and there were hundreds of cynical reporters all over the lawn, drinking beer, wisecracking, and waiting for this thirty-five-story-high rocket.

The countdown came, and then the launch. The first thing you see is this extraordinary orange light, which is just at the limit of what you can bear to look at. Everything is illuminated with this light. Then comes this thing slowly rising up in total silence, because it takes a few seconds for the sound to come across. You hear a "WHOOOOOSH! HHHHMMMM!" It enters right into you.

You can practically hear jaws dropping. The sense of wonder fills everyone in the whole place, as this thing goes up and up. The first stage ignites this beautiful blue flame. It becomes like a star, but you realize there are humans on it. And then there's total silence.

People just get up quietly, helping each other. They're kind. They open doors. They look at one another, speaking quietly and interestedly. These were suddenly moral people because the sense of wonder, the experience of wonder, had made them moral.

When we have a sense of wonder toward God, we too have our lives changed for the better.

Alan W. Steier

(Kindness, Worship)

Dates used:____________

Worship

In his book *Good Morning Merry Sunshine, Chicago Tribune* columnist Bob Greene chronicles his infant daughter's first year of life. When little Amanda began crawling, he records:

This is something I'm having trouble getting used to. I will be in bed reading a book or watching TV. And I will look down at the foot of the bed and there will be Amanda's head staring back at me.

Apparently I've become one of the objects that fascinates her. . . . It's so strange. After months of having to go to her, now she is choosing to come to me. I don't know quite how to react. All I can figure is that she likes the idea of coming in and looking at me. She doesn't expect anything in return. I'll return her gaze and in a few minutes she'll decide she wants to be back in the living room and off she'll crawl again.

The simple pleasure of looking at the one you love is what we enjoy each time we worship God and bask in his presence.

Greg Asimakoupoulos

(Fatherhood, Love)

Dates used:____________

Humor

People think I'm funny. The problem is, they never think I'm funny when I think I'm funny.

Several years ago, I turned to walk through the glass doors at church and smacked into one of the full-length windows instead. As I staggered around the foyer, dazed and confused, everyone, including my wife, just howled. In fact, they still laugh about it. Some people are just sick.

Another time, I was officiating at a wedding in a historic church. As I made my grand entry from the little room behind the platform, the entire door and door frame came off in my hand. I turned to the groom for advice, but he already had that deer-in-the-headlights look. I searched the congregation for help, but they busted up laughing. So I laid the door next to the organ and took my place. Everyone (except the bride and her mother) said it was the most memorable wedding they'd ever attended.

As a result, I hate doors; and there are no door jokes in these humorous selections. What you'll find instead are funny stories and one-liners, topically arranged and cross-referenced so you can check the index to help you locate the appropriate chuckle for the occasion.

From Abstinence to Zeal, you'll find just the right light-hearted illustration to freshen your message and drive home your point. Use them in your bulletin or newsletter. Better yet, buy hundreds of copies of this book for your church; then simply refer to the page number when you use one. Kind of like a humor hymnal.

This section also contains some of our favorite cartoons from *Leadership* and *Christian Reader*. We've even included pastoral humor for the next time you speak at the ministerial alliance or denominational meeting.

We're confident that this humor section will become a valuable asset in your speaking and writing ministry. Not to mention that it will give you a grin.

If you want to inject some levity into your speaking, you can either use this great material, or invite me to speak in your place. Remember, though, I'm a lot harder on the facilities.

Ed Rowell,
with co-editor Bonne L. Steffen

Abstinence

I always scoffed at the idea of a generation gap—until recently, that is. While talking to my preteen daughter, I mentioned how important it was to be chaste.

"But why, Mom?" she asked. "I'd rather do the chasing myself instead of *being* chased."

Janell Wheeler

(Chastity, Purity)

Dates used:____________

Acceptance

Peter Marshall, former chaplain of the U.S. Senate, wrote a little poem worth recalling:

We have the nicest garbage man.
He empties out our garbage can.
He's just as nice as he can be.
He always stops and talks to me.
My mother doesn't like his smell.
But mother doesn't know him well.

Calvin Miller

(Assumptions, Prejudice)

Dates used:____________

Adultery

A third-grade Sunday school teacher was uneasy about the lesson "Thou shalt not commit adultery." By way of introduction she asked, "Would someone please explain what adultery means?"

A young sage answered matter-of-factly, "Adultery is when a kid lies about his age."

Jonathan R. Mutchler

(Age, Ten Commandments)

Dates used:____________

Advent

Advent was one week away, so we thought we'd see what the children remembered from our family devotions the year before. "Who can tell me what the four candles in the Advent wreath represent?" I asked.

Luke jumped in with seven-year-old wisdom and exuberance. "There's love, joy, peace, and . . . and . . ."

"I know!" six-year-old Elise interrupted to finish her brother's sentence: "Peace and quiet!"

Michelle L. Hardie

(Christmas, Peace)

Dates used:____________

Afflictions

A hand-lettered sign nailed to a telephone pole said, "Lost dog with three legs, blind in left eye, missing right ear, tail broken, and recently castrated. Answers to the name of Lucky."

Barbara Johnson

(Attitude, Trouble)

Dates used:____________

An insurance agent was writing a policy for a cowboy. "Have you ever had any accidents?" the agent asked.

"No, not really," replied the cowboy. "A horse kicked in a few of my ribs once. I got bit a couple of times by a rattlesnake, but that's about it."

"Don't you call those accidents?" demanded the agent.

"Oh, no," came the answer, "they did that on purpose."

Herb Miller & Douglas Moore
300 Seed Thoughts: Illustrative Stories for Speakers

(Accidents, Anxiety)

Dates used:____________

You know it's going to be a bad day when:

You wake up in a hospital in traction, and your insurance agent tells you, "Your accident policy covers falling off the roof, but not hitting the ground."

Adapted from Have a Good Day

(Anxiety, Stress)

Dates used:____________

After Hurricane Andrew devastated south Florida, Patricia Christy was waiting in line for food. She vowed she was going to get out of that state. She was going to leave on the first plane out. She was determined to get as far away from the horror of hurricane damage as she possibly could and have a restful vacation.

I have just heard from Patricia Christy. She was standing in line for fresh water on the Hawaiian island of Kauai, having just gone through Hurricane Iniki!

Paul Harvey News

(Stress, Trouble)

Dates used:____________

Aging

Jeanne Calment, at 120 years and counting, is the oldest living human whose birth date can be authenticated. Recently she was asked to describe her vision for the future.

She replied, "Very brief."

Clark Cothern

(Attitude, Sense of Humor)

Dates used:____________

A woman was interviewed by reporters on her 102nd birthday. When asked about the benefits of living past the century mark, she answered, "No peer pressure!"

Win Arn

(Peer Pressure, Sense of Humor)

Dates used:____________

John Fetterman, rector of Grace Episcopal Church in Madison, Wisconsin, told of an elderly woman who died. Having never married, she requested no male pallbearers. In her handwritten instructions for her memorial service, she wrote, "They wouldn't take me out while I was alive; I don't want them to take me out when I'm dead."

Homiletics

(Funerals, Single Adults)

Dates used:____________

A group of senior citizens was lounging on the patio of their retirement community. One looked up as a large flock of birds flew overhead. He nudged a companion who had dozed off. "Frank, you'd better move around a little bit. Those looked like buzzards closing in on us."

(Death, Laziness)

Dates used:____________

Appearances

When my great-niece was five, she asked her grandmother, "Grandma, are you rotten on the inside?"

"No, sweetheart, why?" Grandma answered with some surprise.

"Because when apples are all wrinkled on the outside, they are rotten on the inside."

Shermalee Ochoa

(Aging, Character)

Dates used:____________

Assumptions

In *Point Man*, Steve Farrar tells this story:

The photographer for a national magazine was assigned to shoot a great forest fire. He was told that a small plane would be waiting to take him over the fire.

He arrived at the airstrip just an hour before sundown. Sure enough the Cessna was waiting. He jumped in with his equipment and shouted, "Let's go!" The pilot swung the plane into the wind, and soon they were in the air.

"Fly over the north side of the fire," said the photographer, "and make several low-level passes."

"Why?" asked the nervous pilot.

"Because I'm going to take pictures!" retorted the photographer. "I'm a photographer, and photographers take pictures."

After a long pause, the pilot replied, "You mean, you're not the instructor?"

Ron Willoughby

(Danger, Fear)

Dates used:____________

Attitude

While watching the movie *The Ten Commandments* on television, four-year-old Melissa learned that one of God's names is "I Am That I Am." For days after, true to her contrary style, Melissa strode around the house pronouncing, "I'm not that I'm not!"

Christie Kehn

(Rebellion, Ten Commandments)

Dates used:____________

Way out West, a cowboy was driving down a road, his dog riding in back of the pickup truck, his faithful horse in the trailer behind. He failed to negotiate a curve and had a terrible accident.

Sometime later, a state police officer came upon the scene. An animal lover, he saw the horse first. Realizing the serious nature of its injuries, he drew his service revolver and put the animal out of its misery. He walked around the accident and found the dog, also hurt critically. He couldn't bear to hear it whine in pain, so he ended the dog's suffering as well.

Finally he located the cowboy—who suffered multiple fractures—off in the weeds. "Hey, are you okay?" the cop asked.

The cowboy took one look at the smoking revolver in the trooper's hand and quickly replied, "Never felt better!"

(Complaining, Mercy)

Dates used:____________

Authenticity

In *Becoming a Contagious Christian*, Bill Hybels and Mark Mittelberg tell this story:

A newly promoted colonel had moved into a makeshift office during the Gulf War. He was just getting unpacked when out of the corner of his eye, he noticed a private coming his way with a toolbox.

Wanting to seem important, he grabbed the phone. "Yes, General Schwarzkopf, I think that's an excellent plan." He continued, "You've got my support on it. Thanks for checking with me. Let's touch base again soon, Norm. Good-bye."

"And what can I do for you?" he asked the private.

"Ahhh, I'm just here to hook up your phone," came the rather sheepish reply.

Ron Willoughby

(Deceit, Pride)

Dates used:____________

Baptism

Although I was raised a Methodist, I became active in a Baptist church when I moved to a new community. One day I was helping a group of women clean the church kitchen after a social event. I emptied the large electric coffeepot and handed it to the woman washing dishes.

"Can this be washed like everything else?" she asked.

"No," I replied. "This is a Methodist coffeepot. It says right here, DO NOT IMMERSE."

Jane E. Vajnar

(Denominations, Fellowship)

Dates used:____________

As an adult Sunday school teacher, I'm often given fact sheets on new members so I can invite them to visit our class. While reading about one new member, I chuckled when I read under the "Circumstances of Salvation" this notation: "Accepted Christ in high school. Was baptized but would like to be reimbursed [crossed out] reimmersed."

Steve Page

(God's Gift, Salvation)

Dates used:____________

A congregation installed a new baptistry in the sanctuary as part of an extensive remodeling project. But the county building inspector wouldn't okay its installation. "I can't," he said, "unless it has a separate septic tank."

The trustees couldn't understand why a septic tank would be needed for a baptistry. The building inspector saw their puzzled faces, so he explained, "It's to avoid pollution in the ground."

One of the church trustees finally said with a grin, "I guess it would pollute, with all those sins washed away!"

Helen Daley

(Sanctification, Sin)

Dates used:____________

Our church had finally decided to invest in a P.A. system. As the technician and I made our way around the sanctuary, we studied the best locations for the speakers. When we got to the front, the technician made a beeline for the large opening in the front wall. He leaned over, practically disappearing. I could hear his question echoing from the baptistry, "What's a bathtub doing in a church?"

Quincy Collins

(Confusion, Perspective)

Dates used:____________

Beliefs

My daughter Barb and I were hired to conduct an in-depth survey. After a day of reading questions and writing responses, we were getting weary, but we decided to finish the last two people before calling it a day.

I dropped Barb at her final location and went to mine. I finished early, so I walked in on Barb just as she was finishing the personal data section, which included the question, "Religious Affiliation?"

I knew a hard day's work had finally gotten to Barb when I heard her ask, "And finally, what is your religious affliction?"

Gusty Chartrand

(Church, Faith)

Dates used:____________

Bible

It is truly astonishing what happens in Bible stories when they are retold by young scholars around the world. . . .

God got tired of creating the world, so he took the Sabbath off. Adam and Eve were created from an apple tree. Noah's wife was called Joan of Ark. Lot's wife was a pillar of salt by day, but a ball of fire by night.

Samson was a strongman who let himself be led astray by a Jezebel like Delilah. Samson slayed the Philistines with the axe of the apostles.

Moses led the Hebrews to the Red Sea, where they made unleavened bread made without any ingredients. The Egyptians were all drowned in the desert. Afterward, Moses went up on Mount Cyanide to get the Ten Amendments.

The First Commandment was when Eve told Adam to eat the apple. The Fifth Commandment is to humor thy father and mother. The Seventh Commandment is thou shalt not admit adultery.

Moses died before he ever reached Canada. Then Joshua led the Hebrews in the Battle of Geritol. The greatest miracle in the Bible is when Joshua told his son to stand still and he obeyed him.

David was a Hebrew king skilled at playing the liar. He fought with the Finklesteins, a race of people who lived in biblical times. Solomon, one of David's sons, had three hundred wives and seven hundred porcupines.

Jesus enunciated the Golden Rule, which says to do one to others before they do one to you. The people who followed the Lord were called the Twelve Decibels. The epistles were the wives of the apostles. One of the opossums was St. Matthew who was by profession a taxi man.

St. Paul cavorted to Christianity. He preached holy acrimony, which is another name for marriage. A Christian should have only one wife. This is called monotony.

The things they teach in Sunday School these days!

Roger Moberg

(Inerrancy, Sunday School)

Dates used:____________

Blame

I went to my psychiatrist to be
psychoanalyzed,
To find out why I killed the cat and
blackened my wife's eyes.
He laid me on a downy couch to see
what he could find,
And this is what he dregged up
from my subconscious mind.
When I was one, my mommy locked
my dolly in the trunk,
and so it follows naturally that I am
always drunk.
When I was two, I saw my father kiss
the maid one day.
That is why I suffer now from
kleptoman-e-ay.
When I was three, I suffered from
ambivalence toward my brothers.
That is just the reason why I poisoned
all my lovers.
I'm so glad since I have learned that
lesson so well taught,
That everything I do that's wrong is
someone else's fault.

John Guest

(Guilt, Responsibility)

Dates used:____________

Two kids sat down for lunch. One opened his lunchbox and began to gripe. "Baloney again? This is the fourth day in a row! I'm sick and tired of baloney!"

His friend said, "I bet if you just tell your mom you don't like baloney, she'll fix you something else."

"Mom?" replied the first kid. "I fix my own lunches."

(Complaining, Responsibility)

Dates used:____________

At bedtime, Lillian Holcomb told her two grandsons a Bible story, then asked if they knew what the word sin meant. Seven-year-old Keith spoke up: "It's when you do something bad."

Four-year-old Aaron's eyes widened. "I know a big sin Keith did today."

Annoyed, Keith turned to his little brother: "You take care of your sins, and I'll take care of mine."

Christian Reader

(Responsibility, Sin)

Dates used:____________

A dog food company's newest product was not selling well. The president called in his management staff. "How's our advertising?" he asked.

"Great," replied the advertising executive. "This ad campaign will probably win the industry's top awards this year."

"All right," the president continued. "How about our product design?"

The production manager spoke up. "It's great, boss. Our new label and packaging scored high in every marketing test we ran."

"Hmmm. Well, how's our sales staff? Are they doing their job?"

The sales manager was quick to respond. "Oh, sure. Our people are the best in the business."

There was heavy silence as the president thought about what he'd just heard. "We've got great advertising, great packaging, a top-notch sales force, yet this product is coming in dead last in the dog food market. Does anyone have any idea what the problem might be?"

Everyone looked at each other. Finally, one brave soul spoke up. "It's those stupid dogs, sir. They just won't touch the stuff."

John Maxwell
Developing the Leader Within You

(Confusion, Responsibility)

Dates used:____________

Body of Christ

Carol, a clerk in our local Christian bookstore, often refers to a church as "the body." One week, a number of members of a local "body" had come to the bookstore to buy birthday gifts for their beloved pastor.

Later, that pastor, John, stopped at the store. He told Carol about the surprise party his congregation had given him the night before. Carol's heart was touched. Spontaneously, she exclaimed, "Oh, John, I just love your 'body'!"

The customers in the store burst into laughter, leaving a startled look on John's face—and Carol's, too.

Martha E. Garrett

(Church, Communication)

Dates used:____________

Budgets

The bad news: The average American has just $83.42 in the bank.

The good news: The average American is $4.6 trillion richer than the U.S. government.

Hope Health letter (2/96)

(Debt, Money)

Dates used:____________

Bureaucracy

New Chemical Discovered!

The heaviest element known to science was recently discovered by investigators at a major U.S. research university. The element, tentatively named *administratium*, has no protons or electrons and thus has an atomic weight of 0. However, it does have 1 neutron, 125 assistant neutrons, 75 vice neutrons, and 111 assistant vice neutrons, giving it an atomic mass of 312. These 312 particles are held together by a force that involves a continuous exchange of mesonlike particles called morons.

Since it has no electrons, *administratium* is inert. However, it can be detected chemically as it impedes every reaction it comes in contact with. According to its discoverers, just a minute amount of *administratium* can delay a one-second reaction to over four days.

Administratium has a normal half-life of approximately three years, at which time it does not decay, but instead undergoes a reorganization in which assistant neutrons, vice neutrons, and assistant vice neutrons exchange places. Some studies have shown that the atomic mass actually increases after reorganization.

Unknown

(Boards, Committees)

Dates used:____________

Christmas

It's time to recycle those leftover holiday fruitcakes. That's right. You can have your cake and use it, too.* Just consider the possibilities:

Pothole filler.
Shot put.
Speed bump.
Boat anchor.
Flower press.
Bed warmer (heat to 350 degrees).
Ice pack (chilled for twelve hours).
Chopping block.
Scratching post for your cat.

*User assumes all liability for busted toes, hernias, and other medical ailments resulting therefrom.

Suzanne James
America West *airlines magazine*

(Gifts, Recycling)

Dates used:____________

Church

Seen on a church sign:

> We care about you
> Sundays 10 a.m. Only

Gary Shank

(Fellowship, Visitors)

Dates used:____________

An oxymoron is an apparently self-contradictory expression like *jumbo shrimp, freezer burn*, and *working vacation*. A look around the church will uncover a few more expressions that fit the category.

Take, for example, when a pastor assures us that, due to Communion, he will be delivering a *mini sermon*.

Or the poster that announced the community Easter sunrise service would feature a *unified choir*. Whoever wrote that has obviously never sat in a choir loft.

Then there was the announcement in our bulletin noting that the church was looking for a *volunteer junior high leader*. And the *short business meeting* announced by our board chairman to discuss hiring a *long-term youth pastor*.

Now that I've alerted you to their existence, you'll quickly find other Sunday morning oxymorons. But why take my word for it? I'm a *confirmed skeptic*.

Eutychus in Christianity Today

(Communication, Volunteers)

Dates used:____________

Church and State

It was the Sunday before Election Day, and our music department had just presented a skit, "The Publican and the Sinner." This was followed by prayer led by one of our senior members. In a resonant voice he prayed, "Lord, keep us from becoming like the Republicans we heard about this morning."

Marlene Sims

(Impact, Politics)

Dates used:____________

Cleverness

A man and his wife were checking out of a motel. They discovered the manager had charged them for a fresh basket of fruit put in the room every day. The man said, "How can you charge us for fresh fruit when we never ate any fruit from any basket on any day?"

The manager said, "It's not my fault you didn't eat it. It was there."

So this man took the bill and subtracted $150 from it. The manager said, "What in the world are you doing?"

The man said, "I am charging you $50 a day for kissing my wife."

The manager said, "I didn't kiss your wife."

The husband said, "That's not my fault. She was there."

Larry Moyer

(Bills, Expectations)

Dates used:____________

Comfort

It was one of the worst days of my life: The washing machine broke down, the telephone kept ringing, my head ached, and the mail carrier brought a bill I had no money to pay.

Almost to the breaking point, I lifted my one-year-old into his highchair, leaned my head against the tray, and began to cry.

Without a word, my son took his pacifier out of his mouth and stuck it in mine.

Clara Null

(Compassion, Sharing)

Dates used:____________

Commitment

Several years ago I visited a man who had stopped attending our church. Joe was getting up in years but was in fairly good health.

He greeted me at the door but hesitated to let me in. "Joe," I explained through the screen, "we've missed you in church. Is there any problem I should be aware of?"

"No," he replied. "I'm getting older and am having some trouble getting around. It's just too difficult for me to make church anymore."

"I'm sorry to hear that. There are a lot of steps here and at church. I know you don't have a car, and it's a good mile from here to church. Is there any way we can help?"

"I don't know who I'd ask for a ride," he said, and I detected the implication: *And I don't want you to arrange one, either.*

"How about if I visit you regularly as a shut-in, instead? I could come to your house each month with Communion and a tape recording of one of the services for you to listen to at your convenience. How would you like that?"

Joe's face dropped suddenly, and his eyes averted mine. "That wouldn't work out because I'm gone so much. You'd seldom find me at home."

John E. Kassen

(Excuses, Visitation)

Dates used:____________

Committees

George Will quipped, "Football combines the two worst things about American life. It is violence punctuated by committee meetings."

Robert Byrne

(Sports, Violence)

Dates used:____________

An old legend says that when God created the world, the angels were in awe. As he created the animals, the angels asked to give it a try. God agreed, so the animal-creation committee designed the platypus, a creature with the bill of a duck, the fur of a dog, the tail of a beaver, and the feet of a frog.

Since that day, there have been no committees in heaven.

(Confusion, Vision)

Dates used:____________

Communication

Jonny Hawkins

(Boards, Procrastination)

Dates used:____________

Crystal, our five-year-old daughter, recently met an Amish girl her age. Within a few minutes they were off, hand-in-hand, to play. I caught glimpses of them chattering and giggling. Even though Sylvia, the Amish girl, spoke a Pennsylvania Dutch dialect, she and Crystal got along well.

Later I asked Crystal, "Could you understand anything Sylvia said to you?"

"No," she replied.

"But you played so nicely together. How?"

"Oh, Mommy. We understood each other's giggles."

Bonnie Hellum Brechill

(Harmony, Laughter)

Dates used:____________

Four-year-old Jason was visiting his grandparents. Grandpa was in his study intently reading. Jason walked in carrying a peach, said something Grandpa didn't catch, and handed the peach to him.

Thinking his wife had sent him a snack, Grandpa took it and ate it. Just as he swallowed the last bite, Jason, with lip quivering, said, "But, Pap, I didn't want you to eat it. I just wanted you to get the worm out!"

Sue Hammons

(Help, Listening)

Dates used:____________

The *Los Angeles Times* recently printed a sampling of signs from around the world that attempted to communicate in English.

In a hotel elevator in Paris: *"Please leave your values at the front desk."*

In a hotel in Zurich: *"Because of the impropriety of entertaining guests of the opposite sex in the bedroom, it is suggested that the lobby be used for this purpose."*

On the door of a Moscow inn: *"If this is your first visit to Russia, you are welcome to it."*

Announcement in a Russian newspaper: *"There will be a Moscow exhibition of arts by 15,000 Soviet Republic painters and sculptors. These were executed over the past two years."*

In a Bucharest hotel lobby: *"The lift is being fixed for the next day. During that time we regret that you will be unbearable."*

B. Paul Greene

(Evangelism, Misunderstanding)

Dates used:____________

Communion

When I was a child, our church celebrated the Lord's Supper every first Sunday of the month. At that service, the offering plates were passed twice: before the sermon for regular offerings, and just prior to Communion for benevolences. My family always gave to both, but they passed a dime to me only to put in the regular offering.

One Communion Sunday when I was nine, my mother, for the first time, gave me a dime for the benevolent offering also. A little later when the folks in our pew rose to go to the Communion rail, I got up also. "You can't take Communion yet," Mother told me.

"Why not?" I said. "I paid for it!"

Paul Francisco

(Expectations, Giving)

Dates used:____________

My brother-in-law, who is a minister, responded to a Red Cross appeal for blood donations. When he didn't come home by the time his young son expected him, the boy asked his mother, "Is Dad going around visiting all the sick people?"

His mother replied, "He's giving blood."

"But we know it's really grape juice, don't we, Mom?"

Priscilla Larson

(Example, Sacrifice)

Dates used:____________

Seth, our curious five-year-old, couldn't keep his eyes off us when we were taking Communion. A few seconds later, I stole a peek—he was watching his daddy at prayer after receiving the elements. "Good parental example," I thought.

My gratification was short-lived as Seth leaned over and whispered to me, "What's in that stuff? You eat it and go right to sleep."

Sherri Yates

(Example, Prayer)

Dates used:____________

One weekend my little brother was visiting our grandparents in another town. They took him to church with them, and one Sunday after church, he asked what Communion was all about.

Granddad replied, "That was Jesus' last supper."

My little brother replied, "Boy, they didn't give him much, did they?"

Elaine Borcher

(Last Supper, Stinginess)

Dates used:____________

Community

A three-year-old girl listened intently to the children's sermon. The minister explained that God wants everyone to get along and love each other.

"God wants us all to be one," he said.

To which the little girl replied, "But I don't want to be one. I want to be four!"

Marilyn McCoy

(Age, Communication)

Dates used:____________

Compassion

The instructor from a dog training workshop in Salt Lake City noted that a dog's disposition can be tested by the owner. If the owner will fall down and pretend to be hurt, a dog with a bad temper will tend to bite him. But a good dog will show concern and may lick the fallen owner's face.

Susan Matice attended the class and then decided to test her two dogs. While eating pizza in her living room, she stood up, clutched her heart, screamed, and fell to the floor. Her two dogs looked at her, looked at each other, then raced to the coffee table for her pizza.

Associated Press 1/17/91

(Attitude, Greed)

Dates used:____________

A man finally went to the doctor after weeks of symptoms. The doctor examined him carefully, then called the patient's wife into his office.

"Your husband is suffering from a very rare form of anemia. Without treatment, he'll be dead in a few weeks. The good news is it can be treated with proper nutrition.

"You will need to get up early every morning and fix your husband a hot breakfast—pancakes, bacon, and eggs. He'll need a big, home-cooked lunch every day and then an old-fashioned, meat-and-potatoes dinner every evening. It would be especially helpful if you could bake frequently—cakes, pies, homemade bread—these are the things that will allow your husband to live symptom-free.

"One more thing. His immune system is weak, so it's important that your home be kept spotless at all times. Do you have any questions?"

The wife had none.

"Do you want to break the news, or shall I?" asked the doctor.

"I will," the wife replied.

She walked into the examination room. The husband, sensing the seriousness of his illness, asked her, "It's bad, isn't it?" She nodded, tears welling up in her eyes. "Tell me, what is it?" he asked her.

With a sob, the wife blurted out, "The doctor says you're gonna die!"

(Dedication, Marriage)

Dates used:____________

Competition

The five-year-old ringbearer was obviously worried as he looked down the long aisle of the church where his aunt was to be married the following day. His grandmother had an idea. "I think I'll give a prize to the person who does the best job tomorrow," she told him.

The ringbearer's chin went up. There were fourteen others in the wedding party, not counting the minister. "I still think I can do it," he whispered.

The next day, the church filled, and the organ sounded triumphantly. When it was time, the little boy walked to the front with his head held high.

At the reception, when his grandmother told him he had won the prize, he was both excited and relieved.

"I was pretty sure I had it," he admitted, "until Aunt Dana came in wearing that white dress and the horn was blowing. Then I started thinking—she might win!"

Barbara Lee

(Marriage, Pride)

Dates used:____________

Counseling

"I take it there's something you haven't told me."

Rob Portlock

(Guilt, Privacy)

Dates used:____________

Courtesy

When my father was in the hospital, he had a stream of visitors from the church. One day two men stopped by. Their quiet conversation was interrupted by the other patient's peppery language from behind the curtain. Before leaving, the visitors read some Scripture and prayed.

After they left, the roommate loosed another string of expletives and then sheepishly confessed to Dad, "If I'd known one of those guys was a minister, I'd have watched my language."

"Oh," Dad replied, "they're the deacons in the church. I'm the minister."

Ginny Dow

(Guilt, Profanity)

Dates used:____________

Creation

Seen on a church sign: IF EVOLUTION IS TRUE, HOW COME MOTHERS STILL HAVE ONLY TWO HANDS?

Donna Waldeyer

(Evolution, Motherhood)

Dates used:____________

Crisis

A high-speed train was halted for several hours en route from Paris to Toulouse, France, when the emergency-stop mechanism jammed. An unidentified man had yanked it to stop the train because his wallet had fallen into a toilet, and when he reached to get it, his hand got stuck.

Chuck Shepherd in Pitch Weekly

(Emergencies, Teamwork)

Dates used:____________

Criticism

Winston Churchill was attending an official ceremony in London. Two men behind him recognized him and began to whisper behind his back.

"They say Churchill's quite senile now," said the one.

"Yes, they say he's doing England more harm than good," replied the other.

"They say he should step aside and leave the running of this government to younger, more dynamic people," continued the first man.

Churchill turned and in a loud voice said, "They also say he's quite deaf."

Andrew Carr

(Backbiting, Gossip)

Dates used:____________

Every morning on our way to school, my kids and I pray. When I asked our three-year-old if he wanted to pray, he promptly said, "God, please help Sissy not to suck her thumb."

To which Sissy quickly added, "And, God, please help my brother to stop reminding me."

Linda Pace

(Judging, Sin)

Dates used:____________

Crucifixion

The accounting department of a large insurance company was working on year-end reports when the computers went down. An emergency call was put in to the systems analyst. Busy with other troubleshooting, the man didn't appear until three hours later. Yet even then several clerks cheered, "He's here! Our savior!"

Without a word, the systems analyst turned to leave. Panicked, the accounting manager cried in alarm, "Where are you going?"

"I'm leaving," the analyst said with a smile. "I remember what they did to the last savior."

Marla J. Kiley

(Christ's Suffering, Easter)

Dates used:____________

Death

My five-year-old daughter and I often walked through an old cemetery to reach the local playground. One day she saw someone push a rod into the soil near a gravestone and hang a wreath on it.

"Why did that man put a wreath on the grave?" she asked.

"He wanted to remember the person who died," I replied.

"Will someone do that for me when I die?"

"I'm sure they will," I said, mentally preparing myself for the next question.

We walked in silence for a moment. Then she turned to me and said, "It won't be fair. All I'll see is the stick."

Phoebe A. Johnson

(Fairness, Perspective)

Dates used:____________

Our son was five when his goldfish died. I agreed he could "send the goldfish back to God" any way he wanted. Expecting him to give the goldfish a proper burial in our flower garden, I was surprised to receive a call from our small, rural post office.

"Could you come over?" asked the postmaster. "I want to show you what Ben put in the mail drop." I walked quickly to the post office. She was waiting.

"Glenda, a lot is expected of the post office, but this is the most amazing delivery we have ever been asked to make!" She handed me the envelope, laughing.

On the outside of the envelope, printed in big, blue, capital letters were these words: TO GOD FROM BEN.

Inside the envelope was a very flat, dead goldfish.

Glenda Barbre

(Eternity, Mortality)

Dates used:____________

Decision making

A telemarketer phones a home and says, "I'd like to talk to the person who makes the final purchasing decisions for your family."

The woman replies, "I'm sorry. That person is still at kindergarten and won't be home for another hour."

Hope Health letter

(Children, Influence)

Dates used:____________

Delegation

There are three ways to get something done:

1. Do it yourself.
2. Hire someone else to do it.
3. Forbid your kids to do it.

Homiletics

(Parenting, Workplace)

Dates used:____________

Devotions

During the day I take a few moments to unwind by reading the Bible. After seeing me do this for several years, my four-year-old daughter became concerned: "Aren't you ever going to get finished reading that book?"

Jana Jones

(Bible, Discipleship)

Dates used:____________

Disappointment

An Army Airborne ranger was learning to parachute. The sergeant barked out the orders:

1. Jump when you are told to jump.
2. Count to ten, then pull the rip cord.
3. If the first chute doesn't open, pull the second rip cord.
4. When you land, a truck will take you back to the post.

When the plane got over the landing zone, the soldier jumped when it was his turn. He counted to ten, then pulled the rip cord. Nothing happened. He pulled the second rip cord. Nothing happened.

"Oh great," he complained to himself. "I'll bet the truck won't be waiting for us, either."

(Complaining, Plans)

Dates used:____________

Discipleship

My friend decided it was time to talk to her bright four-year-old son, Benji, about receiving Christ.

"Benji," she asked quietly, "would you like to have Jesus in your heart?"

Benji rolled his blue eyes and answered seriously, "No. I don't think I want the responsibility."

Brenda Goodine

(Evangelism, Responsibility)

Dates used:____________

Discretion

"Forget your wife's warnings—tell the joke."

Dik LaPine

(Influence, Sin)

Dates used:____________

Doubt

The only thing that casts doubt on the miracles of Jesus is that they were all witnessed by fishermen.

A Wisconsin fishing guide

(Inerrancy, Miracles)

Dates used:____________

Easter

My Sunday school class of kindergarteners was studying the creation story. After several weeks, we were ready to review.

"What did God make the first day?" I quizzed. "The second day?" They answered both questions correctly.

"And what happened on the third day?" I asked.

One little child, face shining with enthusiasm, exclaimed, "He rose from the dead!"

Michele L. Hardie

(Creation, Resurrection)

Dates used:____________

Employers

Scott Adams, creator of the *Dilbert* cartoon strip, conducted his Second Annual "Highly Unscientific Dilbert Survey," asking this question:

"If you had a chance to hit your boss in the back of the head with one of the following objects, with no risk of getting caught, which would you use?" Here are the percentages for respondents' answers:

A large bean burrito—19 percent
Nerf ball—17
Ripe melon—14
Framed certificate of appreciation—13
Outdated computer you are forced to use—13
Your last performance review, including the 600-pound filing cabinet you keep it in—13
All your coworkers, bound by duct tape and flung from a huge catapult—8
A Ford Pinto with a full tank of gas—7

"I think the bean burrito won because it would make a really cool sound and it would be messy with or without guacamole," said Adams. Over 64 percent of respondents selected a nonlethal response, knowing if their boss were injured, it would mean more work for them.

Lynn Walford for UPI

(Frustration, Work)

Dates used:____________

A large corporation recently installed a stray dog as a senior vice president. The announcement in the company bulletin read, "His ability to get along with anyone, his prompt response to a pat on the back, his interest in watching others work, and his great knack for looking wise while saying nothing make him a natural for this position."

Quote Digest

(Cooperation, Wisdom)

Dates used:____________

Evangelism

Officer Tori Matthews of the Southern California Humane Society got an emergency call: A boy's pet iguana had been scared up a tree by a neighbor's dog. It then fell from the tree into a swimming pool, where it sank like a brick. Officer Matthews came with her net. She dived into the pool, emerging seconds later with the pet's limp body.

As the *Arizona Republic* (2/14/95) reported, she thought, *Well, you do CPR on a person and a dog, why not an iguana?* So she locked lips with the lizard.

"Now that I look back on it," she said, "it was a pretty ugly animal to be kissing, but the last thing I wanted to do was tell this little boy that his iguana had died." The lizard responded to her efforts and is expected to make a full recovery.

Tori Matthews didn't see a waterlogged reptile; she saw a little boy's beloved pet. We may never see the beauty in some people, but when we realize how much they mean to God, we'll do what we can to keep them from drowning.

(Compassion, Missions)

Dates used:____________

FORMER AMWAY REPRESENTATIVE CLAUDE HOFFENPOPPER TEACHES EVANGELISM

"You don't have to lead anyone to Christ personally;
you just need to sign up ten people who will,
who'll sign up ten more people, who'll . . ."

Steve Phelps

(Recruiting, Witnessing)

Dates used:____________

After listening to Chuck Swindoll on the radio, eight-year-old Debbie asked six-year-old David, "Do you know about Jesus?"

Expecting a new slant on the old story, David replied, "No."

Sister continued, "Sit still because this is really scary." After explaining the gospel as only an eight-year-old could, she popped the question.

"Now, David, when you die, do you want to go to heaven to be with Jesus, God, your Mommy and Daddy, and big sister, or do you want to go to the lake of fire to be with the Devil and bank robbers?"

David thought a moment, then replied, "I want to stay right here."

Jim Abrahamson

(Contentment, Worldliness)

Dates used:____________

A man who was trying to be more diligent about witnessing saw an opportunity when he was standing in the "10 Items or Less" checkout at the grocery store.

"All have sinned," he began, sincerely looking at the clerk scanning his items.

"Including you, Mac," she replied, without looking up. "I count twelve items here."

Mary Chambers

(Honesty, Integrity)

Dates used:____________

The song leader asked the congregation to turn in their hymnals and sing, "Till the Whole World Knows." My daughter whispered, "I think we're going to be here a *long* time."

Melodie Dean

(Missions, Music)

Dates used:____________

A woman bought a parrot to keep her company. She took him home, but returned the bird to the store the next day. "This bird doesn't talk," she told the owner.

"Does he have a mirror in his cage?" asked the owner. "Parrots love mirrors. They see themselves in the mirror and start up a conversation." The woman bought a mirror and left. The next day, she returned. The bird still wasn't talking.

"How about a ladder? Parrots love walking up and down a ladder. A happy parrot is more likely to talk." The woman bought a ladder and left. Sure enough, she was back the next day; the bird still wasn't talking.

"Does your parrot have a swing? If not, that's the problem. He'll relax and talk up a storm." The woman reluctantly bought a swing and left.

When she walked into the store the next day, her countenance had changed. "The parrot died," she said. The pet store owner was shocked.

"I'm so sorry. Tell me, did he ever say a word?" he asked.

"Yes, right before he died," the woman replied. "He said, 'Don't they sell any food at that pet store?'"

(Materialism, Priorities)

Dates used:____________

Example

Our Sunday school teacher was a quiet, godly man with a quick wit. Reflecting on one of the verses in our lesson, "Abstain from all appearance of evil," he said with a chuckle, "But please don't do as I do—do what I say." He then explained with a smile, "I was on my way into the post office when I spotted a beer can on the sidewalk. I picked it up to throw it away. Turning around too fast, I momentarily lost my balance and with the empty beer can clutched in my hand proceeded to stumble and trip the whole way up the front steps."

Betty Traver

(Appearances, Role Models)

Dates used:____________

Faith

We were driving through Pennsylvania Dutch Country with my daughter and her seven-year-old son. We passed an Amish horse and buggy, and my grandson's curiosity was stirred.

"Why do they use horses instead of automobiles?"

My daughter explained that the Amish didn't believe in automobiles.

After a few moments, he asked: "But can't they see them?"

Harold F. Bermel

(Belief, Trust)

Dates used:____________

"I've stopped expecting you to make leaps of faith, but it would be nice to see a hop now and then."

Doug Hall

(Doubt, Pessimism)

Dates used:____________

Fatherhood

Our granddaughter's second-grade class was asked to write about their personal heroes. Her father was flattered to find out that she had chosen him. "Why did you pick me?" he asked her later.

"Because I couldn't spell Arnold Schwarzenegger," she replied.

Jack Eppolito

(Heroes, Honesty)

Dates used:____________

Forgiveness

One Saturday morning I awoke to the delightful smell of waffles and the sound of our two small boys in the kitchen with my husband. Padding down to breakfast, I sat on my husband's lap and gave him a big hug for his thoughtfulness.

Later that day, we were having a heated discussion in our bedroom when our four-year-old, Jacob, stopped us in mid-sentence. Standing in the doorway, he said, "Mommy, try to remember how you felt when you were on Daddy's lap."

Jane Schmidt

(Example, Love)

Dates used:____________

During Sunday school, I was trying to teach the children that we all need God's forgiveness. After the Bible story, I asked one of the girls, "Lisa, when is a time you might need God's forgiveness?"

Her blank stare prompted a response from my son. "It's okay, Lisa. You don't have to tell her."

Then he turned to me and said, "We don't have to tell you our problems. This isn't the Oprah Winfrey Show."

Ranai Carlton

(Confession, Repentance)

Dates used:____________

Free Will

When my daughter was five, she disobeyed me and had been sent to her room. After a few minutes, I went in to have a talk about why she was being punished. Teary-eyed, she asked, "Why do we do wrong things?"

"Well," I said, "sometimes the devil tells us to do something wrong and we listen to him. We need to learn to listen to God instead."

To which she sobbed, "But God doesn't talk loud enough!"

Jo M. Guerrero

(God's Direction, Prayer)

Dates used:____________

Frugality

Save a little money each and every month, and at the end of the year, you'll be surprised at just how little you have.

Ernest Haskins in Quote

(Money, Savings)

Dates used:____________

Fruit of the Spirit

Our young daughter was learning the fruit of the Spirit, so I asked her to recite them to me. "Love, joy, peace, patience, kindness, goodness, faithfulness, gentleness, and *remote* control!" was her reply.

Laura Smith

(Self-control, Television)

Dates used:____________

Giving

For years we lived in a small town with one bank and three churches. Early one Monday morning, the bank called all three churches with the same request: "Could you bring in Sunday's collection right away? We're out of $1 bills."

Clara Null

(Miserliness, Stewardship)

Dates used:____________

God's Call

Having lived in South America as missionaries, my family and I realized that moving to another jungle location meant a lot of work. We knew the discomforts of such things as snakes and bugs.

One morning, a few days after beginning to clean our temporary home, the family and I were taking a short break. While we were drinking tea, a large black beetle suddenly flew through the room with a loud buzzing noise. As it darted between us, my wife let out a startled scream.

Astonished more by her scream than by the beetle, my youngest daughter cried out, "For heaven's sake, Mom!"

My wife resolutely replied, "That's the only reason I'm here."

Patrick Jenkins

(Heaven, Missions)

Dates used:____________

God's Image

My husband admired our six-year-old daughter while she was dancing around the kitchen. Finally, he stopped her with a hug.

"You know," he said, looking Amy in the eyes, "you're cute—just like your father."

Amy was silent for a moment. "You mean my heavenly Father or you?"

Jane Stanford

(Beauty, Fathers)

Dates used:____________

God's Love

My Sunday school class of youngsters had some problems repeating the Lord's Prayer. One child prayed, "Our Father, who art in heaven, how'd you know my name."

Clara Null

(Children, Prayer)

Dates used:____________

In the 1980s, people shelled out thousands of dollars to own a potbellied pig, an exotic house pet imported from Vietnam. Their breeders claimed these minipigs were quite smart and would grow to only 40 pounds. Well, they were half right. The pigs were smart. But they had a tendency to grow to about 150 pounds and become quite aggressive.

What do people do with an unwanted potbellied pig? Fortunately, Dale Riffle came to the rescue. Someone had given Riffle one of these pigs, and he fell in love with it. The pig, Rufus, never learned to use its litter box and developed this craving for carpets and wallpaper and drywall. Yet Riffle sold his suburban home and moved with Rufus to a five-acre farm in West Virginia. He started taking in other unwanted pigs, and before long, the guy was living in hog heaven.

There are currently 180 residents on his farm. According to an article in *U.S. News & World Report*, they snooze on beds of pine shavings. They wallow in mud puddles. They soak in plastic swimming pools and listen to piped-in classical music. And they never need fear that one day they'll become bacon or pork chops. There's actually a waiting list of unwanted pigs trying to get a hoof in the door at Riffle's farm.

Dale Riffle told the reporter, "We're all put on earth for some reason, and I guess pigs are my lot in life." How could anybody in his right mind fall in love with pigs?

I'll tell you something even more amazing. An infinite, perfectly holy, majestic, awesome God is passionately in love with insignificant, sinful, sometimes openly rebellious, frequently indifferent people. God loves people like you and me.

Jim Nicodem in Preaching Today

(Fatherhood, Grace)

Dates used:____________

God's Omniscience

A large bowl of Red Delicious apples was placed at the front of the cafeteria line at Asbury College. The note attached read, "Take only one please, God is watching."

Some prankster attached a note to a tray of peanut butter cookies at the other end of the line that said, "Take all you want. God is watching the apples."

Tom Allen

(College, Greed)

Dates used:____________

God's Wrath

I was listening to my five-year-old son, Matthew, as he worked on his Speak-and-Spell computer. He was concentrating intensely, typing words for the computer to say back to him.

Matthew punched in the word *God*. To his surprise, the computer said, "Word not found."

He tried again with the same reply. With great disgust, he stared at the computer and told it in no uncertain terms, "Jesus is not going to like this!"

Mary Farwell

(Culture, Godlessness)

Dates used:____________

When I was a young, single mom with four children, it was difficult to get them all ready for church on Sunday. One particular Sunday morning as the children started to complain and squabble, I stomped from one room to the other, saying out loud why it was important we go to church as a family and have a good attitude. Suddenly, I noticed all four children huddled together and laughing. "What's so funny?" I asked.

"Mom," they said, "every time you slam down your foot, smoke comes out. It must be the wrath of God!" In reality, it was the powder I had sprinkled in my shoes.

But it worked. We made it to church that morning and practically every Sunday thereafter.

Mary Jane Kurtz

(Parenting, Persuasion)

Dates used:____________

Grace

Heaven goes by favor. If it went by merit, you would stay out, and your dog would go in.

Mark Twain

(Favor, Works)

Dates used:____________

Greed

At a birthday party, it came time to serve the cake. A little boy named Brian blurted out, "I want the biggest piece!"

His mother quickly scolded him. "Brian, it's not polite to ask for the biggest piece."

The little guy looked at her in confusion, and asked, "Well then, how *do* you get it?"

Olive Freeman

(Covetousness, Selfishness)

Dates used:____________

Growth

"Besides calling every Sunday 'Easter,' does anyone else have ideas for improving church attendance?"

Tim Liston

(Committees, Easter)

Dates used:____________

Guilt

After a man died, the attorney said to the man's wife, "He did not leave a will. So we need to know the last words he ever said to you."

She said, "I don't want to tell you."

He said, "Look, he did not leave a will. We need to know the last words he ever said to you."

She said, "I don't want to tell you. It was something between the two of us."

He said, "May I beg you one more time?"

She said, "Well, if you have to know, I'll tell you. The last thing he ever said to me was, 'You don't scare me. You couldn't hit the broad side of a barn with that old gun.'"

Larry Moyer

(Incrimination, Indictment)

Dates used:____________

Hardheartedness

These days, not everyone has compassion. Recently I heard about the Psychiatric Hotline. When I dialed the number, I received the following menu of options:

If you are obsessive-compulsive, please press 1 repeatedly.

If you are codependent, please ask someone to press 2.

If you have multiple personalities, please press 3, 4, 5, and 6.

If you are schizophrenic, listen carefully and a little voice will tell you which number to press.

If you are paranoid-delusional, we know who you are and what you want. Just stay on the line while we trace this call.

James Brown

(Compassion, Helpfulness)

Dates used:____________

Health

Cheerful people resist disease better than glum ones. In other words, the surly bird catches the germ.

Hope Health letter (4/96)

(Attitude, Optimism)

Dates used:____________

Heaven

One Sunday morning the pastor read John 14:2 to the congregation using a modern translation. His version read, "In My Father's house there are many dwelling places" (AMP).

Immediately an elderly lady stood up and said, "I want you to read that Scripture again—from my Bible. I've lived in old, run-down houses all my life, and I'm looking forward to that mansion!"

Carol Reddekop

(Bible, Expectations)

Dates used:____________

My brother and his new wife were escorted to their bridal suite in an elegant hotel in the wee hours of the morning. They were tired from the many hours at their wedding reception and from mingling with their guests. They took a look around their room, taking in the sofa, chairs, and table. But where was the bed? This was the bridal suite?

Then they discovered the sofa was a hide-a-bed, complete with lumpy mattress and springs sagging to the floor. My brother and his new wife spent a fitful night on the hide-a-bed, waking up with sore backs.

The next morning, the new husband went to the hotel desk and gave the management a tongue-lashing for giving them such a terrible room for the bridal suite.

"Did you open the door in the room?" was the response.

When my brother went back up to the room, he opened a door they had thought was the closet. There, complete with fruit baskets and chocolates, was a beautiful bedroom.

Cynthia Thomas

(Abundant Life, Expectations)

Dates used:____________

Home

During World War II when housing was in short supply, a lady in our church told a five-year-old girl, "It's too bad you folks don't have a home."

The child quickly replied, "We have a home. We just don't have a house to put it in!"

Margaret T. Hiscox

(Family, Love)

Dates used:____________

Honesty

A woman leaving the worship service said to the minister, "I enjoyed the sermon."

"Don't thank me. Thank the Lord," said the minister.

"It wasn't *that* good," the lady replied.

Robert S. Smith

(Compliments, Humility)

Dates used:____________

Two brothers had terrorized a small town for decades. They were unfaithful to their wives, abusive to their children, and dishonest in business. Then the younger brother died unexpectedly.

The surviving brother went to the pastor of the local church. "I want you to conduct my brother's funeral," he said, "but it's important to me that during the service, you tell everyone my brother was a saint."

"But he was far from that," the minister countered.

The wealthy brother pulled out his checkbook. "Reverend, I'm prepared to give $100,000 to your church. All I'm asking is that you publicly state that my brother was a saint."

On the day of the funeral, the pastor began his eulogy this way: "Everyone here knows that the deceased was a wicked man, a womanizer, and a drunk. He terrorized his employees and cheated on his taxes." Then he paused.

"But as evil and sinful as this man was, compared to his older brother, he was a saint!"

Greg Asimakoupoulos

(Comparison, Temptation)

Dates used:____________

The *Sweet's Soul Cafe* newsletter included this list of "Top 10 Liars' Lies":

10. We'll stay only five minutes.
9. This will be a short meeting.
8. I'll respect you in the morning.
7. The check is in the mail.
6. I'm from the government, and I'm here to help you.
5. This hurts me more than it hurts you.
4. Your money will be cheerfully refunded.
3. We service what we sell.
2. Your table will be ready in just a minute.
1. I'll start exercising (dieting, forgiving) tomorrow.

Leonard Sweet

(Dishonesty, Lying)

Dates used:____________

Humility

In seminary I was impressed with the way Jesus used unusual means to make powerful points—for instance, riding into Jerusalem on a donkey.

I tried taking my cue from Jesus in my first church after seminary. I figured communication would be enhanced by working with live animals.

Like a turtle. A turtle makes progress only if it dares stick out its neck. That's a pretty good posture for Jesus' disciples, too, I thought.

So, my first week there, I asked the kids to find me a turtle. That week, some girls found a turtle and brought it to church, and an elderly couple, while taking a drive in the country, had to slam on the brakes as a turtle ambled across the road.

Eureka! I had two turtles!

The next Sunday I stood before the congregation, trying to exude proper Princeton decorum. In my black Geneva gown accented by red piping, I called the small fries forward and began my talk.

As I held up one turtle, I tapped on its shell. He ducked into it, obviously not going anywhere. "That's like a person acting as if Jesus weren't walking beside him," I observed.

The turtle, meanwhile, got a bad case of nerves and in front of the whole congregation, urinated all over my new robe.

The congregation howled. I acted as though I were not drenched and quickly returned the turtle to his box, commenting that strange faces do funny things to shy turtles.

Picking up the second turtle, I started again. I tapped on the shell, this time holding it well away from my robe. The turtle ducked inside and . . . held its composure. Relieved, I asked, "What happens to a turtle that refuses to stick out its neck?"

A tyke shot up his hand, exclaiming, "It goes tinkle-tinkle!"

That brought the house down again. I thought my ministry had been destroyed in its second week. But the nervous turtle made people see that their new preacher was all too human.

And they accepted me, stains and all—though they did tend to shy away from my new robe.

Jack R. Van Ens

(Embarrassment, Pride)

Dates used:____________

I once pastored a church that met in a former dance hall. Wanting to save money, our small fellowship used carpet remnants for the center aisle. Over the years, the seams began to loosen, and if you weren't careful, your foot could catch.

My wife told me, "Honey, you should get those fixed before some elderly lady trips and falls." I applied a procedure I had learned from my deacons. I tabled the issue.

A few weeks later before a Sunday morning service, I was meditating in my office at the rear of the church. Realizing I was a few minutes late, I hurried into the sanctuary and briskly walked up the center aisle.

As I reached the front, in full view of the congregation, my foot slipped under a loose seam, and I lunged forward. Fortunately, I caught my balance, but my toupee decided to embark on a journey of its own. I snatched it in midair, deposited it back on my head, and proceeded calmly and coolly to the pulpit.

When I turned around, however, I was greeted with mass hysteria. I had placed my toupee on sideways!

Besides the important lesson of listening to the cautions of your wife, I learned something else: If it's not your own hair, don't wear it.

Jerry Lambert

(Embarrassment, Honesty)

Dates used:____________

A sign on a department store dressing room mirror:

"Objects in mirror may appear bigger than they actually are."

Hope Health letter (12/95)

(Distortion, Spiritual Blindness)

Dates used:____________

Impatience

A young woman's car stalled at a stoplight. She tried to get it started, but nothing would happen. The light turned green, and there she sat, angry and embarrassed, holding up traffic. The car behind could have gone around, but instead the driver added to her anger by laying on his horn.

After another desperate attempt to get the car started, she got out and walked back to the honker. The man rolled down his window in surprise.

"Tell you what," she said. "You go start my car, and I'll sit back here and honk the horn for you."

(Criticism, Patience)

Dates used:____________

Inadequacy

Two cows were grazing in a pasture when they saw a milk truck pass. On the side of the truck were the words, "Pasteurized, homogenized, standardized, Vitamin A added."

One cow sighed and said to the other, "Makes you feel kind of inadequate, doesn't it?"

John Maxwell
The Winning Attitude

(Contentment, Inferiority)

Dates used:____________

Incarnation

One evening my three-year-old son and I were sitting at the dinner table looking outside at the birds. I began telling him interesting facts about our feathered friends.

Suddenly, my son looked me square in the eye and said, "How do you know? Were you a bird once?"

Deb Kallman

(Evangelism, Missions)

Dates used:____________

Innovation

"Pastor, we've put up with praise choruses, worship bands, interpretive dance, and you preaching in blue jeans, but we draw the line at bungee baptisms."

Steve Phelps

(Baptism, Boards)

Dates used:____________

Insensitivity

A cartoon showed a man leaning over a casket, whispering last words to the deceased: "Does this mean you won't be cooking dinner tonight?"

Tim Ayers

(Dependence, Marriage)

Dates used:____________

Jobs

Buffalo Bills offensive lineman Glenn Parker speculated as to why NFL linemen are generally cheerful: "There are not a lot of well-paying jobs for 300-pounders. We found one, and we're happy about it."

Chicago Tribune

(Contentment, Happiness)

Dates used:____________

The human resources director was taken aback by the applicant's salary request. "You certainly expect to be compensated well for a beginner."

The applicant replied, "Well sure. Work's a lot harder when you don't know what you're doing."

(Expectations, Work)

Dates used:____________

A job applicant was asked, "Why were you discharged from your last position?"

The reply, "I was overly ambitious. I wanted to take work home with me."

The next question, "Who was your employer?"

"First National Bank."

(Integrity, Stealing)

Dates used:____________

Judging Others

Not long ago I had a kidney stone but was able to pass it. A few months later, my husband also passed a kidney stone. I made sure to remind him, "The Bible says, 'Let she who is without sin cast the first stone.'"

Judie Larson

(Compassion, Sin)

Dates used:____________

The first assignment for my husband, Cecil, in his art class was to sketch the San Luis Rey mission in Oceanside, California.

Everyone turned in a sketch, and the teacher began his oral critique of each student's work. When he came to Cecil's, he held it up and said, "Who is the figure in the doorway of the mission?"

"That's the padre, sir."

"Well, don't you think your padre looks a little sick?"

"He could be," Cecil responded. "I'm an artist, not a doctor."

Agnes Goddard

(Criticism, Perspective)

Dates used:____________

Knowing God

One day my four-year-old son asked me about God's name. I explained God had many names, including Father, Lord, and Jehovah.

After listening to my long explanation, my son asked, "Can I just call him Steve?"

Vicki Crooks

(God, Intimacy)

Dates used:____________

Leadership

Our church has several pastors, each with a specific title such as Senior Pastor, Pastor of Caring and Fellowship, and so on. When my wife worked in the church office, a woman came in to see the Pastor of Missions. Searching her mind for the exact title, she became momentarily confused and asked the church receptionist, "May I see the Minister of Passion?"

Bo Kaufmann

(Missions, Staff Relations)

Dates used:____________

Legalism

Dieting Religiously

I try to live by the book and when it came to losing those pesky pounds this spring I decided to diet by the book, taking cues from Scripture.

I buffetted my body daily (accompanied by praise tapes).

Locusts and wild honey were out of the question, but I did shun fat ("All fat belongs to the Lord" Lev. 3:16) and chewed each bite 40 times (the number of testing and tribulation).

Boy . . . is that a Spam and jelly sandwich?
I tried fasting, but by supper I was "longing to fill my belly with what the swines were eating." Lk. 15:16
THEN ONE GLORIOUS DAY. . .
"The righteous shall eat to their heart's content, but the stomach of the wicked goes hungry." Prov. 13:25
I got myself a cup of coffee and a donut and just kept reading . . . .
BIBLE
©chambers

Love

A husband asked his wife, "Tell me, Dear, have you ever been in love before?"

She thought a moment and replied, "No, Darling. I once respected a man for his great intelligence. I admired another for his remarkable courage. I was captivated by yet another for his good looks and charm. But with you, well, how else could you explain it, except love?"

(Admiration, Marriage)

Dates used:____________

From the Internet, some advice from kids on love and romance:

How do people in love typically behave?

"Mooshy . . . like puppy dogs . . . except puppy dogs don't wag their tails so much" (Arnold, age ten).

"When a person gets kissed for the first time, they fall down and don't get up for at least an hour" (Wendy, age eight).

Why do people in love hold hands?

"They want to make sure their rings don't fall off because they paid good money for them" (Gavin, age eight).

"They are just practicing for when they might have to walk down the aisle someday and do the holy matchimony thing" (John, age nine).

Confidential opinions about love.

"Love is foolish . . . but I still might try it sometime" (Jill, age six).

"Love will find you even if you're trying to hide from it. I been trying to hide from it since I was five, but the girls keep finding me" (Dave, age eight).

"I'm not rushing into love. Fourth grade is hard enough" (Regina, age ten).

What are some ways to make someone fall in love with you?

"Tell them that you own a whole bunch of candy stores" (Del, age six).

"Don't do things like have smelly, green sneakers. You might get attention, but attention ain't the same thing as love" (Alonzo, age nine).

Tell us your thoughts on kissing.

"You learn it right on the spot when the gooshy feelings get the best of you" (Brian, age seven).

"If it's your mom, you can kiss her anytime. But if it's a new person, you better ask for permission" (Roger, age six).

"I look at it like this: Kissing is fine if you like it, but it's a free country and nobody should be forced to do it" (Billy, age six).

(Romance, Valentine's Day)

Dates used:____________

Marriage

While browsing in a Christian bookstore one day, I discovered a shelf of reduced-price items. Among the gifts was a little figurine of a man and woman, their heads lovingly tilted toward one another. HAPPY 10TH ANNIVERSARY read the inscription. It appeared to be in perfect condition, yet its tag indicated DAMAGED.

Examining it more closely, I found another tag underneath that read WIFE IS COMING UNGLUED.

Gayle Urban

(Commitment, Stress)

Dates used:____________

A young bride complained to her friend, "My husband and I are getting along together fairly well, but he simply can't bear children."

"Oh well," a friend consoled her. "You can't expect men to do everything."

(Children, Parenting)

Dates used:____________

I was issuing a marriage license one day when the bride-to-be exploded.

"You rat! You told me this was your first marriage!"

"It is!"

"Oh yeah? Where it says, 'number of marriages,' you wrote 'two'!"

"Oh . . . I thought that meant how many people were getting married."

Ida M. Pardue

(Divorce, Weddings)

Dates used:____________

The caption of an A. A. McCourt cartoon, in the *National Review*, had the wife speaking to the husband, "There you go again, quoting our marriage vows out of context!"

(Arguing, Disharmony)

Dates used:____________

Men and Women

One little girl sang a slightly different version of the Gloria Patri one Sunday morning:

"World with weird men, Amen! Amen!"

Deanna Hendersen

(Music, Worship)

Dates used:____________

In 1492, Columbus set out for the Orient and ended up in the Caribbean, thus setting a pattern that has continued for over five hundred years. Men still won't stop and ask for directions.

(Pride, Self-reliance)

Dates used:____________

Men's Ministry

"So far, the only thing we have in common is an aversion to singing, socializing, and sharing."

Erik Johnson

(Church, Fellowship)

Dates used:____________

Ministry

A woman answered the knock at her door to find an obviously destitute man who wanted to earn some money by doing odd jobs. She was touched by his need and asked, "Can you paint?"

"Yes," he said. "I'm a pretty good painter."

"Well, here's a gallon of green paint and a brush. Go around the house and you'll see a porch that needs repainting. Be very careful. When you're done, I'll look it over and pay you what it's worth."

It wasn't more than an hour before he knocked again. "All finished," he reported.

"Did you do a good job?" she asked.

"Yes. But lady, there's one thing I'd like to point out to you. That's not a Porsche back there. That's a Mercedes."

We don't always get what we expect when we invest in the lives of others.

Bruce Thielemann

(Communication, Expectations)

Dates used:____________

Missions

At eighteen I went to a remote mission outpost in Africa for a short-term project. Upon our arrival, I was instructed that my sleeping quarters were in the church, so I placed my cot in front of the pulpit and turned in for the night.

Within minutes, several folks had slipped into the church. I lay motionless on my portable bed, staring straight up. Could it be? Yes, there was a service that night. The church was packed!

Finally, the pastor arrived, went behind the pulpit, and started the service, graciously ignoring me. Then a youth ensemble came forward, formed a half-circle just in front of me, and sang.

Soon the service ended. I realized there was nothing I could do, so I sat up in my pajamas and shook hands with the people as they left.

Doug A. Schneider

(Cross-Cultural Ministry, Manners)

Dates used:____________

"You're touching the world with your ministry, Pastor. Your luggage is in Malaysia, your Bible is in China, and your sermon is in Omaha."

Jonny Hawkins

(Ministry, Travel)

Dates used:____________

Many years ago when my brothers were small, one of them said to the other, "I'm going to eat you!"

My mother overheard and said, "Oh, we don't eat people. There are some people who eat other people. We call them cannibals. Someone should tell them about Jesus."

To which David replied, "Well, they'd better tell them over the telephone."

Miriam Martin

(Evangelism, Fear)

Dates used:____________

Mortality

To begin a discussion on values, our youth pastor asked the teens this question: "What would you do if your doctor told you you had only twenty-four hours to live?"

The teens' responses were typically, "Be with friends and family." But the discussion came undone when Jason, our thirteen-year-old, said, "I'd get a second opinion."

Donna Spratt

(Calm, Death)

Dates used:____________

Motherhood

My mother was babysitting my son, Dirk, at her house one day. When I stopped to pick him up, Mom told me that Dirk had followed her into the bedroom as she put some things away in the closet. "Grandma," he asked, "what room is this?"

"This is a closet, Dirk," she explained.

"We don't have a room like this in our house," he said.

"Of course you do," she insisted. "You have lots of closets at your home."

When he again denied having closets at our house, she tried another tack. "Where do you keep all your clothes?" she asked.

He replied, "In the dryer."

Shari Hanson

(Busyness, Tidiness)

Dates used:____________

Musicians

"Pastor just asked me to sing this morning . . . I have a terrible sore throat . . . My dog died this morning before—*sniff*—church . . ."

Steve Phelps

(Excuses, Singing)

Dates used:____________

Neighbors

Upon arriving in our new home in Kentucky, my seven-year-old son, Jason, decided to explore the neighborhood. He was back within the hour proclaiming that he had made some new friends.

"Good. Are they boys or girls?" I asked.

"One is a boy, and one is a girl," he replied.

"That's great," I said. "How old are they?"

"Mom," my son replied, "that would be very rude to ask."

I was puzzled by his response, but about an hour later, Jason was back. "Mom!" he shouted through the screen door. "I found out how old my new friends are. The girl is sixty-five, and the boy is seventy."

Teri Leinbaugh

(Aging, Friendship)

Dates used:____________

New Year's Day

Here are some bold prophecies for the year ahead:

Chuck Swindoll will author a best-selling book.

Significant church-state issues will be debated in the nation's courts.

The head of a major parachurch group will name a family member to succeed him.

A leading television evangelist will appeal for money.

A new, "finally understandable" version of the Bible will be published.

A presidential candidate will try to curry favor among Christians.

Don't ask me how I do it.

Eutychus in Christianity Today

(Certainty, Prophecy)

Dates used:____________

Optimism

An optimist is someone who:

Sets up *all* the folding chairs for Wednesday night Bible study!

Makes plans to meet his spouse at 8:45 after an 8:00 board meeting!

Puts her shoes back on when the minister says, "In conclusion . . ."!

Mary Chambers

(Expectations, Hope)

Dates used:____________

Panic

In *Lead On*, John Haggai tells the story of Mrs. Monroe in Darlington, Maryland. The mother of eight children, she came home one afternoon from the grocery store and noticed it was a bit quieter than usual.

She looked in the living room, and five of her darlings were sitting in a circle. She put down the groceries, walked over, and saw they were playing with five of the cutest skunks you can imagine.

She was instantly terrified, and she screamed, "Run children, run!" Each child grabbed a skunk and ran, in five different directions. Her screams so scared the children that each one squeezed his skunk!

It's always too soon to panic.

(Afflictions, Trials)

Dates used:____________

Parenting

Another Baby?

There's a difference between your first pregnancy and subsequent ones—beginning with how people respond . . .

You're less concerned about "losing your figure" (it's gone) and just looking forward to not holding your stomach in. . . .

You can wear most of your old clothes since you haven't worn a shirt that tucks in or a dress with a waist since before the last baby. . . .

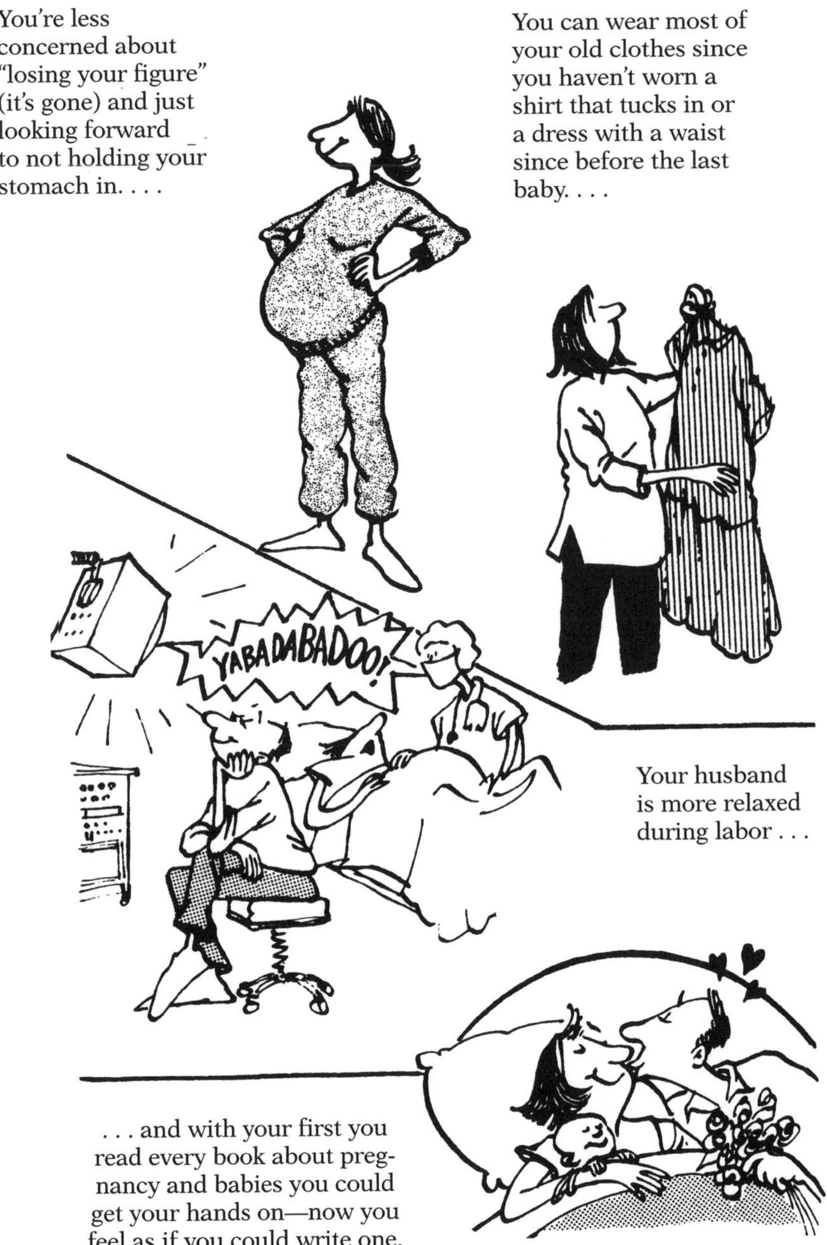

Your husband is more relaxed during labor . . .

. . . and with your first you read every book about pregnancy and babies you could get your hands on—now you feel as if you could write one.

After I had related how tough I had it as a kid, my six-year-old son Jason put his arm around me and said, "It's all right, Dad. You're living with us now."

Jack Eppolito

(Hardships, Reminiscence)

Dates used:____________

Did you know there's a special chain letter for parents? It reads:

Dear Friend: This chain letter is meant to bring relief and happiness to you. Unlike other chain letters, this one does not cost money. Simply send a copy of this letter to six other parents who are tired of their teenagers. Then bundle yours up and send him or her to the parent at the bottom of the list.

In one week, you will receive 16,436 teenagers—and one of them should be worth keeping. Warning: One dad broke the chain and got his own teenager back.

Roger Poupart

(Contentment, Teenagers)

Dates used:____________

Pastoral Care

A troubled parishioner sought counsel from his minister: "Pastor, everyone calls me a liar."

"Oh, come on now," said the pastor. "I can't believe that."

The Light *(Issue 11)*

(Counseling, Lying)

Dates used:____________

Patience

One time a warden asked a man on death row what he would like to eat for his last meal.

The inmate said, "I would like to have a huge piece of watermelon."

The warden said, "You must be kidding? This is December. Watermelons have not been planted, let alone harvested."

The inmate said, "That's okay. I don't mind waiting."

Larry Moyer

(Delay, Procrastination)

Dates used:____________

Peacemaking

When I was a teenager, our family took cross-country car trips each summer. To keep the peace, we each took a turn choosing a cassette to play in the car tape deck. No one was allowed to complain or comment about another's choice.

My mother liked to listen to hymns. I chose contemporary Christian music. My younger brother preferred rock. And Dad? He always thought the best thing was a 90-minute tape that was still blank!

Sharon Fleming

(Respect, Silence)

Dates used:____________

Peer Pressure

The "Just Say No" slogan seems to have caught on and helped the fight against drugs.

I've been so impressed by the concept that I've started a small group in our church based on the same principle: "Just Say No When You Really Want To." The group has attracted a variety of people. The chairman of our Constitutional Revision Subcommittee, the former leader of our "Interpreting Revelation" study, and the chaperones from our "Junior High Goes Crazy" weekend retreat have all been regular attendees. And while no one admits being there to resist financial commitments, the subject of pledging does seem to come up quite often.

Two of our longtime board members and our pastor's wife considered joining for a while, but I think their sense of guilt or commitment was too strong. They started their own "Just Say Maybe" group, and in almost no time, most of our group switched over.

But the "Just Say No" group will go on. After all, there's still me and the judge from last year's Pie Bake.

Eutychus in Christianity Today

(Committees, Small Groups)

Dates used:____________

Perseverance

A young woman from our congregation wrote me from graduate school. She reported on her studies and extracurricular activities, which included participating in a Weight Watchers group.

Determined to lose weight, she had set a goal of losing seventy-eight pounds. In fact, she wrote, she had already lost sixteen. But then she added the Bible reference John 6:9. I checked my Bible and read with a smile, "But what are they among so many?" (KJV).

Guy D. Mattox Jr.

(Dedication, Discipline)

Dates used:____________

I had decided to retire from the ministry, and one Sunday I explained my decision to the congregation: "I wear two hearing aids and trifocal glasses; I have a partial plate, and I sometimes walk with a cane. It seems to me," I concluded, "that the Lord is telling me it's time to retire."

After the service, a white-haired lady told me, "Reverend, you have misinterpreted what the Lord has been saying to you. He's not telling you it's time to retire; he's telling you that if you keep going, he'll keep you patched up."

Ivan P. Downing

(Health, Ministry)

Dates used:____________

Popularity

In April 1993, just after Steve Morrow scored the goal that gave the Arsenal Team England's League Cup soccer championship, his teammates tossed him into the air in ritual celebration of their victory. However, they failed to catch him when he came down, and Morrow was carried off the field on a stretcher with a broken arm and an oxygen mask on his face.

Chuck Shepherd in Pitch Weekly

(Leadership, Recognition)

Dates used:____________

Prayer

When a nightclub opened on Main Street, the only church in that small town organized an all-night prayer meeting. The members asked God to burn down the club. Within a few minutes, lightning struck the club, and it burned to the ground. The owner sued the church, which denied responsibility.

After hearing both sides, the judge said, "It seems that wherever the guilt may lie, the nightclub owner believes in prayer, while the church doesn't."

Herb Miller in Connecting with God

(Faith, Responsibility)

Dates used:____________

My eight-year-old son came home from school with a stuffed animal he had won at the class Valentine party.

"How did that happen?" I asked.

"Well," he explained, "the teacher put all our names together, and then picked one out.

"I cheated, though," he said, looking guilty. "I prayed!"

Davy Troxel

(Intercession, Rewards)

Dates used:____________

My four-year-old daughter and I would always pray before she went to sleep. One night she volunteered to pray. She prayed and prayed and prayed—her voice getting softer and softer and softer, until only her lips were moving. Then she said "Amen."

"Honey," I said, "I didn't hear a word you said."

She answered, "Mama, I wasn't talking to you."

Helen B. Poole

(Eavesdropping, Intercession)

Dates used:____________

A Sunday school teacher came to me with a picture depicting Christ in agonizing prayer in Gethsemane while his disciples slept in the background.

"I showed this picture to my class today," she announced, "and one of the students said, 'That reminds me of Pastor Winger.'"

Naturally, I was quite overwhelmed. While searching for an appropriate comment, I must have failed to catch the twinkle in the teacher's eyes. After I stammered a moment, she asked, "Want to know why this picture reminded my students of you?"

"Yes, of course," I said, trying to sound suitably humble.

"Well, Ronnie pointed to the sleeping disciples and said, 'You see, Jesus was praying so long, just like Pastor Winger does, that the disciples fell asleep!'"

Walter Winger

(Boredom, Patience)

Dates used:____________

Preachers

One day I sat down with my daughter and explained with pride that her grandfather was a preacher, her great-great grandfather was a preacher, and her great-great-great grandfather was a preacher. To which she replied, "Wow! We sure come from a long line of grandfathers."

Linda Click

(Grandparents, Heritage)

Dates used:____________

Pride

With reluctance, my grandson agreed to let his wife sell some of his old ties and suits in her yard sale. He thought they were fine, but she insisted they were outdated.

One shopper came by, picked up one of the old ties and a suit, and exclaimed, "Perfect!"

My grandson quickly gave his wife a smug look—until the woman continued, "These will look terrific on my scarecrow!"

Clara Null

(Appearance, Humility)

Dates used:____________

"It's showtime, baby!"

Rob Portlock

(Servanthood, Ushers)

Dates used:____________

Prophecy

Don't believe the "gloom and doom" experts who want to tell us about the future. Here are three examples of bad predictions:

> "A Japanese attack on Pearl Harbor is a strategic impossibility."
>
> *George Fielding Eliot, 1938*
>
> "Television won't be able to hold on to any market it captures after the first six months. People will soon get tired of staring at a plywood box every night."
>
> *Darryl F. Zanuck, head of 20th Century Fox, 1946*
>
> "Landing and moving around on the moon offers so many serious problems for human beings that it may take science another two hundred years to lick them."
>
> Science Digest, *August 1948*

(Future, Predictions)

Dates used:____________

Noted in a newspaper personal ad:

"Yesterday in this space I predicted that the world would come to an end. It did not, however. I regret any inconvenience this may have caused."

(End Times, Future)

Dates used:____________

Punishment

An irate father phoned the Sunday school superintendent after his daughter had been attending a few weeks. "Our preschooler tells me if she misses Sunday school too often, you'll pitch her into the furnace! What in the world are you teaching in that church?"

Investigating the matter, the superintendent questioned the teacher. At first stumped, they finally put two and two together: Stressing the importance of regular attendance on Sundays, the teacher had told her class that if they missed four consecutive weeks, they would be dropped from the register.

Christian Reader

(Confusion, Sunday School)

Dates used:____________

Relationships

No healthy person would want the neglect I have to offer.

Jerry Seinfeld

(Marriage, Neglect)

Dates used:____________

My neighbor's son, Robert, seemed young to be an usher at a wedding, but he was quickly coached in wedding protocol. A veteran usher instructed Robert to ask the person he was escorting, "Are you a guest of the bride or groom?" to know where to seat them.

Imagine our surprise when we heard Robert ask, as he graciously offered his arm to the first arrival, "Madam, whose side are you on?"

Richard Blake

(Ushers, Weddings)

Dates used:____________

Renewal

My family had gathered at my house for our yearly reunion. While we were in church singing the opening hymn, an earthquake hit. The building shook, and the overhead lights swung back and forth. In true California style we never missed a beat, even though we had to grab the pews in front to steady ourselves.

Following the service, the pastor came over to greet my out-of-town relatives. My son-in-law grinned as he shook the pastor's hand and said, "I've been to a lot of church services in my life, but I can honestly say this was the most moving one I've ever attended."

June Cerza Kolf

(Holy Spirit, Revival)

Dates used:____________

The church was beautifully decorated for Christmas: poinsettias, evergreen boughs, golden bows, and a candle on the sill of each stained-glass window. Amid the beauty, the choir was presenting its cantata.

I wanted to capture this special event, so I asked a fellow churchgoer to videotape the service. He was happy to oblige and after experimenting decided the best place to set up was by the windows.

About fifteen minutes into the service, the cameraman leaned too close to the lit candle on the windowsill, and his suit coat caught fire! Two alert folks hastily snuffed out the blaze. We rejoiced that no one was injured, and, as our minister of music quickly noted, "Finally, somebody was truly on fire for Jesus!"

Tony Foeller

(Christmas, Revival)

Dates used:____________

Repentance

When I was a telephone operator, a customer talked overtime on a long-distance call from a pay telephone booth. Even with my friendly reminders, he refused to deposit his overtime coins. Instead, he slammed down the phone, irate and verbally abusive.

A few seconds later, he was back on my line—somewhat calmer.

"Operator, please let me out of the phone booth—I'll pay, I'll pay, just let me out!"

The customer mistakenly thought I had control of the phone booth's doors and had locked him in! He gladly paid the overtime charge and with my advice gave the booth door a hefty kick to free himself.

Lillian Pearsall

(Atonement, Sin)

Dates used:____________

Resourcefulness

While I was shopping with my eight-year-old, he spotted a toy he wanted but didn't have enough money to buy. Since I wanted to teach him financial responsibility, I told him I couldn't give him the extra money.

In a brilliant display of resourcefulness, he reached into his mouth and, to the astonishment of onlookers, pulled out a loose baby tooth and handed it to me.

He got his toy.

Donna McLean

(Money, Responsibility)

Dates used:____________

Retirement

One woman's definition of retirement: "Twice the husband at half the salary."

(Marriage, Work)

Dates used:____________

Revenge

My friend's four boys were young and bursting with energy, especially in church. But the sermon her minister preached on turning the other cheek got their undivided attention. The minister stressed that no matter what others do to us, we should never try to get even. That afternoon the youngest boy came into the house crying. Between sobs he told his mother he had kicked one of his brothers, who had kicked him in return.

"I'm sorry that you're hurt," his mother said. "But you shouldn't go around kicking people."

The tearful child replied, "But the preacher said he wasn't supposed to kick me back."

Jane Vajnar

(Arguments, Relationships)

Dates used:____________

Sabbath

… and on the 7th day thou shalt clear the platform, check the sound system, replace the broken guitar string, change the microphone battery, select the chorus transparencies, prepare the chord sheets, replace the broken overhead projector lens, tune the piano, attach the new drum heads, lead 2 worship services … and rest.

Robertson

Andy Robertson

(Rest, Worship)

Dates used:____________

Sacrifice

Our seven-year-old daughter had just won $2 for her memory work in Sunday school. After the morning service, the pastor's wife congratulated her.

Our daughter proudly announced, "And I put it all in the morning's offering!"

"My, how wonderful!" the pastor's wife exclaimed. "I'm sure God will be pleased."

"Yes," the child replied, "now maybe God will let me do some of the things I want to do!"

Genia Obal

(Expectations, Giving)

Dates used:____________

My seven-year-old daughter wanted to take violin lessons, so I took her to a music store to rent an instrument. Hoping she would understand the importance of making a commitment to practice, I explained to her that the lessons were expensive. I was willing to make the financial sacrifices if she promised to work hard. "There may be times you'll feel like giving up," I said, "but I want you to hang in there and keep on trying."

She nodded in understanding and then in her most serious voice said, "It will be just like marriage, right, Mom?"

Debra K. Johnson

(Commitment, Marriage)

Dates used:____________

Scripture

The youth in my church had been studying the Book of Esther. I knew my son had been paying attention when we had brussels sprouts for supper. Spearing one and looking at it distastefully, he placed it in his mouth, saying, "If I perish, I perish."

Frankie Roland

(Courage, Fate)

Dates used:_____________

Self-esteem

I like talking to myself because I like dealing with a better class of people.

Jackie Mason

(Pride, Smugness)

Dates used:_____________

"I don't know, Pastor, maybe it's an identity crisis. I just can't seem to shake this feeling that I'm nothing . . . a nobody, just an anonymous speck of dust on this huge planet. I feel totally forgettable."

Jonny Hawkins

(Anonymity, Counseling)

Dates used:____________

Servanthood

My great-great uncle lived to the ripe old age of 106. He was healthy and spry and took joy in chauffering his less able-bodied senior friends around town. On his 100th birthday, his driver's license came up for renewal. When he went to the licensing bureau, the skeptical clerk said, "You're 100 years old! What do you need a driver's license for?"

My uncle, completely nonplussed, replied, "Somebody has to drive the old folks around!"

He continued to have a legal driver's license for the next five years.

Barbara Klassen

(Aging, Attitude)

Dates used:____________

Sharing

Four-year-old Sarah was invited to her first wedding, and she had lots of questions. At the reception, we explained there were two cakes—a groom's cake and a bride's cake.

"What's the matter, Mom," Sarah asked, "haven't they learned to share yet?"

Patti Culver

(Marriage, Weddings)

Dates used:____________

My three-year-old grandson found a quarter in the driveway as the family left for church. When they returned home, he pulled it out of his pocket and handed it to his mother.

"You can have this money, Mommy. I was going to give it to Jesus, but he wasn't there."

Joyce Parson

(Giving, Worship)

Dates used:____________

My grandchild was excited about his parents buying a new home with three bedrooms. He would have his own bedroom for the first time. But he surprised the real estate agent when he blurted, "It's too bad you don't have a house with another bedroom so Mom and Dad don't have to keep sharing a bedroom, too."

Clara Null

(Family, Marriage)

Dates used:____________

Who's afraid of the Small Home Group?

Are you one of the many with ill-founded fears of. . .

Having People in Your Home?
HEY! This guy's got BARNEY sheets.
What if we all sat out here in rows while you talked to us from behind that dresser?
The casual Format?
Well?
Welcome! Glad you could join us. We have a full evening of intense fellowship lined up especially for you, so grab your Bible and chips and stay tuned.
HOME ALONE GROUP
©Chambers

Sin

After telling a class of four- to seven-year-olds the story of Adam and Eve, I began to quiz them. "What was Eve's punishment for disobeying God?" I asked.

A bright-eyed girl raised her hand. "She had to crawl on her belly and eat dirt for the rest of her life."

Ellen Cowan

(Disobedience, Women)

Dates used:____________

I had just finished a lesson on Christian behavior. "Now, Billy," I asked, "tell me what we must do before we can expect to be forgiven for our sins."

Without hesitation, Billy replied, "First we gotta sin."

Clara Null

(Forgiveness, Repentance)

Dates used:____________

Sports

In a never-ending effort to attract the unchurched, some churches have considered translating their unfamiliar terminology into familiar football phrases. Although these definitions are not the best football and certainly not the best theology, they would help initiate football fans into the complexities of church life.

Blocking: Talking endlessly to the pastor at the church door and keeping everyone else from exiting.

Draft choice: The decision to sit close to an air-conditioning vent.

Draw play: What restless children do during a long sermon.

End around: Diaper-changing time in the nursery.

End zone: The pews.

Extra point: What you receive when you tell the preacher his sermon was too short.

Face mask: Smiling and saying everything is fine when it isn't.

Forward motion: The invitation at an evangelistic service.

Fullback: What the choir sees while the sermon is delivered.

Halfback: What the organist sees.

Hash marks: Stains left on the tablecloth after a potluck.

Head linesman: The one who changes the overhead projector transparencies.

Illegal motion: Leaving before the benediction.

Illegal use of hands: Clapping at an inappropriate point in the service.

In the pocket: Where some church members keep God's tithe.

Incomplete pass: A dropped offering plate.

Interference: Talking during the prelude.

Linebacker: A statistic used by a preacher to support a point just made.

Passing game: The maneuver required of latecomers when the person sitting at the end of the pew won't slide to the middle.

Quarterback: What tightwads want after putting fifty cents in the offering.

Running backs: Those who make repeated trips to the rest room.

Through the uprights: Getting things done via the elders or church board.

Touchback: The laying on of hands.

Two-minute warning: The chairman of the board looking at his watch in full view of the preacher.

William Ellis

(Assimilation, Church)

Dates used:____________

Stewardship

Paul Harvey's broadcast (11/22/95) shared this insight:

The Butterball Turkey Company set up a hotline to answer consumer questions about preparing holiday turkeys. One woman called to inquire about cooking a turkey that had been in her freezer for twenty-three years! The operator told her it might be safe if the freezer had been kept below 0 degrees the entire time. But the operator warned the woman that, even if it were safe, the flavor had probably deteriorated, and she wouldn't recommend eating it.

The caller replied, "That's what we thought. We'll just give it to the church."

Rik Danielson

(Generosity, Stinginess)

Dates used:____________

Stress

I was wearing a T-shirt with the words: BE NICE TO ME. I HAD A HARD DAY. Little Eric looked at the words and said, "How can you tell this early in the morning?"

Verna Chambers

(Expectations, Foresight)

Dates used:____________

My friend Dorothy spent several weeks in prayer and special training to lead a Bible discussion group. Finally the big day arrived for the first class. Getting her family of six out the door was more hectic than usual that morning. Breakfast didn't turn out right, and several arguments were going on among the children. Dorothy, quickly getting frazzled, tried to regain her composure. In the midst of the bedlam, her husband entered the kitchen and surveyed the uproar.

"Kids! Settle down!" he admonished. "Your mom has only forty-five minutes until she has to become a radiant Christian."

Roseann Hill

(Example, Lifestyle)

Dates used:____________

Chippie the parakeet never saw it coming. One second he was peacefully perched in his cage singing, the next he was sucked in, washed up, and blown over.

His problem began when his owner decided to clean his cage with a vacuum. She stuck the nozzle in to suck up the seeds and feathers in the bottom of the cage. Then the phone rang. Instinctively she turned to pick it up. She barely said hello when—sswwwwwwppppp! Chippie got sucked in. She gasped, let the phone drop, and snapped off the vacuum. With her heart in her mouth, she unzipped the bag.

There was Chippie—alive, but stunned—covered with heavy black dust. She grabbed him and rushed to the bathtub, turned on the faucet full blast, and held Chippie under a torrent of ice-cold water, power-washing him clean. So she did what any compassionate pet owner would do: She snatched up the hair dryer and blasted the wet, shivering little bird with hot air.

Chippie doesn't sing much anymore.

Chuck Swindoll

(Depression, Trials)

Dates used:____________

"I, too, was saved from a life of addictions.
I was hooked on phonics."

Jonny Hawkins

(Addictions, Salvation)

Dates used:____________

Tactfulness

The elderly pastor's wife was known for her ability to make positive comments about every facet of her husband's ministry. The church choir, however, consisting of seniors in their seventies and eighties, had defied positive but truthful comment.

She finally solved the problem one Sunday morning. As the choir members filed into the choir loft, she leaned over and remarked, "Aren't they walking well this morning?"

Anne Phillips

(Criticism, Diplomacy)

Dates used:____________

As a lady in our church was singing a solo, my four-year-old grandson tugged at my sleeve. "Nana," he said, "she can't sing very well, can she?"

Knowing the deep faith of this wonderful lady, I said, "Chandler, she sings from her heart, so it's good." He nodded with understanding.

Several days later as we were singing along with the car radio, Chandler interrupted me. "Nana," he said, "you sing from your heart too, don't you?"

Barbara McKeever

(Criticism, Diplomacy)

Dates used:____________

In *Be a People Person*, John Maxwell tells this story:

Mr. Myrick had to go to Chicago on business and persuaded his brother to take care of his cat during his absence.

Though he hated cats, the brother agreed. Upon his return, Myrick called from the airport to check on the cat.

"Your cat died," the brother reported, then hung up.

Myrick was inconsolable. His grief was magnified by his brother's insensitivity, so he called again to express his pain. "There was no need for you to be so blunt," he said.

"What was I supposed to say?" asked the perplexed brother.

"You could have broken the news gradually," explained Myrick. "You could have said, 'The cat was playing on the roof.' Then, later in the conversation, you could have said, 'He fell off.' Then you could have said, 'He broke his leg.' Then when I came to pick him up, you could have said, 'I'm so sorry. Your cat passed away during the night.' You've got to learn to be more tactful. . . . By the way, how's Mom?"

After a long pause, the brother replied, "She's playing on the roof."

Mike Neifert

(Criticism, Diplomacy)

Dates used:____________

Ten Commandments

My Sunday school class of first graders was learning the Ten Commandments. When we got to "Thou shalt not commit adultery," I wondered if I would have to explain this to them.

Sure enough, suddenly a seven-year-old girl raised her hand and asked, "What does *commit* mean?"

Clara Null

(Adultery, Sunday School)

Dates used:____________

A third-grade Sunday school teacher was giving a lesson on the commandment, "Honor thy father and mother."

"Now, does anyone know a commandment for brothers and sisters?" she asked.

One sharp girl raised her hand and said, "Thou shalt not kill."

Jack Seberry

(Murder, Parents)

Dates used:____________

A fourth-grade Sunday school completed several lessons on the Ten Commandments by asking the kids, "What is the hardest commandment for you to keep?"

Most responded, "Thou shalt not commit adultery."

She couldn't understand why fourth graders would find that command a problem until a mother quizzed her son on what he meant. Without blinking, the boy replied, "Thou shalt not sass back to adults."

Sheryl Tedder

(Adultery, Sin)

Dates used:____________

While working as the chaplain for the Cub Scouts, I conducted a vesper service at each meeting. One evening the lesson was on the Ten Commandments, so I asked the kids if they could name any. They began to call out a number of them, including, "Don't drink and drive."

James Isenberg

(Alcohol, Sin)

Dates used:____________

Compliments You're Not Sure You Want to Hear When Preaching a Series on the Ten Commandments:

1. Thou shalt have no other gods before me. *"A simply divine sermon, Pastor."*
2. Thou shalt make no graven images. *"You illustrated perfectly what God really looks like."*
3. Thou shalt not take the Lord's name in vain. *"As God is my judge, that was your best sermon ever."*
4. Remember the sabbath, to keep it holy. *"Excellent bit of work, Pastor."*
5. Honor thy father and mother. *"Wish my dad could hear you preach—he could sure use it."*
6. Thou shalt not kill. *"Anyone who slept through that one ought to be shot."*
7. Thou shalt not commit adultery. *"Glad you don't intrude into other people's affairs."*
8. Thou shalt not steal. *"Good sermon, Reverend—you preach it better than Schuller did on TV last week."*
9. Thou shalt not bear false witness. *"I'm literally in heaven when I hear you preach, Pastor."*
10. Thou shalt not covet. *"I really envy your ability to speak well in public."*

David Landegent

(Compliments, Praise)

Dates used:____________

Thankfulness

One Sunday in church, members were praising the Lord for what he had done in their lives that week. Mr. Segault said that the roof of his house had caught on fire, but fortunately, a neighbor had seen it, and the possible disaster was averted with only minor damage.

A minute later, a woman stood up. "I have a praise, too," she said. "I'm Mr. Segault's insurance agent."

Ariana Macksey

(Church, Community)

Dates used:____________

Theology

A new members' class gave some new definitions to theological jargon:

Old nature. Last year's leaves.
Sanctification. What happened to the boat on vacation.
Discipleship. A boat belonging to Peter.
Total Commitment. A covenant to eat one type of breakfast cereal.

Eutychus in Christianity Today

(Insight, Understanding)

Dates used:____________

Thrift

Ronald Warwick, captain of the luxury cruise ship *Queen Elizabeth II*, questioned a passenger who paid full fare for his dog to join them on an around-the-world cruise. (Accommodations ranged from $25,000 to $150,000.) "Wouldn't it have cost less to leave him at home?"

"Oh no," the man said. "When we are away a long time, the dog's psychiatrist fees are so high, it's less expensive to bring him along."

USA Today *(10/25/95)*

(Extravagance, Priorities)

Dates used:____________

Tithing

My five-year-old son was proud that he had graduated from bow ties to a necktie just like Dad's. But one Sunday morning, with his hand clutching the tie tightly, I heard this panicked whisper: "Dad, why did the pastor say they're going to collect the ties and offering?"

G. Brian Manning

(Giving, Sacrifice)

Dates used:____________

Unlike the IRS, the church has always kept its requirements simple: a straight 10 percent off the top. But perhaps church officials should consider engaging in some "Tithe Reform."

The new T-4, Estimated Tithe Declaration Forms, could work like this: On line 1, write down the amount of your regular paycheck. On line 2, enter the number of times you go to church each year. Multiply the number on line 2 by 3.056. Enter the result on line 3. On line 4 enter your age when you first professed Christ. On line 5, enter your pastor's salary. (This can be found on the photocopied budget distributed at your church's annual meeting, which is always held on the day of the Super Bowl.)

Compare line 5 with line 1. Feel guilty. Subtract line 5 from line 1. Take a deep breath and ignore the result. Multiply the amount on line 1 by .10 and enter it on line 6. Throw in a few extra bucks to make you feel better about the minister's salary. And write that check.

Eutychus in Christianity Today

(Generosity, Taxes)

Dates used:____________

Trust

Travel is hard enough without the airline industry scaring us with their terminology.

As I drive to the airport, watching for the signs that indicate what exits to take, I wonder what sadist named the place where you trust your all to a creaking bunch of nuts and bolts *Terminal*.

When I check in at the counter, I remember this particular flight was chosen by my travel agent for one reason—it was the *cheapest available*.

When it's time to land, why does the flight attendant have to remind us that we are making *our final approach*? (On a recent flight, the attendant announced reassuringly, "We will be *in* the ground very shortly.")

When the flight attendant warns us not to move until the plane has reached a *complete stop*, I wonder what an incomplete stop would be like.

Leonard Sweet

(Fear, Travel)

Dates used:____________

Uncertainty

Some questions we'll probably never have answered this side of heaven:

Why isn't *phonetic* spelled the way it sounds?

Why are there interstate highways in Hawaii?

Why are there flotation devices under plane seats, instead of parachutes?

Why are cigarettes sold in gas stations when smoking is prohibited there?

Have you ever imagined a world with no hypothetical situations?

How does the guy who drives the snowplow get to work in the morning?

If 7-Eleven is open 24 hours a day, 365 days a year, why are there locks on the doors?

If nothing ever sticks to Teflon, how do they make Teflon stick to the pan?

Why do we drive on parkways and park on driveways?

Why is it when you transport something by car, it's called a *shipment*, but when you transport something by ship, it's called *cargo*?

(Curiosity, God's Omniscience)

Dates used:____________

Unhappiness

Ten Commandments for an Unhappy Life:

1. Thou shalt wear a grim expression at all times, and thou shalt hold thy body in a stiff and rigid posture, and exercise thy muscles as little as possible.
2. Thou shalt never get too close to anybody.
3. Thou shalt stuff and store all thy feeling in thy gut.
4. Thou shalt put aside play, and shalt inflict upon others that which was once inflicted upon thyself.
5. Thou shalt remain logical and analytical whenever possible.
6. Thou shalt go to as many "all-you-can-eat" buffets as thou canst.
7. Thou shalt not party.
8. Thou shalt not take a vacation.
9. Thou shalt expect the worst in all situations, blame and shame everyone around thyself for everything, and dwell on the feebleness, faults, and fears of others.
10. Thou shalt be in control at all times, no matter what.

Leonard Sweet

(Health, Stress)

Dates used:____________

Unity

Weddings in our church always included the lighting of a unity candle. At one rehearsal I was explaining the symbolism of the candle ceremony.

"After the middle candle is lit, blowing out the two side candles means the two become one," I said.

"Oh," a guest admitted in surprise. "I always thought it meant 'no more flames.'"

Greg Asimakoupoulos

(Marriage, Weddings)

Dates used:____________

Ushers

The Top 10 Reasons It's Great to Be an Usher.

10. You get to wear a badge.
9. You don't have to sit on a hard pew for the whole service.
8. You can slip out to the restroom if you need to, and nobody notices.
7. You get to tell people where to go.
6. You get to take money from people.
5. You don't have to be as friendly as the greeters.
4. You get to eat a lot of breath mints.
3. If a screaming child bothers you, you can do something about it.
2. Preachers preach to the choir, not to the ushers.
1. You get to seat latecomers in the front row.

Jerry Beres, Russell Snyder

(Volunteers, Worship)

Dates used:____________

Vision

A golfer's errant shot ended up on an anthill. He squared up, took a big swing—and missed. Thousands of innocent ants were killed. The hacker took another swing—and missed again. Another wave of ants was destroyed. Panic-stricken insects scurried everywhere.

One ant finally took charge. "Follow me," he cried with authority. Another ant yelled, "But where are we going?"

He pointed to the golf ball sitting in front of them. "There. If we don't get on the ball, we're going to die!"

(Leadership, Mistakes)

Dates used:____________

"It was safe to say that Pastor Mel's vision statement hadn't yet caught fire."

Steve Phelps

(Boards, Enthusiasm)

Dates used:____________

Volunteers

"I'm sorry, could you repeat that? I didn't catch the first four words."

Tim Liston

(Communication, Listening)

Dates used:____________

Weddings

At a wedding, my granddaughter Melissa asked, "Why is a bride always dressed in white?"

"Because white represents happiness, and today is the happiest day of her life," I replied.

Her next question was: "Then why is the groom dressed in black?"

Clara Null

(Happiness, Marriage)

Dates used:____________

I was watching my five-year-old granddaughter play with her toys. At one point, she staged a wedding, first playing the role of the mother who assigned specific duties, then suddenly becoming the bride with her "teddy bear" groom.

She picked him up and said to the "minister" presiding over the wedding, "Now you can read us our rights."

Without missing a beat, she became the minister, who said, "You have the right to remain silent, anything you say may be held against you, you have the right to have an attorney present. You may kiss the bride."

Sonja Ely

(Happiness, Rights)

Dates used:____________

Former Education Secretary William Bennett recently attended a contemporary wedding where the bride and groom pledged, in their wedding vows, to remain together, "as long as love shall last."

"I sent paper plates as my wedding gift," Bennett said.

Detroit News

(Commitment, Marriage)

Dates used:____________

Weight

Medical surveys indicate that 60 percent of Americans are overweight. Of course, those are just round figures.

(Fitness, Health)

Dates used:____________

Work

A TV weather reporter lost her job because her forecasts were never accurate. In an interview for another position, she was asked why she left her last job.

"The climate didn't agree with me," she replied.

(Excuses, Honesty)

Dates used:____________

Worry

Rick Majerus, men's basketball coach at the University of Utah, recently captured a common concern:

"Everyone's worried about the economy this year. Hey, my hairline is in recession, my waistline is in inflation, and altogether, I'm in depression."

Arizona Republic

(Aging, Economy)

Dates used:____________

Worship

A woman entered a Häagen-Dazs store on the Kansas City Plaza for an ice-cream cone. After making her selection, she turned and found herself face-to-face with Paul Newman, in town filming the movie *Mr. & Mrs. Bridge*. He smiled and said hello. Newman's blue eyes caused her knees to shake.

She managed to pay for her cone, then left the shop, heart pounding. When she gained her composure, she realized she didn't have her snack. She started back into the store to get it and met Newman at the door.

"Are you looking for your ice cream?" he asked. She nodded, unable to speak. "You put it in your purse with your change."

When was the last time the presence of God quickened our pulse?

Kansas City Star

(Embarrassment, Idols)

Dates used:____________

Sniglets are words that don't appear in the dictionary, but should. Here are a few words to broaden your worship vocabulary:

Boiked—What an usher feels after going out of his way to take an offering plate to someone alone in a pew, and the person has nothing to contribute.

Pliturgist—The man or woman who is always half a second ahead of the rest of the congregation during a responsive reading.

Jobbling—The gradual rising of the congregation during the final hymn, after the pastor has forgotten to say, "Please rise."

Pleech—A joyful congregant's first note of verse four, when the bulletin said to stop after three.

Scruggles—The scattered, congregational coughs that follow inevitably after someone gets them started.

Grooncher—A 240-pound greeter who thinks his job is to crush hands, not shake them.

Scriggling—The act of wasting one's time thinking up Christian sniglets.

Eutychus in Christianity Today

(Choirs, Ushers)

Dates used:____________

Youth

A recent online discussion followed the question, *Is it appropriate for girls to ask guys out for dates?* One teenage boy wrote, "It would be okay for a girl to ask me out. It would be surprising, but okay."

Campus Life's *Yakety Yak message board*

(Dating, Insecurity)

Dates used:____________

Eighteen-year-old Jennifer Connor, a New York teen with a high hairdo, was diagnosed in 1989 with hearing loss and a "serious" ear infection. Her physician said her ears were clogged with hair spray.

Beyond News of the Weird
by Chuck Shepherd, John J. Kohut, & Roland Sweet

(Beauty, Vanity)

Dates used:____________

Zeal

An unemployed executive answered an intriguing job ad for the regional zoo. The human resources manager explained that the zoo's gorilla had died, and it was cheaper to hire someone to dress in a gorilla's suit than to get another gorilla. The man was desperate for a job, so he took it.

The first day wasn't too bad. He paced the floor, ate the peanuts and bananas thrown to him, and thumped on his chest. The next day, he became bolder and began swinging on the rope tied to an old tree. As he swung, he suddenly lost his grip and fell into the lion's den next door.

He jumped to his feet and began to scream, “Help! Help!” The lion came out of his house to see what the noise was all about, then pounced on the man in the gorilla suit.

“Shhh! If you don’t shut up, we’ll both lose our jobs!”

(Pretense, Workplace)

Dates used:____________

Pastor to Pastor

Let's face it. Your peers can be a tough audience. Women and men who communicate professionally hold a higher standard for one of their own.

That's why we've included this "Pastor to Pastor" section. When speaking to fellow pastors, whether at the local ministerial alliance or the big national conference, fresh humor is the quickest way to disarm your critics and energize your colleagues.

Here, from the archives of *Leadership*, are some of the funniest stories we've heard about life in the ministry.

Bad Days

It's a bad day when . . .

- You call the groom by the bride's former boyfriend's name.
- Your personal parking spot gets relocated—to the Denny's Restaurant three blocks away.
- You forget to turn off the cordless microphone while using the restroom.
- The church begins exploring the possibility of a missionary trip for you—to Libya.
- The organist is asked to play while you preach.
- The church votes to change your day off to Sunday.
- You preach the same sermon for the second week—and nobody notices.
- You get assigned to nursery duty—during the morning service.

Bruce Hoppe, Dwight Dally, Dave Maurer, Ron Saari

(Discouragement, Mistakes)

Dates used:____________

You know you're having *another* bad day when . . .

- You finally remember the name of that person you promised to visit in the hospital—while reading the obituaries.
- The groundskeeper accidentally waters your study along with the flower bed.
- You can't find Obadiah while leading a Bible study.
- In the pulpit you notice your sermon notes this week are for last week's sermon.
- The youth pastor urgently asks you about the church's liability insurance.
- Your church treasurer sends you a postcard from Geneva.
- The manse redecoration committee gets "a great deal" on used chartreuse carpet.
- You are informed that the youth group used steel wool sponges for their car wash.
- The couple you married a year ago calls to ask about a warranty.
- You are elected pastor emeritus—and you're only twenty-eight.

James D. Berkley

(Discouragement, Mistakes)

Dates used:____________

You know you're having *yet another bad day* when . . .

- You're the only one at the potluck dinner.
- You ask your secretary to "Take a letter" and she chooses Q.
- Before the annual meeting, the church treasurer asks if you know of a copier that copies in red.
- A church in Haiti wants to send its youth group to renovate your building.
- The city designates the next-door lot as a landfill site.

Dave Veerman

(Church, Trials)

Dates used:____________

"Where's my husband this morning?
Right where you buried him last week."

Mary Chambers

(Funerals, Mistakes)

Dates used:____________

Church Planting

You know you're in church planting when . . .

- A baby sneezes in the nursery, and the mother leaves the service to check his health.
- You discover you've preached three sermons in the past month on "Commitment and Faithfulness through Church Attendance."
- Your spouse is ill—and attendance dips 20 percent.
- Your hymnals (copyright 1895), your pulpit (ninth-grade shop quality), your (dented) Communion set, and your core members are all castoffs from Old First Church.
- Your attendance matches the temperature—in January.
- Soloists always use taped accompaniment.
- Your first visitor in two months comes on the Sunday three families are gone—and you're preaching on tithing.
- Your services, held in a hotel conference room, are interrupted by passersby looking for the Baseball Card and Comic Book Convention.
- You find the three missing families at the convention.
- Anything that breathes is counted in Sunday attendance.
- Your donated organ has built-in percussion for the rhumba and cha-cha.
- Your favorite Bible verse is "Where two or three are gathered together . . ."
- You say, "Will the usher please come forward?"
- You awake from a dream in which everyone who has ever visited your church comes back.
- The phone number of the church and parsonage are the same.
- A board member asks, "Why do we need a budget?"
- Every piece of furniture has to be put away after the service.

- Even buckets of air freshener on Sundays cannot remove the smell of smoke and sweat remaining in the rented sanctuary from the other six days.
- You need to speak to the church chairman, Sunday school superintendent, and treasurer—but he's gone this week.
- Infants can crawl from the nursery to the pulpit in 19.3 seconds.

Rich Geigert

(Humility, Small Church)

Dates used:____________

Church Talk

Sometimes the church seems to have a language of its own. While insiders understand it well, the uninitiated may not understand the subtle nuances of Churchese. Perhaps a glossary would help:

Statement: "We'll sing only the first verse of our closing hymn."
Definition: "I preached too long."

Statement: "It's VBS time again."
Definition: "Start saving Legg's containers, Popsicle sticks, egg cartons, and baby food jars."

Statement: "This is the best book I've read on the subject."
Definition: "This is the only book I've read on the subject."

Statement: "Everybody is saying . . ."
Definition: "My wife told me . . ."

Statement: "Our church is close-knit."
Definition: "We haven't had a new member in five years."

David E. Steverson

(Church, Discernment)

Dates used:____________

The word *oxymoron* comes from the Greek words for "sharp fool." That's the only way to describe phrases like "jumbo shrimp," "deafening silence," and "freezer burn." You may have heard these oxymorons at church:

10. Board consensus
9. Creative worship
8. Brief treasurer's report
7. Work party
6. Junior high sleepover
5. Men's fellowship
4. Close-knit staff
3. Simple request
2. Bus ministry
1. My final point

Ronald T. Habermas and Gary Habermas

(Church, Confusion)

Dates used:____________

Computers

Here, for the terminologically impaired, are some handy definitions of commonly used computer terms.

Shareware: A common Communion chalice.

Cyberspace: Where people go when we preach on stuff like supralapsarianism.

Hardware: The ugly necktie your kids gave you last Father's Day.

Download: To dump unpleasant tasks on the youth pastor.

Hard drive: A twelve-hour bus trip to junior high camp.

Co-processor: When your wife edits your sermons.

Modem: What you did to the flowers Mrs. Grinch planted in front of the church.

Database: Old Mrs. Weemster who remembers the names and shortcomings of every pastor in the 120-year history of your church.

PC: "Please Come"—an eschatological plea by those who can't find their sermon notes on the computer when it's time to print them Sunday morning.

Online: Where your job will be when you step up to the pulpit with nothing to say.

Ed Rowell

(Church, Technology)

Dates used:____________

Counseling

Not every pastor enjoys counseling. But other than by skipping town, how can you decrease the demand? Here, based on specious clinical research, are a dozen methods guaranteed to keep counseling off your to-do list.

1. Recite tales of people who are a lot worse off, and call the counselee a crybaby.
2. Engage the counselee's mother-in-law as a cotherapist.
3. Don't put a door on your office.
4. Sing songs such as "Put On a Happy Face" and "Don't Worry; Be Happy" to counselees.
5. Step out of the office and start laughing uproariously.
6. Tell the counselee that although you can't figure out a solution to the problem, you'll bring it up in the sermon on Sunday and see if anybody has any ideas.
7. Casually catch up on your reading while counselees bare their deepest problems.
8. Tell the counselee you are videotaping the session for replay on the local cable program *Candid Clergy*.
9. Put a bumper sticker on your car: I'D RATHER NOT BE COUNSELING.
10. Refer them to a helpful article in your favorite professional journal: the *National Enquirer*.
11. Suggest counseling by fax machine.
12. In front of the counselee, phone your spouse and ask for his or her opinion on what to do.

Paul Bailey

(Hardheartedness, Pastoral Care)

Dates used:____________

Definitions

Have you ever noticed church phenomena for which there should be a term, yet none exists? No longer. Introducing . . . *The Living Lexicon: Church Terms That Oughta Be*.

Biblidue: The buildup of bookmarks, bulletins, notes, and other miscellanea that collects in one's Bible.

Clivaholic: One who can no longer control the compulsion to quote C. S. Lewis in every sermon, lesson, or conversation.

Hymnastics: The entertaining body language of the song leader.

Narthexegesis: Unsolicited postsermon commentary given the preacher by armchair biblical theologians.

Pewtrify: To occupy a precise spot in the sanctuary for more than fifteen years without once showing signs of sentient life.

Ministereotype: A common myth or misconception about any ordained person.

Pulpituitary: That phenomenon familiar to those seated on the front pew, during which a preacher produces hazardous conditions with alliterative *P*'s.

Deaconscript: An unwilling church officer cajoled into a position of leadership.

Hi-litaholic: One who cannot resist highlighting Bible verses until the entire volume is a multihued mass of Day-Glo vibrancy.

Hymnprovisation: The abrupt and unannounced transition from one song to another, usually a chorus unfamiliar to most present.

Rob Suggs

(Church, Discernment)

Dates used:____________

A district superintendent often assists local churches in their search for new pastors. If the D.S. calls you as a potential candidate, the D.S. will try to give you a feel for the congregation. To help pastors translate these assessments, we submit the following list:

When the District Superintendent says, *"I just need someone to go in there and love the people."*
What the D.S. means is, This group is on the verge of a major church split.

"This church simply needs an injection of new life."
The senior adult class constitutes 90 percent of the membership.

"There's a good core of young marrieds in the church."
The young marrieds Sunday school class has been going for forty-two years, and they haven't bothered to change their name.

"This congregation has an involved, well-mobilized laity."
They've demanded recall votes of the last six pastors.

"With a little bit of time, this church could bust loose."
The most cantankerous church boss is experiencing health problems and may die soon.

"This church offers a competitive salary package."
It's on par with what the cashier at Wal-Mart makes.

"This church features uplifting music."
The organist is so bad she makes your hair stand on end.

"The building is highly visible."

The property is located so far off the beaten path that there's open space for miles around.

"The leadership is very, very stable."

The last time there was turnover on the church board was during the Eisenhower administration.

"You won't believe the benefits."

There are none.

"I know you're the one for the job."

Please take this assignment so I can spend more time on the golf course.

Brad Edgbert, Joe Shreffler,
Scott Thornton, John Whitsett

(Church, Discernment)

Dates used:____________

Exercise

Who says ministry is a sedentary occupation? Now you can keep track of the energy expended by such routine pastoral tasks as:

Jumping to conclusions—10 calories
Bending over backward—25 calories
Bowing to pressure—25 calories
Climbing the walls—50 calories
Gnashing teeth—50 calories
Going the second mile—50 calories
Putting your hand to the plow—60 calories
Reaping what you sow—75 calories
Turning the other cheek—90 calories
Casting the first stone—90 calories
Throwing your weight around—50 to 300 calories (depending on your weight)
Making mountains out of molehills—150 calories
Moving mountains—200 calories
Digging into the Greek—110 calories
Eating crow—75 calories
Riding a hobby horse—20 calories
Pushing programs—300 calories
Bending an ear—60 calories
Casting pearls before swine—80 calories
Carrying the weight of the world—200 calories
Laying up treasure in heaven—250 calories
Upholding the church in prayer—275 calories
Talking to the board chairman—300 calories
Listening to the board chairman—2 calories

Terry C. Muck, Dean Merrill, Marshall Shelley

(Ministry, Pastoral Care)

Dates used:____________

Guest Speakers

You know you're in trouble when the guest speaker begins with . . .

A funny thing happened on the way to the church this morning . . .

Unaccustomed as I am to public speaking . . .

Did you hear the one about the three ministers on an airplane . . .

Here are the notes for the sermon I was going to give, but I've decided not to give that message and simply say some things that need to be said . . .

As I was eating lunch with (insert big name) last week . . .

Webster defines (insert any word) as . . .

Yesterday's Cubs game has many parallels to this morning's text . . .

My wife doesn't like this sermon, but I decided to go ahead with it anyway . . .

This morning's message has twenty points . . .

Last night I had a dream—of footprints in the sand . . .

Cereal boxes don't usually lead to sermon ideas, but this morning . . .

There are some topics that thirty minutes just can't do justice . . .

I was digging through some old seminary class notes this week . . .

At first glance, variants between the Septuagint and the Masoretic Text don't seem all that interesting, but . . .

Over the last few months, while struggling with my sexual identity . . .

I normally prepare my sermons in advance, but today . . .

Kevin A. Miller

(Impressions, Preaching)

Dates used:____________

Good News

Good News: You baptized four people today.

Bad News: You lost two others in the swift river current.

Good News: The Women's Association voted to send you a get-well card.

Bad News: It passed 31 to 30.

Good News: The church board accepted your job description the way you wrote it.

Bad News: They also formed a search committee to find somebody capable of filling the position.

Good News: Your stand on nuclear disarmament has won the respect and admiration of many people.

Bad News: None of them is remotely connected to your church.

Good News: You finally found a choir director who approaches things your way.

Bad News: The choir mutinied.

Good News: Seventy junior high students showed up last Thursday.

Bad News: The meeting was on Wednesday.

Good News: Your women's softball team won their first game.

Bad News: They beat your men's softball team.

Good News: The trustees finally voted to add more church parking.

Bad News: They want to blacktop the front lawn of the manse.

James D. Berkley

(Disappointment, Perspective)

Dates used:____________

Illustrations

A Pastor's Top Ten Favorite Illustrations:

10. Someone else's big mistake.
9. The bumper sticker I read on the way to church.
8. My last vacation.
7. My kid's darling, off-the-cuff remark.
6. Anything from *Reader's Digest* found while waiting for the doctor.
5. An old joke, which magically becomes "something that happened to a friend of mine."
4. The story of my only fishing trip, made to sound like a *National Geographic* expedition.
3. The day I won "the big game."
2. The day I lost "the big game."
1. The day I finally told the truth about "the big game."

Michael E. Phillips

(Jokes, Stories)

Dates used:____________

Last Words

Here are the most frequent phrases in ministry that become preludes to a fast farewell:

10. I think I've earned the right to say this.
9. Thank you for the unanimous vote of confidence.
8. We'll incorporate a seeker-sensitive approach into our present worship service.
7. In ancient Israel, the people *danced* before the Lord.
6. Recently, I've been reading about the importance of publicly confessing your own sins, so today . . .
5. I'll show the church secretary who's boss around here!
4. I'm sure I can trust you to keep this confidential.
3. Then there are no hard feelings, right?
2. I'm sure Mrs. Jones will agree that she's been our organist long enough.
1. They need to realize this kitchen belongs to everyone.

Bob Moeller and the Leadership *editors*

(Conflict, Leadership)

Dates used:____________

Prayer

I pastor a young church that still meets in temporary facilities. During the usual chaos of setting up for worship, I heard one of my parishioners complain about back pain. Just before the service, his wife explained that Jack was recovering from surgery.

During the pastoral prayer, Jack's name came to mind. I asked God to help him recover from surgery and to "restore him to full function." I heard a gasp and some muffled laughter.

I found out after the service that Jack's surgery was a vasectomy.

Mike Coglan

(Embarrassment, Pastoral Care)

Dates used:____________

Pulpit Committees

It's important to read between the lines of what the pulpit committee says, so you know what it really means.

When the pulpit committee says, *"Our church is in a delightful rural setting."*
What the pulpit committee means is, No visitors will ever find it.

"The parsonage is conveniently located to the church."
It's right next door, so you'll never have a moment's quiet.

"We have 246 members on the roll."
Sunday morning worship attendance is 20.

"We want to reach the unchurched in our area."
We want a pastor who will evangelize for us.

"Church members are active in community affairs."
Good luck finding volunteers to teach Sunday school.

"We're seeking someone to revitalize the church."
The church needs to be painted.

"We'll be glad to review your performance periodically."
You can expect to get a phone call every Sunday afternoon.

"We'd like a hardworking pastor."
You get one day off a month.

"We want to build a strong youth program."
Our last addition to the cradle roll was in 1959.

"We'd like our pastor to be a family person."

We hope your children can help set up chairs and your spouse can type the bulletin.

Jack and Ann Wald

(Expectations, Honesty)

Dates used:____________

Resumes

Have you ever wondered why your pastoral resume doesn't evoke more enthusiasm? Here, as a public service, are some statements you might want to edit out of your next resume:

"I believe empathy is overrated."

"In the five churches I have faithfully served over the past two years . . ."

"My hobbies are pit bulls and automatic weapons."

"I am willing to sacrifice my family for the sake of the ministry. I am also willing to sacrifice yours."

"I have learned to cope with financial crisis at every church I've served."

"I require an attractive secretary and/or organist."

"My extensive counseling of church members has proved a rich source of sermon illustrations."

"I've been told that every sermon I preach is better than the next."

"My personality has provided me ample opportunity to develop conflict-resolution skills."

Dave Wilkinson

(Disclosure, Perspective)

Dates used:____________

"And never, ever look at serving the church as burdensome."

Jonny Hawkins

(Bondage, Obligation)

Dates used:____________

Spiritual Gifts

Seven True Spiritual Gifts for Today's Church:

1. *Nursery worker.* This is based on Mark 10:14, "Suffer the little children to come unto me" (KJV). Anyone who believes this verse is or should be in the Bible has nursery worker for his or her dominant gift.

2. *Giving.* This is the dominant gift for anybody who makes more money than I do. Michael Jordan, for example, would fit in this category if he came to my church. In fact, he's thinking about coming to my church, so he's asked me to tell everybody else's church to get off his back about it.

3. *Criticism.* Although not actually mentioned in the text, this is in fact the most widely practiced spiritual gift in the church today, so the academy has finally voted that it be officially recognized.

4. *Amway.* Discretion forbids me to say more.

5. *Wedding Hostess.* You don't really need the inventory for this one, since anyone with this gift could be identified blindfolded. These are people who in other life circumstances would have grown up to be General Patton or Turkish prison guards. In churches that are truly gift based, the wedding hostess actually functions as senior pastor.

6. *Kitchen Hostess.* This is to wedding hostess what minor leagues are to the majors: a place where promising rookies can get experience and fading veterans can enjoy a last fling at playing the game before it's time to hang up the spikes.

7. *Helping People Discover Their Spiritual Gifts.*

John Ortberg

(Recruiting, Training)

Dates used:____________

Meet your church staff

Dik LaPine

(Perception, Relationships)

Dates used:____________

Dik LaPine

(Attitude, Relationships)

Dates used:____________

Theology

Here is a valuable tool to help with your congregation, board, even your peers. When in need of additional class or clout, simply select any three-digit number at random. Instantly you have the words to impress and inspire.

For example, a "567" would be an "Ingenuous theoretical gratuity." Such verbosity can go a long way toward substantiating your position on anything—especially since no one would dare admit he didn't understand what you said.

0 Veracious	0 Ecclesiastical	0 Tenet
1 Reverential	1 Canonical	1 Doctrine
2 Integrated	2 Theological	2 Concept
3 Preferential	3 Spiritual	3 Assurance
4 Consecrated	4 Intangible	4 Credence
5 Ingenuous	5 Incorporeal	5 Speculation
6 Comparable	6 Theoretical	6 Dogma
7 Systematized	7 Patristic	7 Gratuity
8 Balanced	8 Sacerdotal	8 Piety
9 Transitional	9 Ecumenical	9 Perception

Boyce Mouton

(Egotism, Intimidation)

Dates used:____________

Index

Index

Index

Ed Rowell is senior pastor of Tri-Lakes Chapel in Monument, Colorado. A former editor at *Leadership Journal* and *Preaching Today*, Ed has written six books, including a novel, *Emma's Journal*.